THE STORY OF MY LIFE

Ellen Terry (1847–1928) was the most magical figure of
the Victorian stage. She wrote these memoirs in 1908, at
the end of her main stage career, though her last stage
appearance was in 1925. She tells her story very simply
and unaffectedly, beginning with her childhood as a
travelling player (she first appeared on stage at the age of
nine), her ill-fated marriage to the painter G. F. Watts
when she was sixteen, her return to the stage and to a series
of triumphant successes in London and New York, particularly during her time at the Lyceum with Henry
Irving. Her wry and humorous self-portrait is matched by
vivid sketches of the great actors and actresses she worked
with, and of her wide circle of friends among artists and
writers of the time. Her character study of Irving himself,
spendthrift and prodigious in all he did, is in itself enough
to ensure the book's place among the classics of the
theatre.

'*The Story of My Life* is one of the jolliest, most friendly
and entertaining, by which I mean the best, theatre auto-
biographies I know.'

IAN MCKELLEN

THE STORY OF MY LIFE

Ellen Terry

SCHOCKEN BOOKS · NEW YORK

First American edition published by Schocken Books 1982
10 9 8 7 6 5 4 3 2 1   82 83 84 85

Published by agreement with
The Boydell Press, Woodbridge, Suffolk

Photoset in Great Britain by
Galleon Photosetting, Ipswich, Suffolk
and printed by Nene Litho, Wellingborough, Northants

ISBN 0–8052–3814–X (hardback)
     0–8052–0721–X (paperback)

Library of Congress Cataloging in Publication Data

Terry, Ellen, Dame, 1848 – 1928.
   The Story of my Life.

   1. Terry, Ellen, Dame, 1848 – 1928.
2. Actors -- Great Britain -- Biography. I. Title.
PN2598.T4A3 1982 792'.028'0924 [B] 82 – 3330 AACR2

Contents

Contents

INTRODUCTION

When I read the book, the biography famous,
And is this then (said I) what the author calls a man's life?
And so will some one when I am dead and gone write my life?
(As if any man really knew aught of my life!)
Why even I myself, I often think, know little or nothing of my real life?
Only a few hints—a few diffused faint clues and indirections I seek . . . to
   trace out here

WALT WHITMAN.

FOR years I have contemplated telling this story, and for years I have
put off telling it. While I have delayed, my memory has not improved,
and my recollections of the past are more hazy and fragmentary than
when it first occurred to me that one day I might write them down.

My bad memory would matter less if I had some skill in writing—the
practised writer can see possibilities in the most ordinary events—or if I
had kept a systematic and conscientious record of my life. But although
I was at one time conscientious and diligent enough in keeping a diary,
I kept it for use at the moment, not for future reference. I kept it with
paste-pot and scissors as much as with a pen. My method was to cut bits
out of the newspapers and stick them into my diary day by day. Before
the end of the year was reached Mr. Letts would have been ashamed to
own his diary. It had become a bursting, groaning dustbin of information, for the most part useless. The biggest elastic band made could
hardly encircle its bulk, swelled by photographs, letters, telegrams,
dried flowers—the whole making up a confusion in which every one
but the owner would seek in vain to find some sense or meaning.

About six years ago I moved into a smaller house in London, and I
burnt a great many of my earlier diaries as unmovable rubbish. The few
passages which I shall quote in this book from those which escaped
destruction will prove that my bonfire meant no great loss!

Still, when it was suggested to me in the year of my stage jubilee that
I ought to write down my recollections, I longed for those diaries! I
longed for anything which would remind me of the past and make it live
again for me. I was frightened. Something would be expected of me,
since I could not deny that I had had an eventful life, packed full of
incident, and that by the road I had met many distinguished and
interesting men and women. I could not deny that I had been fifty years
on the stage, and that this meant enough material for fifty books, if only
the details of every year could be faithfully told. But it is not given to all
of us to see our lives in relief as we look back. Most of us, I think, see
them in perspective, of which our birth is the vanishing point. Seeing,

too, is only half the battle. How few people can describe what they see!

While I was thinking in this obstructive fashion and wishing that I could write about my childhood like Tolstoi, about my girlhood like Marie Bashkirtseff, and about the rest of my days and my work like many other artists of the pen, who merely, by putting black upon white, have had the power to bring before their readers not merely themselves "as they lived", but the most homely and intimate details of their lives, the friend who had first impressed on me that I ought not to leave my story untold any longer, said that the beginning was easy enough: "What is the first thing you remember? Write that down as a start."

But for my friend's practical suggestion it is doubtful if I should ever have written a line! He relieved my anxiety about my powers of compiling a stupendous autobiography, and made me forget that writing was a new art, to me, and that I was rather old to try my hand at a new art. My memory suddenly began to seem not so bad after all. For weeks I had hesitated between Othello's "Nothing extenuate, nor write down aught in malice", and Pilate's "What is truth?" as my guide and my apology. Now I saw that both were too big for my modest endeavour. I was not leaving a human document for the benefit of future psychologists and historians, but telling as much of my story as I could remember to the good, living public which has been considerate and faithful to me for so many years.

How often it has made allowances for me when I was nervous on first nights! With what patience it has waited long and uncomfortable hours to see me! Surely its charity would quickly cover my literary sins.

I gave up the search for a motto which should express my wish to tell the truth so far as I know it, to describe things as I see them, to be faithful according to my light, not dreading the abuse of those who might see in my light nothing but darkness.

I shut up "Othello" and did not try to verify the remark of "jesting" Pilate. The only instruction that I gave myself was to "begin at the beginning".

E.T.

I

A CHILD OF THE STAGE

1848–1856

THIS is the first thing that I remember.

In the corner of a lean-to whitewashed attic stood a fine, plain, solid oak bureau. By climbing up on to this bureau I could see from the window the glories of the sunset. My attic was on a hill in a large and busy town, and the smoke of a thousand chimneys hung like a grey veil between me and the fires in the sky. When the sun had set, and the scarlet and gold, violet and primrose, and all those magic colours that have no names, had faded into the dark, there were other fires for me to see. The flaming forges came out and terrified while they fascinated my childish imagination.

What did it matter to me that I was locked in and that my father and mother, with my elder sister Kate, were all at the theatre? I had the sunset, the forges, and the oak bureau.

I cannot say how old I was at this time, but I am sure that it wasn't long after my birth (which I can't remember, although I have often been asked to decide in which house at Coventry I was born!) At any rate, I had not then seen a theatre, and I took to the stage before many years had passed over my head.

Putting together what I remember, and such authentic history as there is of my parents' movements, I gather that this attic was in theatrical lodgings in Glasgow. My father was an actor, my mother an actress, and they were at this time on tour in Scotland. Perhaps this is the place to say that father was the son of an Irish builder, and that he eloped in a chaise with mother, who was the daughter of a Scottish minister. I am afraid I know no details of their romance. As for my less immediate ancestry, it is "wropt in mystery". Were we all people of the stage? There was Daniel Terry who was not only a famous actor in his day, but a friend of Sir Walter Scott's. There was an Eliza Terry, an actress whose portrait appears in *The Dramatic Mirror* in 1847. But so far as I know I cannot claim kinship with either Eliza or Daniel.

I have a very dim recollection of anything that happened in the attic, beyond the fact that when my father and mother went to the theatre every night, they used to put me to bed, and that directly their backs were turned and the door locked, I used to jump up and go to the window. My "bed" consisted of the mattress pulled off their bed and laid on the floor—on father's side. Both my father and my mother were very kind and devoted parents (though severe at times, as all good parents are), but

1

while mother loved all her children too well to make favourites, I was, I believe, my father's particular pet. I used to sleep all night holding his hand.

One night I remember waking up to find a beautiful face bending over me. Father was holding a candle so that the visitor might see me better, and gradually I realised that the face belonged to some one in a brown silk dress—the first silk dress that I had ever seen. This being from another world had brown eyes and brown hair, which looked to me very dark, because we were a white lot, very fair indeed. I shall never forget that beautiful vision of this well-dressed woman with her lovely complexion and her gold chain round her neck. It was my Aunt Lizzie.

I hold very strongly that a child's earliest impressions mould its character perhaps more than either heredity or education. I am sure it is true in my case. What first impressed me? An attic, an oak bureau, a lovely face, a bed on the floor. Things have come and gone in my life since then, but they have been powerless to efface those early impressions. I adore pretty faces. I can't keep away from shops where they sell good old furniture like my bureau. I like plain rooms with low ceilings better than any other rooms; and for my afternoon siesta, which is one of my institutions, I often choose the floor in preference to bed or sofa.

What we remember in our childhood and what we are told afterwards often become inextricably confused in our minds, and after the bureau and Aunt Lizzie, my memory is a blank for some years. I can't even tell you when it was first decided that I was to go on the stage, but I expect it was when I was born, for in those days theatrical folk did not imagine that their children *could* do anything but follow their parents' profession.

I must depend now on hearsay for certain facts. The first fact is my birth, which should, perhaps, have been mentioned before anything else. To speak by the certificate, I was born on the 27th of February, 1848, at Coventry. Many years afterwards, when people were kind enough to think that the house in which I was born deserved to be discovered, there was a dispute as to which house in Market Street could claim me. The dispute was left unsettled in rather a curious way. On one side of the narrow street a haberdasher's shop bore the inscription, "Birthplace of Ellen Terry". On the other, an eating-house declared itself to be "the original birthplace"! I have never been able to arbitrate in the matter, my statement that my mother had always said that the house was "on the right-hand side, coming from the market-place", being apparently of no use. I have heard lately that one of the birthplaces has retired from the competition, and that the haberdasher has the field to himself. I am glad, for the sake of those friends of mine who have bought his handkerchiefs and ties as souvenirs. There is, however, nothing very attractive about the house itself. It is better built than a house of the same size would be built now, and it has a certain old-fashioned respectability, but that is the end of its praises. Coventry itself makes up for the deficiency. It is a delightful town, and it was a happy chance that made me a native of Warwickshire, Shakespeare's own county. Sarah Kemble married Mr. Siddons at Coventry too—another happy omen.

I have acted twice in my native town in old days, but never in recent years. In 1904 I planned to act there again, but unfortunately I was taken ill at Cambridge, and the doctors would not allow me to go to Coventry. The morning my company left Cambridge without me, I was very miserable. It is always hateful to disappoint the public, and on this occasion I was compelled to break faith where I most wished to keep it. I heard afterwards from my daughter (who played some of my parts instead of me) that many of the Coventry people thought I had never meant to come at all. If this should meet their eyes, I hope they will believe that this was not so. My ambition to play at Coventry again shall be realised yet.[1]

At one time nothing seemed more unlikely than that I should be able to act in another Warwickshire town, a town whose name is known all over the world. But time and chance and my own great wish succeeded in bringing about my appearance at Stratford-on-Avon.

I can well imagine that the children of some strolling players used to have a hard time of it, but my mother was not one to shirk her duties. She worked hard at her profession and yet found it possible not to *drag* up her children, to live or die as it happened, but to bring them up to be healthy, happy, and wise—theatre-wise, at any rate. When her babies were too small to be left at the lodgings (which she and my father took in each town they visited as near to the theatre as possible), she would bundle us up in a shawl and put us to sleep in her dressing-room. So it was, that long before I spoke in a theatre, I slept in one.

Later on, when we were older and mother could leave us at home, there was a fire one night at our lodgings, and she rushed out of the theatre and up the street in an agony of terror. She got us out of the house all right, took us to the theatre, and went on with the next act as if nothing had happened. Such fortitude is commoner in our profession, I think, than in any other. We "go on with the next act" whatever happens, and if we know our business, no one in the audience will ever guess that anything is wrong—that since the curtain last went down some dear friend has died, or our children in the theatrical lodgings up the street have run the risk of being burnt to death.

My mother had eleven children altogether, but only nine survived their infancy, and of the nine, my eldest brother, Ben, and my sister Florence have since died. My sister Kate, who left the stage at an age

[1] Since I wrote this, I have again visited my native town—this time to receive its civic congratulations on the occasion of my jubilee, and as recently as March of the present year I acted at the new Empire Theatre.

when most of the young women of the present day take to it for the first time, and made an enduring reputation in a few brilliant years, was the eldest of the family. Then came a sister, who died, and I was the third. After us came Ben, George, Marion, Flossie, Charles, Tom, and Fred. Six out of the nine have been on the stage, but only Marion, Fred, and I are there still.

Two or three members of this large family, at the most, were in existence when I first entered a theatre in a professional capacity, so I will leave them all alone for the present. I had better confess at once that I don't remember this great event, and my sister Kate is unkind enough to say that it never happened—to me! The story, she asserts, was told of *her*. But without damning proofs she is not going to make me believe it! Shall I be robbed of the only experience of my first eight years of life? Never.

During the rehearsals of a pantomime in a Scottish town (Glasgow, I think. Glasgow has always been an eventful place to me!), a child was wanted for the Spirit of the Mustard-pot. What more natural than that my father should offer my services? I had a shock of pale yellow hair, I was small enough to be put into the property mustard-pot, and the Glasgow stage manager would easily assume that I had inherited talent. My father had acted with Macready in the stock seasons both at Edinburgh and Glasgow, and bore a very high reputation with Scottish audiences. But the stage manager and father alike reckoned without their actress! When they tried to put me into the mustard-pot, I yelled lustily and showed more lung-power than aptitude for the stage.

"Pit your child into the mustard-pot, Mr Terry," said the stage manager.

"D——n you and your mustard-pot, sir!" said my mortified father. "I won't frighten my child for you or any one else!"

But all the same he was bitterly disappointed at my first dramatic failure, and when we reached home he put me in the corner to chasten me. "*You'll* never make an actress!" he said, shaking a reproachful finger at me.

It is *my* mustard-pot, and why Kate should want it, I can't think! She hadn't yellow hair, and she couldn't possibly have behaved so badly. I have often heard my parents say significantly that they had no trouble with *Kate!* Before she was four, she was dancing a hornpipe in a sailor's jumper, a rakish little hat, and a diminutive pair of white ducks! Those ducks, marked "Kate Terry", were kept by mother for years as a precious relic, and are, I hope, still in the family archives!

I stick to the mustard-pot, but I entirely disclaim the little Duke of York in Richard III, which some one with a good memory stoutly insists he saw me play before I made my first appearance as Mamilius. Except for this abortive attempt at Glasgow, I was never on any stage even for a rehearsal until 1856, at the Princess's Theatre, when I appeared with Charles Kean in "A Winter's Tale".

The man with the memory may have seen Kate as one of the Princes in the Tower, but he never saw me with her. Kate was called up to London in 1852 to play Prince Arthur in Charles Kean's production of "King John", and after that she acted in all his plays, until he gave up management in 1859. She had played Arthur during a stock season at Edinburgh, and so well that some one sang her praises to Kean and advised him to engage her. My mother took Kate to London, and I was left with my father in the provinces for two years. I can't recall much about those two years except sunsets and a great mass of shipping looming up against the sky. The sunsets followed me about everywhere; the shipping was in Liverpool, where father was engaged for a considerable time. He never ceased teaching me to be useful, alert, and quick. Sometimes he hastened my perceptive powers with a slipper, and always he corrected me if I pronounced any word in a slipshod fashion. He himself was a beautiful elocutionist, and if I now speak my language well it is in no small degree due to my early training.

It was to his elocution that father owed his engagement with Macready, of whom he always spoke in terms of the most affectionate admiration in after years, and probably it did him a good turn again with Charles Kean. An actor who had supported Macready with credit was just the actor likely to be useful to a manager who was producing a series of plays by Shakespeare. Kate had been a success at the Princess's, too, in child parts, and this may have reminded Mr. Kean to send for Kate's father! At any rate he was sent for towards the end of the year 1853 and left Liverpool for London. I know I cooked his breakfasts for him in Liverpool, but I haven't the slightest recollection of the next two years in London. As I am determined not to fill up the early blanks with stories of my own invention, I must go straight on to 1856, when rehearsals were called at the Princess's Theatre for Shakespeare's "Winter's Tale".

THE CHARLES KEANS

1856

The Charles Keans, from whom I received my first engagement, were both remarkable people, and at the Princess's Theatre were doing very remarkable work. Kean the younger had not the fire and genius of his wonderful father, Edmund, and but for the inherited splendour of his name it is not likely that he would ever have attained great eminence as an actor. His Wolsey and his Richard (the Second, not the Third) were his best parts, perhaps because in them his beautiful diction had full scope and his limitations were not noticeable. But it is more as a stage reformer

5

than as an actor that he will be remembered. The old happy-go-lucky way of staging plays, with its sublime indifference to correctness of detail and its utter disregard of archaeology, had received its first blow from Kemble and Macready, but Charles Kean gave it much harder knocks and went further than either of them in the good work.

It is an old story and a true one that when Edmund Kean made his first great success as Shylock, after a long and miserable struggle as a strolling player, he came home to his wife and said: "You shall ride in your carriage," and then, catching up his little son, added, "and Charley shall go to Eton!" Well, Charley did go to Eton, and if Eton did not make him a great actor, it opened his eyes to the absurd anachronisms in costumes and accessories which prevailed on the stage at that period, and when he undertook the management of the Princess's Theatre, he turned his classical education to account. In addition to scholarly knowledge, he had a naturally refined taste and the power of selecting the right men to help him. Planché, the great authority on historical costume, was one of his ablest coadjutors, and Mr. Bradshaw designed all the properties. It has been said lately that I began my career on an unfurnished stage, when the play was the thing, and spectacle was considered of small importance. I take this opportunity of contradicting that statement most emphatically. Neither when I began nor yet later in my career have I ever played under a management where infinite pains were not given to every detail. I think that far from hampering the acting, a beautiful and congruous background and harmonious costumes, representing accurately the spirit of the time in which the play is supposed to move, ought to help and inspire the actor.

Such thoughts as these did not trouble my head when I acted with the Keans, but, child as I was, the beauty of the productions at the Princess's Theatre made a great impression on me, and my memory of them is quite clear enough, even if there were not plenty of other evidence, for me to assert that in some respects they were even more elaborate than those of the present day. I know that the bath-buns of one's childhood always seem in memory much bigger and better than the buns sold nowadays, but even allowing for the natural glamour which the years throw over buns and rooms, places and plays alike, I am quite certain that Charles Kean's productions of Shakespeare would astonish the modern critic who regards the period of my first appearance as a sort of dark-age in the scenic art of the theatre.

I have alluded to the beauty of Charles Kean's diction. His voice was also of a wonderful quality—soft and low, yet distinct and clear as a bell. When he played Richard II the magical charm of this organ was alone enough to keep the house spell-bound. His vivid personality made a strong impression on me. Yet others only remember that he called his wife "Delly", though she was Nelly, and always spoke as if he had a cold

6

in his head. How strange! If I did not understand what suggested impressions so different from my own, they would make me more indignant.

> Now who shall arbitrate?
> Ten men love what I hate,
> Shun what I follow, slight what I receive.
> Ten who in ears and eyes
> Match me; they all surmise,
> They this thing, and I that:
> Whom shall my soul believe?

What he owed to Mrs. Kean, he would have been the first to confess. In many ways she was the leading spirit in the theatre; at the least, a joint ruler, not a queen-consort. During the rehearsals Mr. Kean used to sit in the stalls with a loud-voiced dinner-bell by his side, and when anything went wrong on the stage, he would ring it ferociously, and everything would come to a stop, until Mrs. Kean, who always sat on the stage, had set right what was wrong. She was more formidable than beautiful to look at, but her wonderful fire and genius were none the less impressive because she wore a white handkerchief round her head and had a very beaky nose! How I admired and loved and feared her! Later on the fear was replaced by gratitude, for no woman ever gave herself more trouble to train a young actress than did Mrs. Kean. The love and admiration, I am glad to say, remained and grew. It is rare that it falls to the lot of anyone to have such an accomplished teacher. Her patience and industry were splendid.

It was Mrs. Kean who chose me out of five or six other children to play my first part. We were all tried in it, and when we had finished, she said the same thing to us all: "That's very nice! Thank you, my dear. That will do."

We none of us knew at the time which of us had pleased her most.

At this time we were living in the upper part of a house in the Gower Street region. That first home in London I remember chiefly by its fine brass knocker, which mother kept beautifully bright, and by its being the place to which was sent my first part! Bound in green American cloth, it looked to me more marvellous than the most priceless book has ever looked since! I was so proud and pleased and delighted that I danced a hornpipe for joy!

Why was I chosen, and not one of the other children, for the part of Mamilius? some one may ask. It was not mere luck, I think. Perhaps I was a born actress, but that would have served me little if I had not been able to *speak*! It must be remembered that both my sister Kate and I had been trained almost from our birth for the stage, and particularly

7

in the important branch of clear articulation. Father, as I have already said, was a very charming elocutionist, and my mother read Shakespeare beautifully. They were both very fond of us and saw our faults with the eyes of love, though they were unsparing in their corrections. In these early days they had need of all their patience, for I was a most troublesome, wayward pupil. However, "the labour we delight in physics pain", and I hope, too, that my more staid sister made it up to them!

The rehearsals for "A Winter's Tale" were a lesson in fortitude. They taught me once and for all that an actress's life (even when the actress is only eight) is not all beer and skittles, or cakes and ale, or fame and glory. I was cast for the part of Mamilius in the way I have described, and my heart swelled with pride when I was told what I had to do, when I realised that I had a real Shakespeare part—a possession that father had taught me to consider the pride of life!

But many weary hours were to pass before the first night. If a company has to rehearse four hours a day now, it is considered a great hardship, and players must lunch and dine like other folk. But this was not Kean's way! Rehearsals lasted all day, Sundays included, and when there was no play running at night, until four or five the next morning! I don't think any actor in those days dreamed of luncheon. (Tennyson, by the way, told me to say "luncheon"—not "lunch".) How my poor little legs used to ache! Sometimes I could hardly keep my eyes open when I was on the stage, and often when my scene was over, I used to creep into the greenroom and forget my troubles and my art (if you can talk of art in connection with a child of eight) in a delicious sleep.

At the dress-rehearsals I did not want to sleep. All the members of the company were allowed to sit and watch the scenes in which they were not concerned, from the back of the dress-circle. This, by the way, is an excellent plan, and in theatres where it is followed the young actress has reason to be grateful. In these days of greater publicity when the press attend rehearsals, there may be strong reasons against the company being "in front", but the perfect loyalty of all concerned would dispose of these reasons. Now, for the first time, the beginner is able to see the effect of the weeks of thought and labour which have been given to the production. She can watch from the front the fulfilment of what she has only seen as intention and promise during the other rehearsals. But I am afraid that beginners now are not so keen as they used to be. The first wicked thing I did in a theatre sprang from excess of keenness. I borrowed a knife from a carpenter and made a slit in the canvas to watch Mrs. Kean as Hermione!

Devoted to her art, conscientious to a degree in mastering the spirit and details of her part, Mrs. Kean also possessed the personality and force to chain the attention and indelibly imprint her rendering of a part on the imagination. When I think of the costume in which she played Hermione, it seems marvellous to me that she could have produced the impression that she did. This seems to contradict what I have said about the magnificence of the production. But not at all! The designs of the dresses were purely classic; but then, as now, actors and actresses seemed unable to keep their own period and their own individuality out of the clothes directly they got them on their backs. In some cases the original design was quite swamped. No matter what the character that Mrs. Kean was assuming, she always used to wear her hair drawn flat over her forehead and twisted tight round her ears in a kind of circular sweep—such as the old writing-masters used to make when they attempted an extra grand flourish. And then the amount of petticoats she wore! Even as Hermione she was always bunched out by layer upon layer of petticoats, in defiance of the fact that classical parts should not be dressed in a superfluity of raiment. But if the petticoats where full of starch, the voice was full of pathos—and the dignity, simplicity, and womanliness of Mrs. Charles Kean's Hermione could not have been marred by a far more grotesque costume.

There is something, I suppose, in a woman's nature which always makes her remember how she was dressed at any specially eventful moment of her life, and I can see myself, as though it were yesterday, in the little red-and-silver dress I wore as Mamilius. Mrs. Grieve, the dresser—"Peter Grieve-us," as we children called her—had pulled me into my very pink tights (they were by no means *tight* but very baggy, according to the pictures of me), and my mother had arranged my hair in sausage curls on each side of my head in even more perfect order and regularity than usual. Besides my clothes, I had a beautiful "property" to be proud of. This was a go-cart, which had been made in the theatre by Mr. Bradshaw, and was an exact copy of a child's toy as depicted on a Greek vase. It was my duty to drag this little cart about the stage, and on the first night, when Mr. Kean as Leontes told me to "go play", I observed his instructions with such vigour that I tripped over the handle and came down on my back! A titter ran through the house, and I felt that my career as an actress was ruined for ever. Even now I remember how bitterly I wept, and how deeply humiliated I felt. But the little incident, so mortifying to me, did not spoil my first appearance altogether. *The Times* of May 1, 1856 was kind enough to call me "vivacious and precocious", and "a worthy relative of my sister Kate", and my parents were pleased (although they would not show it too much), and Mrs. Kean gave me a pat on the back. Father and Kate were both in the cast, too, I ought to have said, and the Queen, Prince Albert, and the Princess Royal were all in a box on the first night.

To act for the first time in Shakespeare, in a theatre where my sister

9

had already done something for our name, and before royalty, was surely a good beginning!

From April 28, 1856, I played Mamilius every night for one hundred and two nights. I was never ill, and my understudy, Clara Denvil, a very handsome, dark child with flaming eyes, though quite ready and longing to play my part, never had the chance.

I had now taken the first step, but I had taken it without any notion of what I was doing. I was innocent of all art, and while I loved the actual doing of my part, I hated the labour that led up to it. But the time was soon to come when I was to be fired by a passion for work. Meanwhile I was unconsciously learning a number of lessons which were to be most useful to me in my subsequent career.

TRAINING IN SHAKESPEARE

1856–1859

From April 1856 until 1859 I acted constantly at the Princess's Theatre with the Keans, spending the summer holidays in acting at Ryde. My whole life was the theatre, and naturally all my early memories are connected with it. At breakfast father would begin the day's "coaching". Often I had to lay down my fork and say my lines. He would conduct these extra rehearsals anywhere—in the street, the 'bus—we were never safe! I remember vividly going into a chemist's shop and being stood upon a stool to say my part to the chemist! Such leisure as I had from my profession was spent in "minding" the younger children—an occupation in which I delighted. They all had very pretty hair, and I used to wash it and comb it out until it looked as fine and bright as floss silk.

It is argued now that stage life is bad for a young child, and children are not allowed by law to go on the stage until they are ten years old—quite a mature age in my young days! I cannot discuss the whole question here, and must content myself with saying that during my three years at the Princess's I was a very strong, happy, and healthy child. I was never out of the bill except during the run of "A Midsummer Night's Dream", when, through an unfortunate accident, I broke my toe. I was playing Puck, my second part on any stage, and had come up through a trap at the end of the last act to give the final speech. My sister Kate was playing Titania that night as understudy to Carlotta Leclercq. Up I came—but not quite up, for the man shut the trap-door too soon and caught my toe. I screamed. Kate rushed to me and banged her foot on the stage, but the man only closed the trap tighter, mistaking the signal.

"Oh, Katie! Katie!" I cried. "Oh, Nelly! Nelly!" said poor Kate helplessly. Then Mrs. Kean came rushing on and made them open the trap and release my poor foot.

"Finish the play, dear," she whispered excitedly, "and I'll double your salary!" There was Kate holding me up on one side and Mrs. Kean on the other. Well, I did finish the play in a fashion. The text ran something like this—

> If we shadows have offended (Oh, Katie, Katie!)
> Think but this, and all is mended, (Oh, my toe!)
> That you have but slumbered here,
> While these visions did appear. (I can't, I can't!)
> And this weak and idle theme,
> No more yielding but a dream, (Oh, dear! oh, dear!)
> Gentles, do not reprehend; (A big sob)
> If you pardon, we will mend. (Oh, Mrs. Kean!)

How I got through it, I don't know! But my salary was doubled—it had been fifteen shillings, and it was raised to thirty—and Mr. Skey, President of St. Bartholomew's Hospital, who chanced to be in a stall that very evening, came round behind the scenes and put my toe right. He remained my friend for life.

I was not chosen for Puck because I had played Mamilius with some credit. The same examination was gone through, and again I came out first. During the rehearsals Mrs. Kean taught me to draw my breath in through my nose and begin a laugh—a very valuable accomplishment! She was also indefatigable in her lessons in clear enunciation, and I can hear her now lecturing the ladies of the company on their vowels. "A, E, I, O, U, my dear," she used to say, "are five distinct vowels, so don't mix them all up together as if you were making a pudding. If you want to say, 'I am going on the river,' say it plainly and don't tell us you are going on the 'riv*ah!*' You must say *her*, not *har*; it's *God*, not *Gud*: rem*on*strance, not rem*un*strance," and so forth. No one ever had a sharper tongue or a kinder heart than Mrs. Kean. Beginning with her, I have always loved women with a somewhat hard manner! I have never believed in their hardness, and have proved them tender and generous in the extreme.

Actor-managers are very proud of their long runs nowadays, but in Shakespeare, at any rate, they do not often eclipse Charles Kean's two hundred and fifty nights of "A Midsummer Night's Dream" at the Princess's. It was certainly a very fascinating production, and many of the effects were beautiful. I, by the way, had my share in marring one of these during the run. When Puck was told to put a girdle round the earth in forty minutes, I had to fly off the stage as swiftly as I could, and a dummy Puck was whirled through the air from the point where I disappeared. One night the dummy, while in full flying action, fell on the stage, whereupon in great concern for its safety, I ran on, picked it up in my arms, and ran off with it amid roars of laughter! Neither of the Keans was acting in this production, but there was some one in authority to give me a sound cuff. Yet I had such excellent intentions. 'Tis ever thus!

I revelled in Puck and his impish pranks, and unconsciously realised that it was a part in which the imagination could run riot. I believe I played it well, but I did not *look* well, and I must contradict emphatically the kind assumption that I must have been a "delightful little fairy". As Mamilius I was really a sweet little thing, but while I was playing Puck I grew very gawky—not to say ugly! My hair had been cut short, and my red cheeks stuck out too much. I was a sight!

The parts we play influence our characters to some extent, and Puck made me a bit of a romp. I grew vain and rather "cocky", and it was just as well that during the rehearsals for the Christmas pantomime in 1857 I was tried for the part of the Fairy Dragonetta and rejected. I believe that my failure was principally due to the fact that Nature had not given me flashing eyes and raven hair—without which, as every one knows, no bad fairy can hold up her head and respect herself. But at the time I felt distinctly rebuffed, and only the extreme beauty of my dress as the maudlin "good fairy" Goldenstar consoled me. Milly Smith (afterwards Mrs. Thorn) was Dragonetta, and one of her speeches ran like this:

> Ungrateful Simple Simon! (darting forward) You thought no doubt to spite me!
> That to this Royal Christening you did not invite me!
> BUT—(Mrs. Kean: *"You must plaster that 'but' on the white wall at the back of the gallery."*)—
> But on this puling brat revenged I'll be!
> My fiery dragon there shall have her broiled for tea!

At Ryde during the previous summer my father had taken the theatre, and Kate and I played in several farces which the Keeleys and the great comedian Robson had made famous in London. My performances as Waddilove and Jacob Earwig had provoked some one to describe me as "a perfect little heap of talent!" To fit my Goldenstar, I must borrow that phrase and describe myself as a perfect little heap of vanity!

It was that dress! It was a long dress, though I was still a baby, and it was as pink and gold as it was trailing. I used to think I looked *beautiful* in it. I wore a trembling star on my forehead, too, which was enough to upset any girl!

One of the most wearisome, yet essential details of my education is connected with my first long dress. It introduces, too, Mr. Oscar Byrn, the dancing-master and director of crowds at the Princess's. One of his lessons was in the art of walking with a flannel blanket pinned in front and trailing six inches on the floor. My success in carrying out this manoeuvre with dignity won high praise from Mr. Byrn. The other children used to kick at the blanket and progress in jumps like young kangaroos, but somehow I never had any difficulty in moving gracefully. No wonder then that I impressed Mr. Byrn, who had a theory that "an actress was no actress unless she learned to dance early". Whenever he was not actually putting me through my paces, I was busy watching him teach the others. There was the minuet, to which he used to attach great importance, and there was "walking the plank". Up and down one of the long planks, extending the length of the stage, we had to walk first slowly and then quicker and quicker until we were able at a considerable pace to walk the whole length of it without deviating an inch from the straight line. This exercise, Mr. Byrn used to say, and quite truly, I think, taught us uprightness of carriage and certainty of step.

"Eyes right! Chest out! Chin tucked in!" I can hear the dear old man shouting at us as if it were yesterday; and I have learned to see of what value all his drilling was, not only to deportment, but to clear utterance. It would not be a bad thing if there were more "old fops" like Oscar Byrn in the theatres of today. That old-fashioned art of "deportment" is sadly neglected.

The pantomime in which I was the fairy Goldenstar was very frequently preceded by "A Midsummer Night's Dream", and the two parts on one night must have been fairly heavy work for a child, but I delighted in it.

In the same year (1858) I played Karl in "Faust and Marguerite", a jolly little part with plenty of points in it, but not nearly as good a part as Puck. Progress on the stage is often crab-like, and little parts, big parts, and no parts at all must be accepted as "all in the day's work". In these days I was cast for many a "dumb" part. I walked on in "The Merchant of Venice" carrying a basket of doves; in "Richard II" I climbed up a pole in the street scene; in "Henry VIII" I was "top angel" in the vision, and I remember that the heat of the gas at that dizzy height made me sick at the dress-rehearsal! I was a little boy "cheering" in several other productions. In "King Lear" my sister Kate played Cordelia. She was only fourteen, and the youngest Cordelia on record. Years after I played it at the Lyceum when I was over forty!

The production of "Henry VIII" at the Princess's was one of Charles Kean's best efforts. I always refrain from belittling the present at the expense of the past, but there were efforts here which I have never seen surpassed, and about this my memory is not at all dim. At this time I seem to have been always at the side watching the acting. Mrs. Kean's Katherine of Aragon was splendid, and Charles Kean's Wolsey, his best part after, perhaps, his Richard II. Still, the lady who used to stand ready with a tear-bottle to catch his tears as he came off after his last scene rather overdid her admiration. My mental criticism at the time was "What rubbish!" When I say in what parts Charles Kean was "best", I don't mean to be assertive. How should a mere child be able to decide? I "think back" and remember in what parts I liked him best, but I may be quite wide of the mark.

In those days audiences liked plenty for their money, and a Shakespeare play was not nearly long enough to fit the bill. English playgoers in the early 'fifties did not emulate the Japanese, who go to the theatre early in the morning and stay there until late at night, still less the Chinese, whose plays begin one week and end the next, but they thought nothing of sitting in the theatre from seven to twelve. In one of the extra pieces which these hours necessitated, I played a "tiger", one of those youthful grooms who are now almost a bygone fashion. The pride that I had taken in my trembling star in the pantomime was almost equalled now by my pride in my top-boots! They were too small and caused me insupportable suffering, but I was so afraid that they would be taken away if I complained, that every evening I used to put up valorously with the torture. The piece was called "If the Cap Fits", but my boots were the fit with which I was most concerned!

Years later the author of the little play, Mr. Edmund Yates, the editor of The World—wrote to me about my performance as the tiger:

> When on June 13, 1859 (to no one else in the world would I breathe the date!) I saw a very young lady play a tiger in a comedietta of mine called "If the Cap Fits", I had no idea that the precocious child had in her the germ of such an artist as she has since proved herself. What I think of her performance of Portia she will see in The World.

In "The Merchant of Venice", though I had no speaking part, I was firmly convinced that the basket of doves which I carried on my shoulder was the principal attraction of the scene in which it appeared. The other little boys and girls in the company regarded those doves with eyes of bitter envy. One little chorus boy, especially, though he professed a personal devotion of the tenderest kind for me, could never quite get over those doves, and his romantic sentiments cooled considerably when I gained my proud position as dove-bearer. Before, he had shared his sweets with me, but now he transferred both sweets and affections to some more fortunate little girl. Envy, after all, is the death of love!

Mr. Harley was the Launcelot Gobbo in "The Merchant of Venice"—

an old gentleman, and almost as great a fop as Mr. Byrn. He was always smiling; his two large rows of teeth were so *very* good! And he had pompous, grandiloquent manners, and wore white gaiters and a long hanging eye-glass. His appearance I should never have forgotten anyhow, but he is also connected in my mind with my first experience of terror.

It came to me in the greenroom, the window-seat of which was a favourite haunt of mine. Curled up in the deep recess I had been asleep one evening, when I was awakened by a strange noise, and, peeping out, saw Mr. Harley stretched on the sofa in a fit. One side of his face was working convulsively, and he was gibbering and mowing the air with his hand. When he saw me, he called out: "Little Nelly! oh, little Nelly!" I stood transfixed with horror. He was still dressed as Launcelot Gobbo, and this made it all the more terrible. A doctor was sent for, and Mr. Harley was looked after, but he never recovered from his seizure and died a few days afterwards.

Although so much of my early life is vague and indistinct, I can always see and hear Mr. Harley as I saw and heard him that night, and I can always recollect the view from the greenroom window. It looked out on a great square courtyard, in which the spare scenery, that was not in immediate use, was stacked. For some reason or other this courtyard was a favourite playground for a large company of rats. I don't know what the attraction was for them, except that they may have liked nibbling the paint off the canvas. Out they used to troop in swarms, and I, from my perch on the window-seat, would watch and wonder. Once a terrible storm came on, and years after, at the Lyceum, the Brocken Scene in "Faust" brought back the scene to my mind—the thunder and lightning and the creatures crawling on every side, the *greyness* of the whole thing.

All "calls" were made from the greenroom in those days, and its atmosphere was, I think, better than that of the dressing-room in which nowadays actors and actresses spend their time during the waits. The greenroom at the Princess's was often visited by distinguished people, among them Planché, the archaeologist, who did so much for Charles Kean's productions, and Macready. One night, as with my usual impetuosity I was rushing back to my room to change my dress, I ran right into the white waistcoat of an old gentleman! Looking up with alarm, I found that I had nearly knocked over the great Mr. Macready.

"Oh, I *beg* your pardon!" I exclaimed in eager tones. I had always heard from father that Macready was the greatest actor of all, and this was our first meeting. I was utterly abashed, but Mr. Macready, looking down with a very kindly smile, only answered: "Never mind! You are a very polite little girl, and you act very earnestly and speak very nicely."

I was too much agitated to do anything but continue my headlong course to my dressing-room, but even in those short moments the strange attractiveness of his face impressed itself on my imagination. I remember distinctly his curling hair, his oddly coloured eyes full of fire, and his beautiful, wavy mouth.

When I first described this meeting with Macready, a disagreeable person wrote to the papers and said that he did not wish to question my veracity, but that it was utterly impossible that Macready could ever have brought himself to go to the Princess's at this time, because of the rivalry between him and Charles Kean. I know that the two actors were not on speaking terms, but very likely Macready had come to see my father or Mr. Harley or one of the many members of Kean's company who had once served under him.

The period when I was as vain as a little peacock had come to an end before this. I think my part in "Pizarro" saw the last of it. I was a Worshipper of the Sun, and, in a pink feather, pink swathings of muslin, and black arms, I was again struck by my own beauty. I grew quite attached to the looking-glass which reflected that feather! Then suddenly there came a change. *I began to see the whole thing.* My attentive watching of other people began to bear fruit, and the labour and perseverance, care and intelligence which had gone to make these enormous productions dawned on my young mind. *One must see things for oneself.* Up to this time I had loved acting because it was great fun, but I had not loved the grind. After I began to rehearse Prince Arthur in "King John", a part in which my sister Kate had already made a great success six years earlier, I understood that if I did not work, I could not act. And I wanted to work. I used to get up in the middle of the night and watch my gestures in the glass. I used to try my voice and bring it down and up in the right places. And all the vanity fell away from me. At the first rehearsals of "King John" I could not do anything right. Mrs. Kean stormed at me, slapped me. I broke down and cried, and then, with all the mortification and grief in my voice, managed to express what Mrs. Kean wanted and what she could not teach me by doing it herself.

"That's right, that's right!" she cried excitedly, "you've got it! Now remember what you did with your voice, reproduce it, remember everything, and do it!"

When the rehearsal was over, she gave me a vigorous kiss. "You've done very well," she said. "That's what I want. You're a very tired little girl. Now run home to bed." I shall never forget the relief of those kind words after so much misery, and the little incident often comes back to me now when I hear a young actress say, "I can't do it!" If only she can cry with vexation, I feel sure that she will then be able to make a good attempt at doing it!

There were oppositions and jealousies in the Keans' camp, as in most theatres, but they were never brought to my notice until I played Prince Arthur. Then I saw a great deal of Mr. Ryder, who was the Hubert of the production, and discovered that there was some soreness between him and his manager. Ryder was a very pugnacious man—an admirable actor, and in appearance like an old tree that has been struck by lightning, or a greenless, barren rock; and he was very strong in his likes and dislikes, and in his manner of expressing them.

"D'ye suppose he engaged me for my powers as an actor?" he used to say of Mr. Kean. "Not a bit of it! He engaged me for my d——d archaeological figure!"

One night during the run of "King John", a notice was put up that no curtain calls would be allowed at the end of a scene. At the end of my scene with Hubert there was tremendous applause, and when we did not appear, the audience began to shout and yell and cheer. I went off to the greenroom, but even from there I could still hear the voices: "Hubert! Arthur!" Mr. Kean began the next scene, but it was of no use. He had to give in and send for us. Meanwhile old Ryder had been striding up and down the greenroom in a perfect fury. "Never mind, ducky!" he kept on saying to me; and it was really quite unnecessary, for "ducky" was just enjoying the noise and thinking it all capital fun. "Never mind! When other people are rotting in their graves, ducky, you'll be up there!" (with a terrific gesture indicative of the dizzy heights of fame). When the message came to the greenroom that we were to take the call, he strode across the stage to the entrance, I running after him and quite unable to keep up with his long steps.

In "Macbeth" I was again associated with Ryder, who was the Banquo when I was Fleance, and I remember that after we had been dismissed by Macbeth: "Good repose the while", we had to go off up a flight of steps. I always stayed at the top until the end of the scene, but Mr. Ryder used to go down the other side rather heavily, and Mr. Kean, who wanted perfect quiet for the dagger speech, had to keep on saying: "Ssh! ssh!" all through it.

"Those carpenters at the side are enough to ruin any acting," he said one night when he came off.

"I'm a heavy man, and I can't help it," said Ryder.

"Oh, I didn't know it was *you*," said Mr. Kean—but I think he did! One night I was the innocent cause of a far worse disturbance. I dozed at the top of the steps and rolled from the top to the bottom with a fearful crash! Another night I got into trouble for not catching Mrs. Kean when, as Constance, in "King John", she sank down on to the ground.

"Here is my throne, bid kings come bow to it!"

I was, for my sins, looking at the audience, and Mrs. Kean went down with a *run*, and was naturally very angry with me!

17

In 1860 the Keans gave up the management of the Princess's Theatre and went to America. They travelled in a sailing vessel, and, being delayed by a calm, had to drink water caught in the sails, the water supply having given out. I believe that although the receipts were wonderful, Charles Kean spent much more than he made during his ten years of management. Indeed, he confessed as much in a public announcement. The Princess's Theatre was not very big, and the seats were low-priced. It is my opinion, however, that no manager with high artistic aims, resolute to carry them out in his own way, can ever make a fortune.

Of the other members of the company during my three years at the Princess's, I remember best Walter Lacy, who was the William Terriss of the time. He knew Madame Vestris, and had many entertaining stories about her. Then there were the Leclercqs, two clever sisters, Carlotta and Rose, who did great things later on. Men, women and children alike worked hard, and if the language of the actors was more Rabelaisian than polite, they were good fellows and heart and soul devoted to their profession. Their salaries were smaller and their lives were simpler than is the case with actors now.

Kate and I had been hard at work for some years, but our parents had no notion of our resting. We were now to show what our training had done for us in "A Drawing-room Entertainment".

II

ON THE ROAD

1859–1861

FROM July to September every year the leading theatres in London and
the provincial cities were closed for the summer vacation. This plan is
still adhered to more or less, but in London, at any rate, some theatres
keep their doors open all the year round. During these two months most
actors take their holiday, but when we were with the Keans we were not
in a position to afford such a luxury. Kate and I were earning good
salaries for our age,[1] but the family at home was increasing in size, and
my mother was careful not to let us think that there never could be any
rainy days. I am bound to say that I left questions of thrift, and what we
could afford and what we couldn't entirely to my parents. I received
sixpence a week pocket-money, with which I was more than content for
many years. Poor we may have been at this time, but, owing to my
mother's diligent care and cleverness, we always looked nice and neat.
One of the few early dissipations I can remember was a Christmas party
in Half Moon Street, where our white muslin dresses were equal to any
present. But more love and toil and pride than money had gone to make
them. I have a very clear vision of coming home late from the theatre to
our home in Stanhope Street, Regent's Park, and seeing my dear mother
stitching at those pretty frocks by the light of one candle. It was no
uncommon thing to find her sewing at that time, but if she was tired, she
never showed it. She was always bright and tender. With the callousness
of childhood, I scarcely realised the devotion and ceaseless care that she
bestowed on us, and her untiring efforts to bring us up as beautifully as
she could. The knowledge came to me later on when, all too early in my
life, my own responsibilities came on me and quickened my perceptions.
But I was a heartless little thing when I danced off to that party! I
remember that when the great evening came, our hair, which we still
wore down our backs, was done to perfection, and we really looked fit to
dance with a king. As things were, I *did* dance with the late Duke of
Cambridge! It was the most exciting Christmas Day of my life!

Our summer holidays as I have said, were spent at Ryde. We stayed at
Rose Cottage (for which I sought in vain when I revisited the place the

[1]Of course, all salaries are bigger now than they were then. The "stars" in old days
earned large sums—Edmund Kean received two hundred and fifty pounds for four
performances—but the ordinary members of a company were paid at a very moderate rate.
I received fifteen shillings a week at the Princess's until I played Puck, when my salary was
doubled.—E.T.

other day), and the change was pleasant, even though we were working hard. One of the pieces father gave at the theatre to amuse the summer visitors was a farce called "To Parents and Guardians". I played the fat, naughty boy Waddilove, a part which had been associated with the comedian Robson in London, and I remember that I made the unsophisticated audience shout with laughter by entering with my hands covered with jam! Father was capital as the French usher Tourbillon; and the whole thing went splendidly. Looking back, it seems rather audacious for such a child to have attempted a grown-up comedian's part, but it was excellent practice for that child! It was the success of these little summer ventures at Ryde which made my father think of our touring in "A Drawing-room Entertainment" when the Keans left the Princess's.

The entertainment consisted of two little plays "Home for the Holidays" and "Distant Relations", and they were written, I think, by a Mr. Courtney. We were engaged to do it first at the Royal Colosseum, Regent's Park, by Sir Charles Wyndham's father, Mr. Culverwell. Kate and I played all the parts in each piece, and we did quick changes at the side worthy of Fregoli! The whole thing was quite a success, and after playing it at the Colosseum we started on a round of visits.

In "Home for the Holidays", which came first on our little programme, Kate played Letitia Melrose, a young girl of about seventeen, who is expecting her young brother "home for the holidays". Letitia, if I remember right, was discovered soliloquising somewhat after this fashion: "Dear little Harry! Left all alone in the world, as we are, I feel such responsibility about him. Shall I find him changed, I wonder, after two years' absence? He has not answered my letters lately. I hope he got the cake and toffee I sent him, but I've not heard a word". At this point I entered as Harry, but instead of being the innocent little schoolboy of Letitia's fond imagination, Harry appears in loud peg-top trousers (peg-top trousers were very fashionable in 1860), with a big cigar in his mouth, and his hat worn jauntily on one side. His talk is all of racing, betting, and fighting. Letty is struck dumb with astonishment at first, but the awful change, which two years have effected, gradually dawns on her. She implores him to turn from his idle, foolish ways. Master Harry sinks on his knees by her side, but just as his sister is about to rejoice and kiss him, he looks up in her face and bursts into loud laughter. She is much exasperated, and, threatening to send some one to him who will talk to him in a very different fashion, she leaves the stage. Master Hopeful thereupon dons his dressing-gown and smoking cap, and, lying full length upon the sofa, begins to have a quiet smoke. He is interrupted by the appearance of a most wonderful and grim old woman in blue spectacles—Mrs. Terrorbody. This is no other than "Sister Letty", dressed up in order to frighten the youth out of his wits. She talks and talks, and, after painting vivid pictures of what will become of him unless he alters his "vile ways", leaves him, but not before she succeeds in making him shed tears, half of fright and half of anger. Later on, Sister Letty, looking from the window, sees a grand fight going on between Master Harry and a butcher-boy, and then Harry enters with his coat off, his sleeves tucked up, explaining in a state of blazing excitement that he "*had* to fight that butcher-boy, because he had struck a little girl in the street". Letty sees that the lad has a fine nature in spite of his folly, and appeals to his heart and the nobility of his nature — this time not in vain.

"Distant Relations" was far more inconsequent, but it served to show our versatility, at any rate. I was all things by turns, and nothing long! First I was the page boy who admitted the "relations" (Kate in many guises). Then I was a relation myself—Giles, a rustic. As Giles, I suddenly asked if the audience would like to hear me play the drum, and "obliged" with a drum solo, in which I had spent a great deal of time perfecting myself. Long before this I remember dimly some rehearsal when I was put in the orchestra and taken care of by "the gentleman who played the drum", and how badly I wanted to play it too! I afterwards took lessons from Mr. Woodhouse, the drummer at the Princess's. Kate gave an imitation of Mrs. Kean as Constance so beautifully that she used to bring tears to my eyes, and make the audience weep too.

Both of us, even at this early age, had dreams of playing all Mrs. Kean's parts. We knew the words, not only of them, but of every female part in every play in which we had appeared at the Princess's. "Walking on is so dull", the young actress says sometimes to me now, and I ask her if she knows all the parts of the play in which she is "walking on". I hardly ever find that she does. "I have no understudy", is her excuse. Even if a young woman has not been given an understudy, she ought, if she has any intention of taking her profession as an actress seriously, to constitute herself an understudy to every part in the piece! Then she would not find her time as a "super" hang heavy on her hands.

Some of my readers may be able to remember the "Stalactite Caverns" which used to form one of the attractions at the Colosseum. It was there that I first studied the words of Juliet. To me the gloomy horror of the place was a perfect godsend! Here I could cultivate a creepy, eerie sensation, and get into a fitting frame of mind for the potion scene. Down in this least imposing of subterranean abodes I used to tremble and thrill with passion and terror. Ah, if only in after years, when I played Juliet at the Lyceum, I could have thrilled an audience to the same extent!

After a few weeks at the Colosseum, we began our little tour. It was a very merry, happy time. We travelled a company of five, although only two of us were acting. There were my father and mother, Kate and myself, and Mr. Sydney Naylor, who played the very important part of orchestra. With a few exceptions we made the journeys in a carriage. Once we tramped from Bristol to Exeter. Oh, those delightful journeys on the open road! I tasted the joys of the strolling player's existence, without its miseries. I saw the country for the first time . . . When they asked me what I was thinking of as we drove along, I remember answering: "Only that I should like to run wild in a wood for ever!" At night we stayed in beautiful little inns which were ever so much more cheap and comfortable than the hotels of today. In some of the places we were asked out to tea and dinner and very much fêted. An odd little troupe we were! Father was what we will call for courtesy's sake "Stage Manager", but in reality he set the stage himself, and did the work which generally falls to the lot of the stage manager and an army of carpenters combined. My mother used to coach us up in our parts, dress us, make us go to sleep part of the day so that we might look "fresh" at night, and look after us generally. Mr. Naylor, who was not very much more than a boy, though to my childish eyes his years were quite venerable, besides discoursing eloquent music in the evenings, during the progress of the "Drawing-room Entertainment", would amuse us—me most especially— by being very entertaining himself during our journeys from place to place. How he made us laugh about—well, mostly about nothing at all.

We travelled in this way for nearly two years, visiting a new place every day, and making, I think, about ten to fifteen pounds a performance. Our little pieces were very pretty, but very slight, too; and I can only suppose that the people thought that "never anything can be amiss when simpleness and duty tender it", for they received our entertainment very well. The time had come when my little brothers had to be sent to school, and our earnings came in useful.

When the tour came to an end in 1861, I went to London with my father to find an engagement, while Kate joined the stock company at Bristol. We still gave the "Drawing-room Entertainment" at Ryde in the summer, and it still drew large audiences.

In London my name was put on an agent's books in the usual way, and presently he sent me to Madame Albina de Rhona, who had not long taken over the management of the Royal Soho Theatre and changed its name to the Royalty. The improvement did not stop at the new play. French workmen had swept and garnished the dusty, dingy place and transformed it into a theatre as dainty and pretty as Madame de Rhona herself. Dancing was Madame's strong point, but she had been very successful as an actress too, first in Paris and Petersburg, and then in London at the St. James's and Drury Lane. What made her go into management on her own account I don't know. I suppose she was ambitious, and rich enough for the enterprise.

At this time I was "in standing water", as Malvolio says of Viola when she is dressed as a boy. I was neither child nor woman—a long-legged girl of about thirteen, still in short skirts, and feeling that I ought to have long ones. However, when I set out with father to see Madame de Rhona, I

22

was very smart. I borrowed Kate's new bonnet—pink silk trimmed with black lace—and thought I looked nice in it. So did father, for he said on the way to the theatre that pink was my colour. In fact, I am sure it was the bonnet that made Madame de Rhona engage me on the spot!

She was the first Frenchwoman I had ever met, and I was tremendously interested in her. Her neat and expressive ways made me feel very "small", or rather *big* and clumsy, even at the first interview. A quick-tempered, bright, energetic little woman, she nearly frightened me out of my wits at the first rehearsal by dancing round me on the stage in a perfect frenzy of anger at what she was pleased to call my stupidity. Then something I did suddenly pleased her, and she overwhelmed me with compliments and praise. After a time these became the order of the day, and she soon won my youthful affections. "Gross flattery", as a friend of mine says, "is good enough for me!" Madame de Rhona was, moreover, very kind-hearted and generous. To her generosity I owed the first piece of jewellery I ever possessed—a pretty little brooch, which, with characteristic carelessness, I promptly lost! Besides being flattered by her praise and grateful for her kindness, I was filled with great admiration for her. She was a wee thing—like a toy, and her dancing was really exquisite. When I watched the way she moved her hands and feet, despair entered my soul. It was all so precise, so "express and admirable". Her limbs were so dainty and graceful—mine so big and unmanageable! "How long and gaunt I am," I used to say to myself, "and what a pattern of prim prettiness she is!" I was so much ashamed of my large hands, during this time at the Royalty, that I kept them tucked up under my arms! This subjected me to unmerciful criticism from Madame Albina at rehearsals.

"Take down your hands," she would call out. "*Mon Dieu!* It is like an ugly young *poulet* going to roost!"

In spite of this, I did not lose my elegant habit for many years! I was only broken of it at last by a friend saying that he supposed I had very ugly hands, as I never showed them! That did it! Out came the hands to prove that they were not so *very* ugly, after all! Vanity often succeeds where remonstrance fails.

The greenroom at the Royalty was a very pretty little place, and Madame Albina sometimes had supper-parties there after the play. One night I could not resist the pangs of curiosity, and I peeped through the keyhole to see what was going on! I chose a lucky moment! One of Madame's admirers was drinking champagne out of her slipper! It was even worth the box on the ear that mother gave me when she caught me. She had been looking all over the theatre for me, to take me home.

My first part at the Royalty was Clementine in "Attar Gull". Of the play, adapted from a story by Eugene Sue, I have a very hazy recollection, but I know that I had one very effective scene in it. Clementine, an ordinary fair-haired ingénue in white muslin, has a great horror of snakes, and, in order to cure her of her disgust, some one suggests that a dead snake should be put in her room, and she be taught how harmless the thing is for which she had such an aversion. An Indian servant, who, for some reason or other, has a deadly hatred for the whole family, substitutes a live reptile. Clementine appears at the window with the venomous creature coiled round her neck, screaming with wild terror. The spectators on the stage think that the snake is dead, and that she is only screaming from "nerves", but in reality she is being slowly strangled. I began screaming in a frantic, heartrending manner, and continued screaming, each cry surpassing the last in intensity and agony. At rehearsal I could not get these screams right for a long time. Madame de Rhona grew more and more impatient and at last flew at me like a wild-cat and shook me. I cried, just as I had done when I could not get Prince Arthur's terror right, and then the wild, agonised scream that Madame de Rhona wanted came to me. I *reproduced* it and enlarged it in effect. On the first night the audience applauded the screaming more than anything in the play. Madame de Rhona assured me that I had made a sensation, kissed me and said I was a genius! How sweet and pleasant her flattering words sounded in my young and inexperienced ears I need hardly say.

Looking back to it now, I know perfectly well why I, a mere child of thirteen, was able to give such a realistic display of horror. I had the emotional instinct to start with, no doubt, but if I did it well, it was because I was able to imagine what would be *real* in such a situation. I had never *observed* such horror, but I had previously *realised* it, when as Arthur, I had imagined the terror of having my eyes put out.

Imagination! imagination! I put it first years ago, when I was asked what qualities I thought necessary for success upon the stage. And I am still of the same opinion. Imagination, industry, and intelligence—"the three I's"—are all indispensable to the actress, but of these three the greatest is, without any doubt, imagination.

After this "screaming" success, which, however, did not keep "Attar Gull" in the bill at the Royalty for more than a few nights, I continued to play under Madame de Rhona's management until February 1862. During these few months new plays were being constantly put on, for Madame was somehow not very fortunate in gauging the taste of the public. It was in the fourth production—"The Governor's Wife", that, as Letty Briggs, I had my first experience of what is called "stage fright". I had been on the stage more than five years, and had played at least sixteen parts, so there was really no excuse for me. I suspect now that I had not taken enough pains to get word-perfect. I know I had five new parts to study between November 21 and December 26.

Stage fright is like nothing else in the world. You are standing on the stage apparently quite well and in your right mind, when suddenly you feel as if your tongue had been dislocated and was lying powerless in your mouth. Cold shivers begin to creep downwards from the nape of your neck and all up you at the same time, until they seem to meet in the small of your back. About this time you feel as if a centipede, all of whose feet have been carefully iced, has begun to run about in the roots of your hair. The next agreeable sensation is the breaking out of a cold sweat all over. Then you are certain that some one has cut the muscles at the back of your knees. Your mouth begins to open slowly, without giving utterance to a single sound, and your eyes seem inclined to jump out of your head over the footlights. At this point it is as well to get off the stage as quickly as you can, for you are far beyond human help.

Whether everybody suffers in this way or not I cannot say, but it exactly describes the torture I went through in "The Governor's Wife". I had just enough strength and sense to drag myself off the stage and seize a book, with which, after a few minutes, I reappeared and ignominiously read my part. Whether Madame de Rhona boxed my ears or not, I can't remember, but I think it is very likely she did, for she was very quick-tempered. In later years I have not suffered from the fearsome malady, but even now, after fifty years of stage-life, I never play a new part without being overcome by a terrible nervousness and a torturing dread of forgetting my lines. Every nerve in my body seems to be dancing an independent jig on its own account.

It was at the Royalty that I first acted with Mr. Kendal. He and I played together in a comedietta called "A Nice Quiet Day". Soon after, my engagement came to an end, and I went to Bristol, where I gained the experience of my life with a stock company.

LIFE IN A STOCK COMPANY

1862–1863

"I think anything, naturally written, ought to be in everybody's way that pretends to be an actor." This remark of Colley Cibber's long ago struck me as an excellent motto for beginning on the stage. The ambitious boy thinks of Hamlet, the ambitious girl of Lady Macbeth or Rosalind, but where shall we find the young actor and actress whose heart is set on being useful?

Usefulness! It is not a fascinating word, and the quality is not one of which the aspiring spirit can dream o' nights, yet on the stage it is the first thing to aim at. Not until we have learned to be useful can we afford to do what we like. The tragedian will always be a limited tragedian if he has not learned how to laugh. The comedian who cannot weep will never touch the highest levels of mirth.

It was in the stock companies that we learned the great lesson of usefulness; we played everything—tragedy, comedy, farce, and burlesque. There was no question of parts "suiting" us; we had to take what we were given.

The first time I was cast for a part in a burlesque I told the stage manager I couldn't sing and I couldn't dance. His reply was short and to the point. "You've got to do it," and so I did it in a way—a very funny way at first, no doubt. It was admirable training, for it took all the self-consciousness out of me to start with. To end with, I thought it capital fun, and enjoyed burlesque as much as Shakespeare.

What was a stock company? I forget that in these days the question may be asked in all good faith, and that it is necessary to answer it. Well, then, a stock company was a company of actors and actresses brought together by the manager of a provincial theatre to support a leading actor or actress—"a star"—from London. When Edmund Kean, the Kembles, Macready, or Mrs. Siddons visited provincial towns, these companies were ready to support them in Shakespeare. They were also ready to play burlesque, farce, and comedy to fill out the bill. Sometimes the "stars" would come for a whole season; if their magnitude were of the first order, for only one night. Sometimes they would rehearse with the stock company, sometimes they wouldn't. There is a story of a manager visiting Edmund Kean at his hotel on his arrival in a small provincial town, and asking the great actor when he would rehearse.

"Rehearse! I'm not going to rehearse—I'm going to sleep!"

"Have you any instructions?"

"Instructions! No! Tell 'em to keep at a long arm's length away from me and do their d——d worst!"

At Bristol, where I joined Mr. J. H. Chute's stock company in 1861, we had no experience of that kind, perhaps because there was no Kean alive to give it to us. And I don't think that our "worst" would have been so very bad. Mr. Chute, who had married Macready's half-sister, was a splendid manager, and he contrived to gather round him a company which was something more than "sound".

Several of its members distinguished themselves greatly in after years. Among these I may mention Miss Marie Wilton (now Lady Bancroft) and Miss Madge Robertson (now Mrs. Kendal).

Lady Bancroft had left the company before I joined it, but Mrs. Kendal was there, and so was Miss Henrietta Hodson (afterwards Mrs. Labouchere). I was much struck at that time by Mrs. Kendal's singing. Her voice was beautiful. As an example of how anything can be twisted to make mischief, I may quote here an absurd tarradiddle about Mrs. Kendal never forgetting in after years that in the Bristol stock company she had to play the singing fairy to my Titania, in "A Midsummer Night's Dream". The simple fact, of course, was that she had the best voice in the company, and was of such infinite value in singing parts that

26

no manager in his senses would have taken her out of them. There was no question of my taking precedence of her, or of her playing second fiddle to me.

Miss Hodson was a brilliant burlesque actress, a good singer, and a capital dancer. She had great personal charm, too, and was an enormous favourite with the Bristol public. I cannot exactly call her a "rival" of my sister Kate's for Kate was the "principal lady" or "star", and Henrietta Hodson the "soubrette", and, in burlesque, the "principal boy". Nevertheless, there were certainly rival factions of admirers, and the friendly antagonism between the Hodsonites and the Terryites used to amuse us all greatly.

We were petted, spoiled, and applauded to our heart's content, but I don't think it did us any harm. We all had scores of admirers, but their youthful ardour seemed to be satisfied by tracking us when we went to rehearsal in the morning and waiting for us outside the stage-door at night.

When Kate and I had a "benefit" night, they had an opportunity of coming to rather closer quarters, for on these occasions tickets could be bought from members of the company, as well as at the box-office of the theatre.

Our lodgings in Queen Square were besieged by Bristol youths who were anxious to get a glimpse of the Terrys. The Terrys demurely chatted with them and sold them tickets. My mother was most vigilant in her rôle of duenna, and from the time I first went on the stage until I was a grown woman I can never remember going home unaccompanied by either her or by my father.

The leading male members of Mr. Chute's stock company were Arthur Wood (an admirable comedian), William George Rignold, W. H. Vernon, and Charles Coghlan. At this time Charles Coghlan was acting magnificently, and dressing each of his characters so correctly and so perfectly that most of the audience did not understand it. For instance, as Glavis, in "The Lady of Lyons", he looked a picture of the Directoire fop. He did not compromise in any single detail, but wore the long straggling hair, the high cravat, the eye-glass, bows, jags, and tags, to the infinite amusement of some members of the audience, who could not imagine what his quaint dress meant. Coghlan's clothes were not more perfect than his manner, but both were a little in advance of the appreciation of Bristol playgoers in the 'sixties.

At the Princess's Theatre I had gained my experience of long rehearsals. When I arrived in Bristol I was to learn the value of short ones. Mr. Chute took me in hand, and I had to wake up and be alert with brains and body. The first part I played was Cupid in "Endymion". To this day I can remember my lines. I entered as a blind old woman in what is known in theatrical parlance as a "disguise cloak". Then, throwing it off, I said:

27

Pity the poor blind—what no one here?
Nay then, I'm not so blind as I appear,
And so to throw off all disguise and sham,
Let me at once inform you who I am!
I'm Cupid!

Henrietta Hodson as Endymion and Kate as Diana had a dance with me which used to bring down the house. I wore a short tunic which in those days was considered too scanty to be quite nice, and carried the conventional bow and quiver.

In another burlesque, "Perseus and Andromeda", I played Dictys; it was in this piece that Arthur Wood used to make people laugh by punning on the line: "Such a mystery (Miss Terry) here!" It was an absurd little joke, but the people used to cheer and applaud.

At the end of my first season at Bristol I returned to London for a time to play at the Haymarket under Mr. Buckstone, but I had another season at Bristol in the following year. While my stage education was progressing apace, I was, through the influence of a very wonderful family whose acquaintance we made, having my eyes opened to beautiful things in art and literature. Mr. Godwin, the architect and archaeologist, was living in Bristol when Kate and I were at the Theatre Royal, and we used to go to his house for some of the Shakespeare readings in which our Bristol friends asked us to take part. This house, with its Persian rugs, beautiful furniture, its organ, which for the first time I learned to love, its sense of design in every detail, was a revelation to me, and the talk of its master and mistress made me *think*. At the theatre I was living in an atmosphere which was developing my powers as an actress and teaching me what work meant, but my mind had begun to grasp dimly and almost unconsciously that I must do something for myself—something that all the education and training I was receiving in my profession could not do for me. I was fourteen years old at Bristol, but I now felt that I had never really lived at all before. For the first time I began to appreciate beauty, to observe, to feel the splendour of things, to *aspire*!

I remember that in one of the local papers there had appeared under the headline "Jottings" some very wonderful criticisms of the performances at the theatre. The writer, whoever he was, did not indulge in flattery, and in particular he attacked our classical burlesques on the ground that they were ugly. They were discussing "Jottings" one day at the Godwins' house, and Kate said it was absurd to take a burlesque so seriously. "Jottings" was all wrong.

"I don't know," said our host. "Even a burlesque can be beautiful."

Afterwards he asked me what I thought of "Jottings", and I confessed that there seemed to me a good deal of truth in what had been said. I had cut out all that he had written about us, read it several times, and thought it all very clever, most amusing—and generally right. Later on I found that Mr. Godwin and "Jottings" were one and the same!

At the Godwins' I met Mr. Barclay, Mr. Hine, William Burges the architect, and many other people who made an impression on my young mind. I accepted their lessons eagerly, and found them of the greatest value later on.

In March 1863 Mr. Chute opened the Theatre Royal, Bath, when, besides a specially written play symbolic of the event, his stock company performed "A Midsummer Night's Dream". Titania was the first Shakespeare part I had played since I left Charles Kean, but I think even in those early days I was more at home in Shakespeare than anything else. Mr. Godwin designed my dress, and we made it at his house in Bristol. He showed me how to damp it and "wring" it while it was wet, tying up the material as the Orientals do in their "tie and dry" process, so that when it was dry and untied, it was all crinkled and clinging. This was the first lovely dress that I ever wore, and I learned a great deal from it.

Almost directly after that appearance at Bath I went to London to fulfil an engagement at the Haymarket Theatre, of which Mr. Buckstone was still the manager and Sothern the great attraction. I had played Gertrude Howard in "The Little Treasure" during the stock season at Bristol, and when Mr. Buckstone wanted to do the piece at the Haymarket, he was told about me. I was fifteen at this time, and my sense of humour was as yet ill-developed. I was fond of "larking" and merry enough, but I hated being laughed *at*! At any rate, I could see no humour in Mr. Sothern's jokes at my expense. He played my lover in "The Little Treasure", and he was always teasing me—pulling my hair, making me forget my part and look like an idiot. But for dear old Mr. Howe, who was my "father" in the same piece, I should not have enjoyed acting in it at all, but he made amends for everything. We had a scene together in which he used to cry, and I used to cry—oh, it was lovely!

Why I should never have liked Sothern, with his wonderful hands and blue eyes, Sothern, whom every one found so fascinating and delightful, I cannot say, and I record it as discreditable to me, not to him. It was just a case of "I do not like thee, Dr. Fell". I admired him—I could not help doing that—but I dreaded his jokes, and thought some of them very cruel.

Another thing I thought cruel at this time was the scandal which was talked in the theatre. A change for the better has taken place in this respect—at any rate, in conduct. People behave better now, and in our profession, carried on as it is in the public eye, behaviour is everything.

At the Haymarket there were simply no bounds to what was said in the greenroom. One night I remember gathering up my skirts (we were, I think, playing "The Rivals" at the time), making a curtsey, as Mr. Chippendale, one of the best actors in old comedy I ever knew, had taught me, and sweeping out of the room with the famous line from another Sheridan play: "Ladies and gentlemen, I leave my character behind me!"

I see now that this was very priggish of me, but I am quite as uncompromising in my hatred of scandal now as I was then. Quite recently I had a line to say in "Captain Brassbound's Conversion", which is a very helpful reply to any tale-bearing. "As if any one ever knew the whole truth about anything!" That is just the point. It is only the whole truth which is informing and fair in the long run, and the whole truth is never known.

I regard my engagement at the Haymarket as one of my lost opportunities, which in after years I would have given much to have over again. I might have learned so much more than I did. I was preoccupied by events outside the theatre. Tom Taylor, who had for some time been a good friend to both Kate and me, had introduced us to Mr. Watts, the great painter, and to me the stage seemed a poor place when compared with the wonderful studio where Kate and I were painted as "The Sisters". At the Taylors' house, too, the friends, the arts, the refinements had an enormous influence on me, and for a time the theatre became almost distasteful. Never at any time in my life have I been ambitious, but at the Haymarket I was not even passionately anxious to do my best with every part that came my way—a quality which with me has been a good substitute for ambition. I was just dreaming of and aspiring after another world, a world full of pictures and music and gentle, artistic people with quiet voices and elegant manners. The reality of such a world was Little Holland House, the home of Mr. Watts.

So I confess quite frankly that I did not appreciate until it was too late, my advantages in serving at the Haymarket with comrades who were the most surpassingly fine actors and actresses in old comedy that I have ever known. There were Mr. Buckstone, the Chippendales, Mr. Compton, Mr. Farren. They one and all thoroughly understood Sheridan. Their bows, their curtseys, their grand manner, the indefinable *style* which they brought to their task were something to see. We shall never know their like again, and the smoothest old-comedy acting of this age seems rough in comparison. Of course, we suffer more with every fresh decade that separates us from Sheridan. As he gets farther and farther away, the traditions of the performances which he conducted become paler and paler. Mr Chippendale knew these traditions backwards. He might even have known Sheridan himself. Charles

Reade's mother did know him, and sat on the stage with him while he rehearsed "The School for Scandal" with Mrs. Abingdon, the original Lady Teazle in the part.

Mrs. Abingdon, according to Charles Reade, who told the story, had just delivered the line, "How dare you abuse my relations?" when Sheridan stopped the rehearsal.

"No, no, that won't do at all! It mustn't be *pettish*. That's shallow—shallow. You must go up stage with, 'You are just what my cousin Sophy said you would be,' and then turn and sweep down on him like a volcano. 'You are a great bear to abuse my relations! How *dare* you abuse my relations!'"

I want to refrain, in telling the story of my life, from praising the past at the expense of the present. It is at best the act of a fogey and always an easy thing to do, as there are so few people who can contradict one. Yet even the fear of joining hands with the people who like every country but their own, and every age except that in which they live, shall not deter me from saying that although I have seen many improvements in actors and acting since I was at the Haymarket, I have never seen artificial comedy acted as it was acted there.

Not that I was much good at it myself. I played Julia in "The Rivals" very ill; it was too difficult and subtle for me—ungrateful into the bargain—and I even made a blunder in bringing down the curtain on the first night. It fell to my lot to finish the play—in players' language, to speak the "tag". Now, it has been a superstition among actors for centuries that it is unlucky to speak the "tag" in full at rehearsal. So during the rehearsals of "The Rivals", I followed precedent and did not say the last two or three words of my part and of the play, but just "mum, mum, mum!" When the first night came, instead of dropping my voice with the last word in the conventional and proper manner, I ended with an upward inflection, which was right for the sense, but wrong for the curtain.

This unexpected innovation produced utter consternation all round me. The prompter was so much astounded that he thought there was something more coming and did not give the "pull" for the curtain to come down. There was a horrid pause while it remained up, and then Mr. Buckstone, the Bob Acres of the cast, who was very deaf and had not heard the upward inflection, exclaimed loudly and irritably: "Eh! eh! What does this mean? Why the devil don't you bring down the curtain?" And he went on cursing until it did come down. This experience made me think more than ever of the advice of an old actor: "Never leave your stage effects to *chance*, my child, but *rehearse*, and find out all about it!"

How I wished I had rehearsed that "tag" and taken the risk of being unlucky!

For the credit of my intelligence I should add that the mistake was a technical one, not a stupid one. The line was a question. It *demanded* an upward inflection; but no play can end like that.

It was not all old comedy at the Haymarket. "Much Ado About Nothing" was put on during my engagement, and I played Hero to Miss Louisa Angell's Beatrice. Miss Angell was a very modern Beatrice, but I, though I say it "as shouldn't", played Hero beautifully! I remember wondering if I should ever play Beatrice. I just *wondered*, that was all. It was the same when Miss Angell played Letitia Hardy in "The Belle's Stratagem", and I was Lady Touchwood. I just wondered! I never felt jealous of other people having bigger parts; I never looked forward consciously to a day when I should have them myself. There was no virtue in it. It was just because I wasn't ambitious.

Louise Keeley, a pretty little woman and clever, took my fancy more than any one else in the company. She was always merry and kind, and I admired her dainty, vivacious acting. In a burlesque called "Buckstone at Home" (in which I played Britannia and came up a trap in a huge pearl, which opened and disclosed me) Miss Keeley was delightful. One evening the Prince and Princess of Wales (now our King and Queen) came to see "Buckstone at Home". I believe it was the very first time they had appeared at a theatre since their marriage. They sat far back in the royal box, the ladies and gentlemen of their suite occupying the front seats. Miss Keeley, dressed as a youth, had a song in which she brought forward by the hand some well-known characters in fairy tales and nursery rhymes—Cinderella, Little Boy Blue, Jack and Jill, and so on, and introduced them to the audience in a topical verse. One verse ran:

> Here's the Prince of Happyland,
> Once he dwelt at the Lyceum;
> Here's another Prince at hand,
> But being *invisible*, you can't see him!

Probably the Prince of Wales must have wished the singer at—well, not at the Haymarket Theatre; but the next minute he must have been touched by the loyal greeting that he received. When the audience grasped the situation, every one—stalls, boxes, circle, pit, gallery—stood up and cheered and cheered again. Never was there a more extraordinary scene in a playhouse—such excitement, such enthusiasm! The action of the play came to a full stop, but not the cheers. They grew louder and louder, until the Prince came forward and bowed his acknowledgements. I doubt if any royal personage has ever been so popular in England as he was. Of course he is popular as King too, but as Prince of Wales he came nearer the people. They had more opportunity of seeing him, and they appreciated his untiring efforts to make up by his many public appearances for the seclusion in which the Queen lived.

In the middle of the run of "The American Cousin" I left the stage and married. Mary Meredith was the part, and I played it vilely. I was not quite sixteen years old, too young to be married even in those days, when every one married early. But I was delighted, and my parents were delighted, although the disparity of age between my husband and me was very great. It all seems now like a dream—not a clear dream, but a fitful one which in the morning one tries in vain to tell. And even if I could tell it, I would not. I was happy, because my face was the type which the great artist who married me loved to paint. I remember sitting to him in armour for hours and never realising that it was heavy until I fainted!

The day of my wedding it was very cold. Like most women, I always remember what I was wearing on the important occasions of my life. On that day I wore a brown silk gown which had been designed by Holman Hunt, and a quilted white bonnet with a sprig of orange-blossom, and I was wrapped in a beautiful Indian shawl. I "went away" in a sealskin jacket with coral buttons, and a little sealskin cap. I cried a great deal, and Mr. Watts said, "Don't cry. It makes your nose swell". The day I left home to be married, I "tubbed" all my little brothers and sisters and washed their fair hair.

Little Holland House, where Mr. Watts lived, seemed to me a paradise, where only beautiful things were allowed to come. All the women were graceful, and all the men were gifted. The trio of sisters—Mrs. Prinsep—(mother of the painter), Lady Somers, and Mrs. Cameron, who was the pioneer in artistic photography as we know it today—were known as Beauty, Dash, and Talent. There were two more beautiful sisters, Mrs. Jackson and Mrs. Dalrymple. Gladstone, Disraeli and Browning were among Mr. Watts's visitors. At Freshwater, where I went soon after my marriage, I first saw Tennyson.

As I write down these great names I feel almost guilty of an imposture! Such names are bound to raise high anticipations, and my recollections of the men to whom some of the names belong are so very humble.

I sat, shrinking and timid, in a corner—the girl-wife of a famous painter. I was, if I was anything at all, more of a curiosity, a side-show, than hostess to these distinguished visitors. Mr. Gladstone seemed to me like a suppressed volcano. His face was pale and calm, but the calm was the calm of the grey crust of Etna. To look into the piercing dark eyes was like having a glimpse into the red-hot crater beneath. Years later, when I met him again at the Lyceum and became better acquainted with him, this impression of a volcano at rest again struck me. Of Disraeli I carried away even a scantier impression. I remember that he wore a blue tie, a brighter blue tie than most men would dare to wear, and that his straggling curls shook as he walked. He looked the great Jew before everything. But "there is the noble Jew", as George Meredith writes somewhere, "as well as the bestial Gentile". When I first saw Henry Irving made up as Shylock, my thoughts flew back to the garden-party at Little Holland House, and Disraeli. I know I must have admired him greatly, for the only other time I ever saw him he was walking in Piccadilly, and I crossed the road, just to get a good look at him. I even went the length of bumping into him on purpose. It was a *very little* bump! My elbow just touched his, and I trembled. He took off his hat, muttered, "I beg your pardon," and passed on, not recognising me, of course; but I had had my look into his eyes. They were very quiet eyes, and didn't open wide.

I love Disraeli's novels—like his tie, brighter in colour than any one else's. It was "Venetia" which first made me see the real Lord Byron, the real Lady Byron, too. In "Tancred" I recall a description of a family of strolling players which seems to me more like the real thing than anything else of the kind in fiction. It is strange that Dizzy's novels should be neglected. Can any one with a pictorial sense fail to be delighted by their pageantry? Disraeli was a heaven-born artist, who, like so many of his race, on the stage, in music, and elsewhere, seems to have had an unerring instinct for the things which the Gentile only acquires by labour and training. The world he shows us in his novels is big and swelling, but only to a hasty judgment is it hollow.

Tennyson was more to me than a magic-lantern shape, flitting across the blank of my young experience, never to return. The first time I saw him he was sitting at the table in his library, and Mrs. Tennyson, her very slender hands hidden by thick gloves, was standing on a step-ladder handing him down some heavy books. She was very frail, and looked like a faint tea-rose. After that one time I only remember her lying on a sofa.

In the evenings I went walking with Tennyson over the fields, and he would point out to me the differences in the flight of different birds, and tell me to watch their solid phalanxes turning against the sunset, the compact wedge suddenly narrowing sharply into a thin line. He taught me to recognise the barks of trees and to call wild flowers by their names. He picked me the first bit of pimpernel I ever noticed. Always I was quite at ease with him. He was so wonderfully simple.

A hat that I wore at Freshwater suddenly comes to my remembrance. It was a brown straw mushroom with a dull red feather round it. It was tied under my chin, and I still had my hair down.

It was easy enough to me to believe that Tennyson was a poet. He showed it in everything, although he was entirely free from any assumption of the poetical rôle. That Browning, with his carefully brushed hat, smart coat, and fine society manners was a poet, always seemed to me far more incomprehensible than his poetry, which I think most people would have taken straightforwardly and read with a fair amount of ease, if certain enthusiasts had not founded societies for making his crooked places plain, and (to me) his plain places very crooked. These societies have terrorised the ordinary reader into leaving Browning alone. The same thing has been tried with Shakespeare, but fortunately the experiment in this case has proved less successful. Coroners' inquests by learned societies can't make Shakespeare a dead man.

At the time of my first marriage, when I met these great men, I had never had the advantage—I assume that it *is* an advantage!—of a single day's schooling in a *real school*. What I have learned outside my own profession I have learned from my environment. Perhaps it is this which makes me think environment more valuable than a set education, and a stronger agent in forming character even than heredity. I should have written the *externals* of character, for primal, inner feelings are, I suppose, always inherited.

Still, my want of education may be partly responsible for the unsatisfactory blankness of my early impressions. As it takes two to make a good talker, so it takes two to make a good hero—in print, at any rate. I was meeting distinguished people at every turn, and taking no notice of them. At Freshwater I was still so young that I preferred playing Indians and Knights of the Round Table with Tennyson's sons, Hallam and Lionel, and the young Camerons, to sitting indoors noticing what the poet did and said. I was mighty proud when I learned how to prepare his daily pipe for him. It was a long churchwarden, and he liked the stem to be steeped in a solution of sal volatile, or something of that kind, so that it did not stick to his lips. But he and all the others seemed to me very old. There were my young knights waiting for me; and jumping gates, climbing trees, and running paper-chases are pleasant when one is young.

It was not to inattentive ears that Tennyson read his poems. His reading was most impressive, but I think he read Browning's "Ride from Ghent to Aix" better than anything of his own, except, perhaps "The Northern Farmer". He used to preserve the monotonous rhythm of the galloping horses in Browning's poem, and made the words come out sharply like hoofs upon a road. It was a little comic until one got used to it, but that fault lay in the ear of the hearer. It was the right way and the fine way to read this particular poem, and I have never forgotten it.

In after years I met Tennyson again, when with Henry Irving I acted in two of his plays at the Lyceum. When I come to those plays, I shall have more to say of him. Gladstone, too, came into my later life. Browning I saw once or twice at dinner-parties, but knew him no better than in this early period, when I was Nelly Watts, and heedless of the greatness of great men. "To meet an angel and not to be afraid is to be impudent." I don't like to confess to it, but I think I must have been, according to this definition, *very* impudent!

One charming domestic arrangement at Freshwater was the serving of the dessert in a separate room from the rest of the dinner. And such a dessert it always was!—fruit piled high on great dishes in Veronese fashion, not the few nuts and an orange of some English households.

It must have been some years after the Freshwater days, yet before the production of "The Cup", that I saw Tennyson in his carriage outside a jeweller's shop in Bond Street.

"How very nice you look in the daytime," he said. "Not like an actress!"

I disclaimed my singularity, and said I thought actresses looked *very* nice in the daytime.

To him and to the others my early romance was always the most interesting thing about me. When I saw them in later times, it seemed as if months, not years, had passed since I was Nelly Watts.

Once, at the dictates of a conscience perhaps over fastidious, I made a bonfire of my letters. But a few were saved from the burning, more by accident than design. Among them I found yesterday a kind little note from Sir William Vernon Harcourt, which shows me that I must have known him, too, at the time of my first marriage and met him later on when I returned to the stage.

> You cannot tell how much pleased I am to hear that you have been as happy as you deserve to be. The longer one lives, the more one learns not to despair, and to believe that nothing is impossible to those who have courage and hope and youth—I was going to add beauty and genius." [*This is the sort of thing that made me blush—and burn my letters before they shamed me!*]
>
> My little boy is still the charm and consolation of my life. He is now twelve years old, and though I say it that should not, is a perfect child, and wins the hearts of all who know him.

That little boy, now in His Majesty's Government, is known as the Right Honourable Lewis Harcourt. He married an American lady, Miss Burns of New York.

Many inaccurate stories have been told of my brief married life, and I have never contradicted them—they were so manifestly absurd. Those who can imagine the surroundings into which I, a raw girl, undeveloped in all except my training as an actress, was thrown, can imagine the situation.

Of one thing I am certain. While I was with Signor— the name by which Mr. Watts was known among his friends—I never had one single pang of regret for the theatre. This may do me no credit, but it is *true*.

I wondered at the new life, and worshipped it because of its beauty. When it suddenly came to an end, I was thunderstruck; and refused at first to consent to the separation, which was arranged for me in much the same way as my marriage had been.

The whole thing was managed by those kind friends whose chief business in life seems to be the care of others. I don't blame them. There are cases where no one is to blame. "There do exist such things as honest misunderstandings," as Charles Reade was always impressing on me at a later time. There were no vulgar accusations on either side, and the words I read in the deed of separation, "incompatibility of temper"—a mere legal phrase—*more* than covered the ground. Truer still would have been "incompatibility of *occupation*", and the interference of well-meaning friends. We all suffer from that sort of thing. Pray God one be not a well-meaning friend one's self!

"The marriage was not a happy one," they will probably say after my death, and I forestall them by saying that it in many ways was very happy indeed. What bitterness there was effaced itself in a very remarkable way.

I saw Mr. Watts but once face to face after the separation. We met in the street at Brighton, and he told me that I had grown! I was never to speak to him again. But years later, after I had appeared at the Lyceum and had made some success in the world, I was in the garden of a house which adjoined Mr. Watts's new Little Holland House, and he, in his garden, saw me through the hedge. It was then that I received from him the first letter that I had had for years. In this letter he told me that he had watched my success with eager interest, and asked me to shake hands with him in spirit. "What success I may have," he wrote, "will be very incomplete and unsatisfactory if you cannot do what I have long been hesitating to ask. If you cannot, keep silence. If you can, one word, 'Yes,' will be enough."

I answered simply, "Yes".

After that he wrote to me again, and for two or three years we corresponded, but I never came into personal contact with him.

As the past is now to me like a story in a book that I once read, I can speak of it easily. But if by doing so I thought that I might give pain or embarrassment to any one else, I should be silent about this long-forgotten time. After careful consideration it does not seem to me that it can be either indiscreet or injurious to let it be known that this great artist honoured and appreciated my efforts and strife in my art; that this great man could not rid himself of the pain of feeling that he "had spoiled my life" (a chivalrous assumption of blame for what was, I think, a natural, almost inevitable, catastrophe), and that long after all personal relation had been broken off, he wrote to me gently, kindly,—

as sympathetically ignoring the strangeness of the position, as if, to use his own expression, "we stood face to face on the brink of a universal grave".

When this tender kindness was established between us he sent me a portrait-head that he had done of me when I was his wife. I think it a very beautiful picture. He did not touch it except to mend the edges, thinking it better not to try to improve it by the work of another time.

In one of these letters he writes that "there is nothing in all this that the world might not know". Surely the world is always the better for having a little truth instead of a great deal of idle inaccuracy and falsehood. That is my justification for publishing this, if justification be needed.

If I did not fulfil his too high prophecy that "in addition to your artistic eminence, I feel that you will achieve a solid social position, make yourself a great woman, and take a noble place in the history of your time", I was the better for his having made it.

If I had been able to look into the future, I should have been less rebellious at the termination of my first marriage. Was I so rebellious, after all? I am afraid I *showed* about as much rebellion as a sheep. But I was miserable, indignant, unable to understand that there could be any justice in what had happened. In a little more than two years I returned to the stage. I was practically *driven* back by those who meant to be kind—Tom Taylor, my father and mother, and others. *They* looked ahead and saw clearly it was for my good.

It *was* a good thing, but at the time I hated it. And I hated going back to live at home. Mother furnished a room for me, and I thought the furniture hideous. Poor mother!

For years Beethoven always reminded me of mending stockings, because I used to struggle with the large holes in my brothers' stockings upstairs in that ugly room, while downstairs Kate played the "Moonlight Sonata". I caught up the stitches in time to the notes! This was the period when, though every one was kind, I hated my life, hated everyone and everything in the world more than at any time before or since.

III

ROSSETTI, BERNHARDT, IRVING

1865–1867

MOST people know that Tom Taylor was one of the leading playwrights of the 'sixties as well as the dramatic critic of *The Times*, editor of *Punch*, and a distinguished Civil Servant, but to us he was more than this—he was an institution! I simply cannot remember when I did not know him. It is the Tom Taylors of the world who give children on the stage their splendid education. We never had any education in the strict sense of the word, yet, through the Taylors and others, we *were* educated. Their house in Lavender Sweep was lovely. I can hardly bear to go near that part of London now, it is so horribly changed. Where are its green fields and its chestnut-trees? We were always welcome at the Taylors', and every Sunday we heard music and met interesting people—Charles Reade among them. Mrs. Taylor had rather a hard outside—she was like Mrs. Charles Kean in that respect—and I was often frightened out of my life by her; yet I adored her. She was in reality the most tender-hearted, sympathetic woman, and what an admirable musician! She composed nearly all the music for her husband's plays. Every Sunday there was music at Lavender Sweep—quartet playing with Madame Schumann at the piano.

Tom Taylor was one of the most benign and gentle of men, a good and a loyal friend. At first he was more interested in my sister Kate's career than in mine, as was only natural; for, up to the time of my first marriage, Kate had a present, I only a future. Before we went to Bristol and played with the stock company, she had made her name. At the St. James's Theatre, in 1862, she was playing a small part in a version of Sardou's "Nos Intimes", known then as "Friends and Foes", and in a later day and in another version as "Peril".

Miss Herbert—the beautiful Miss Herbert, as she was appropriately called—had the chief part in the play (Mrs. Union), and Kate, although not the understudy, was called upon to play it at a few hours' notice. She had from childhood acquired a habit of studying every part in every play in which she was concerned, so she was as ready as though she had been the understudy. Miss Herbert was not a remarkable actress, but her appearance was wonderful indeed. She was very tall, with pale gold hair and the spiritual, ethereal look which the aesthetic movement loved. When mother wanted to flatter me very highly, she said that I looked like Miss Herbert! Rossetti founded many of his pictures on her, and she and Mrs. "Janie" Morris were his favourite types. When any one was the object of Rossetti's devotion, there was no extravagant length to which he would not go in demonstrating it. He bought a white bull because it had "eyes like Janie Morris", and tethered it on the lawn of his home in Chelsea. Soon there was no lawn left—only the bull! He invited people to meet it, and heaped favours on it until it kicked everything to pieces, when he reluctantly got rid of it.

His next purchase was a white peacock, which, very soon after its arrival, disappeared under the sofa. In vain did Rossetti "shoo" it out. It refused to budge. This went on for days.

"The lovely creature won't respond to me," said Rossetti pathetically to a friend.

The friend dragged out the bird.

"No wonder! It's *dead*!"

"Bulls don't like me," said Rossetti a few days later, "and peacocks aren't homely."

It preyed on his mind so much that he tried to repair the failure by buying some white dormice. He sat them up on tiny bamboo chairs, and they looked sweet. When the winter was over, he invited a party to meet them and congratulate them upon waking up from their long sleep.

"They are awake now," he said, "but how quiet they are! How full of repose!"

One of the guests went to inspect the dormice more closely, and a peculiar expression came over his face. It might almost have been thought that he was holding his nose.

"Wake up, little dormice," said Rossetti, prodding them gently with a quill pen.

"They'll never do *that*," said the guest. "They're *dead*. I believe they have been dead some days!"

Do you think Rossetti gave up live stock after this? Not a bit of it. He tried armadillos and tortoises.

"How are the tortoises?" he asked his man one day, after a long spell of forgetfulness that he had any.

"Pretty well, sir, thank you. . . . That's to say, sir, there ain't no tortoises!"

The tortoises, bought to eat the beetles, had been eaten themselves. At least, the shells were found full of beetles.

And the armadillos? "The air of Chelsea don't suit them," said Rossetti's servant. They had certainly left Rossetti's house, but they had not left Chelsea. All the neighbours had dozens of them! They had burrowed, and came up smiling in houses where they were far from welcome.

This by the way. Miss Herbert, who looked like the Blessed Damosel leaning out "across the bar of heaven", was not very well suited to the line of parts that she was playing at the St. James's, but she was very much admired. During the run of "Friends and Foes" she fell ill. Her illness was Kate's opportunity. From the night that Kate played Mrs. Union, her reputation was made.

It was a splendid chance, no doubt, but of what use would it have been to any one who was not ready to use it? Kate, though only about nineteen at this time, was a finished actress. She had been a perfect Ariel, a beautiful Cordelia, and had played at least forty other parts of importance since she had appeared as a tiny Robin in the Keans' production of "The Merry Wives of Windsor". She had not had her head turned by big salaries, and she had never ceased working since she was four years old. No wonder that she was capable of bearing the burden of a piece at a moment's notice. The Americans cleverly say that "the lucky cat *watches*". I should add that the lucky cat *works*. Reputations on the stage—at any rate, enduring reputations—are not made by chance, and to an actress who has not worked hard the finest opportunity in the world will be utterly useless.

My own opinion of my sister's acting must be taken for what it is worth—and that is very little. I remember how she looked on the stage—like a frail white azalea—and that her acting, unlike that of Adelaide Neilson, who was the great popular favourite before Kate came to the front, was scientific. She knew what she was about. There was more ideality than passionate womanliness in her interpretations. For this reason, perhaps, her Cordelia was finer than her Portia or her Beatrice.

She was engaged at one time to a young actor called Montagu. If the course of that love had run smooth, where should I have been? Kate would have been the Terry of the age. But Mr. Montagu went to America, and, after five years of life as a matinée idol, died there. Before that, Arthur Lewis had come along. I was glad because he was rich, and during his courtship I had some riding, of which in my girlhood I was passionately fond.

Tom Taylor had an enormous admiration for Kate, and during her second season as a "star" at Bristol he came down to see her play Juliet and Beatrice and Portia. This second Bristol season came in the middle of my time at the Haymarket, but I went back, too, and played Nerissa and Hero. Before that I had played my first leading Shakespeare part, but only at one matinée.

An actor named Walter Montgomery was giving a matinée of "Othello" at the Princess's (the theatre where I made my first appearance) in the June of 1863, and he wanted a Desdemona. The agents sent for me. It was Saturday, and I had to play it on Monday! But for my training, how could I have done it? At this time I knew the words and had *studied* the words—a very different thing—of every woman's part in Shakespeare. I don't know what kind of performance I gave on that memorable afternoon, but I think it was not so bad. And Walter Montgomery's Othello? Why can't I remember something about it? I only remember that the unfortunate actor shot himself on his wedding-day!

Any one who has come with me so far in my life will realise that Kate Terry was much better known than Ellen at the time of Ellen's first retirement from the stage. From Bristol my sister had gone to London to become Fechter's "leading lady", and from that time until she made her last appearance in 1867 as Juliet at the Adelphi, her career was a blaze of triumph.

Before I came back to take part in her farewell tour (she became engaged to Mr. Arthur Lewis in 1866), I paid my first visit to Paris. I saw the Empress Eugénie driving in the Bois, looking like an exquisite waxwork. Oh, the beautiful *slope* of women at this period! They sat like lovely half-moons, lying back in their carriages. It was an age of elegance—in France particularly—an age of luxury. They had just laid down asphalt for the first time in the streets of Paris, and the quiet of the boulevards was wonderful after the rattling London streets. I often went to three parties a night; but I was in a difficult position, as I could not speak a word of the language. I met Tissot and Gambard, who had just built Rosa Bonheur's house at Nice.

I liked the Frenchmen because they liked me, but I didn't admire them.

I tried to learn to smoke, but I never took kindly to it and soon gave it up.

What was the thing that made me homesick for London? *Household Words*. The excitement in the 'sixties over each new Dickens can be understood only by people who experienced it at the time. Boys used to sell *Household Words* in the streets, and they were often pursued by an eager crowd, for all the world as if they were carrying news of the "latest winner".

Of course I went to the theatre in Paris. I saw Sarah Bernhardt for the first time, and Madame Favart, Croisette, Delaunay, and Got. I never thought Croisette—a superb animal—a "patch" on Sarah, who was at this time as thin as a harrow. Even then I recognised that Sarah was not a bit conventional, and would not stay long at the Comédie. Yet she did not put me out of conceit with the old school. I saw "Les Précieuses Ridicules" finely done, and I said to myself then, as I have often said since: "Old school—new school? What does it matter which, so long as it is *good enough*?"

Madame Favart I knew personally, and she gave me many useful hints. One was never to black my eyes *underneath* when "making up". She pointed out that although this was necessary when the stage was lighted entirely from beneath, it had become ugly and meaningless since the introduction of top-lights.

42

The friend who took me everywhere in Paris landed me one night in the dressing-room of a singer. I remember it because I heard her complain to a man of some injustice. She had not got some engagement that she had expected.

"It serves you damn right!" he answered. "You can't sing a bit." For the first time I seemed to realise how brutal it was of a man to speak to a woman like that, and I *hated* it.

Long afterwards, in the same city, I saw a man sitting calmly in a *fiacre*, a man of the "gentlemanly" class, and ordering the *cocher* to drive on, although a woman was clinging to the side of the carriage and refusing to let go. She was a strong, splendid creature of the peasant type, bareheaded, with a fine open brow, and she was obviously consumed by resentment of some injustice—mad with it. She was dragged along in one of the busiest streets in Paris, the little Frenchman sitting there smiling, easy. How she escaped death I don't know. Then he became conscious that people were looking, and he stopped the cab and let her get in. Oh, men!

Paris! Paris! Young as I was, I fell under the spell of your elegance, your cleanness, your well-designed streets, your nonchalant gaiety. I drank coffee at Tortoni's. I visited the studio of Meissonier. I stood in the crowd that collected round Rosa Bonheur's "Horse Fair", which was in the Salon that year. I grew dead sick of the endless galleries of the Louvre. I went to the Madeleine at Easter time, all purple and white lilies, and fainted from trying to imagine ecstasy when the Host was raised . . . I never fainted again in my life, except once from *anger*, when I heard some friends whom I loved slandering another friend whom I loved more.

Good-bye to Paris and back to London, where I began acting again with only half my heart. I did very well, they said, as Helen in "The Hunchback", the first part I played after my return; but I cared nothing about my success. I was feeling wretchedly ill, and angry, too, because they insisted on putting my married name on the bills.

After playing with Kate at Bristol and at the Adelphi in London, I accepted an engagement to appear in a new play by Tom Taylor, called "The Antipodes". It was a bad play, and I had a bad part, but Telbin's scenery was lovely. Telbin was a poet, and he has handed on much of his talent to his son, who is alive now, and painted most of our Faust scenery at the Lyceum—he and dear Mr. Hawes Craven, who so loved his garden and could paint the flicker of golden sunshine for the stage better than any one. I have always been friendly with the scene-painters, perhaps because I have always taken pains about my dresses, and consulted them beforehand about the colour, so that I should not look wrong in their scenes, nor their scenes wrong with my dresses.

Telbin and Albert Moore together did up the New Queen's Theatre,

Long Acre, which was opened in October 1867, under the ostensible management of the Alfred Wigans. I say "ostensible", because Mr. Labouchere had something to do with it, and Miss Henrietta Hodson, whom he afterwards married, played in the burlesques and farces without which no theatre bill in London at that time was complete. The Wigans offered me an engagement, and I stayed with them until 1868, when I again left the stage. During this engagement I acted with Charles Wyndham and Lionel Brough, and, last but not least, with Henry Irving.

Mrs. Wigan, *née* Leonora Pincott, did me the honour to think that I was worth teaching, and took nearly as much pains to improve me as Mrs. Kean had done at a different stage in my artistic growth. Her own accomplishments as a comedy actress impressed me more than I can say. I remember seeing her as Mrs. Candour, and thinking to myself, "This is absolutely perfect". If I were a teacher I would impress on young actresses never to move a finger or turn the eye without being quite certain that the movement or the glance *tells* something. Mrs. Wigan made few gestures, but each one quietly, delicately indicated what the words which followed expressed. And while she was speaking she never frittered away the effect of that silent eloquence.

One of my besetting sins was—nay, still is—the lack of repose. Mrs. Wigan at once detected the fault, and at rehearsals would work to make me remedy it. *"Stand still!"* she would shout from the stalls. "Now you're of value!" "Motionless! Just as you are! *That's* right."

A few years later she came to see me at the Court Theatre, where I was playing in "The House of Darnley", and afterwards wrote me the following very kind and encouraging letter:

December 7, 1877.

DEAR MISS TERRY, You have a very difficult part in "The House of Darnley". I know no one who could play it as well as you did last night— but *you* could do it much better. You would vex me much if I thought you had no ambition in your art. You are the one young actress of my day who can have her success entirely in her own hands. You have all the gifts for your noble profession, and, as you know, your own devotion to it will give you all that can be learned. I'm very glad my stage direction was useful and pleasant to you, and any benefit you have derived from it is overpaid by your style of acting. You cannot have a "groove"; you are too much of an artist. Go on and prosper, and if at any time you think I can help you in your art, you may always count on that help from your most sincere well-wisher.

LEONORA WIGAN.

Another service that Mrs. Wigan did me was to cure me of "fooling" on the stage. "*Did* she?" I thought I heard some one interrupt me unkindly at that point! Well, at any rate, she gave me a good fright one night, and I never forgot it, though I will not say I never laughed again. I think it was in "The Double Marriage", the first play put on at the New Queen's. As Rose de Beaurepaire, I wore a white muslin Directoire dress and looked absurdly young. There was one "curtain" which used to convulse Wyndham. He had a line, "Whose child is this?" and there was I, looking a mere child myself, and with a bad cold in my head too, answering: "It's *bine!*" The very thought of it used to send us off into fits of laughter. We hung on to chairs, helpless, limp, and incapable. Mrs. Wigan said if we did it again, she would go in front and hiss us, and she carried out her threat. The very next time we laughed, a loud hiss rose from the stage-box. I was simply paralysed with terror.

Dear old Mrs. Wigan! The stories that have been told about her would fill a book! She was exceedingly plain, rather like a toad, yet, perversely, she was more vain of her looks than of her acting. In the theatre she gave herself great airs and graces, and outside it hobnobbed with duchesses and princesses.

This fondness for aristocratic society gave additional point to the story that one day a blear-eyed old cabman in capes and muffler descended from the box of a disreputable-looking growler, and inquired at the stage-door for Leonora Pincott.

"Any lady 'ere of that name?"

"No."

"Well, I think she's married, and changed her name, but she's 'ere right enough. Tell 'er I won't keep 'er a minute. I'm 'er —— old father!"

In "Still Waters Run Deep" I was rather good as Mrs. Mildmay, and the rest of the cast were admirable. Mrs. Wigan was, of course, Mrs. Sternhold. Wyndham, who was afterwards to be such a splendid Mildmay, played Hawksley, and Alfred Wigan was Mildmay, as he had been in the original production. When the play is revived now, much of it seems very old-fashioned, but the office scene strikes one as freshly and strongly as when it was first acted. I don't think that any drama which is vital and *essential* can ever be old-fashioned.

MY FIRST IMPRESSIONS OF HENRY IRVING

One very foggy night in December 1867—it was Boxing Day, I think— I acted for the first time with Henry Irving. This ought to have been a great event in my life, but at the time it passed me by and left "no wrack behind". Ever anxious to improve on the truth, which is often devoid of all sensationalism, people have told a story of Henry Irving promising that if he ever were in a position to offer me an engagement I

45

should be his leading lady. But this fairy story has been improved on since. The newest tale of my first meeting with Henry Irving was told during my jubilee. Then, to my amazement, I read that on the famous night when I was playing Puck at the Princess's, and caught my toe in the trap, "a young man with dark hair and a white face rushed forward from the crowd and said: 'Never mind, darling. Don't cry! One day you will be queen of the stage.' It was Henry Irving!"

In view of these legends, I ought to say all the more stoutly that, until I went to the Lyceum Theatre, Henry Irving was nothing to me and I was nothing to him. I never consciously thought that he would become a great actor. He had no high opinion of *my* acting! He has said since that he thought me at the Queen's Theatre charming and individual as a woman, but as an actress *hoydenish*! I believe that he hardly spared me even so much definite thought as this. His soul was not more surely in his body than in the theatre, and I, a woman who was at this time caring more about love and life than the theatre, must have been to him more or less unsympathetic. He thought of nothing else, cared for nothing else; worked day and night; went without his dinner to buy a book that might be helpful in studying, or a stage jewel that might be helpful to wear. I remember his telling me that he once bought a sword with a jewelled hilt, and hung it at the foot of his bed. All night he kept getting up and striking matches to see it, shifting its position, rapt in admiration of it.

He had it all in him when we acted together that foggy night, but he could express very little. Many of his defects sprang from his not having been on the stage as a child. He was stiff with self-consciousness; his eyes were dull and his face heavy. The piece we played was Garrick's boiled-down version of "The Taming of the Shrew", and he, as Petruchio, appreciated the humour and everything else far more than I did, as Katherine; yet he played badly, nearly as badly as I did; and how much more to blame I was, for I was at this time much more easy and skilful from a purely technical point of view.

Was Henry Irving impressive in those days? Yes and no. His fierce and indomitable will showed itself in his application to his work. Quite unconsciously I learned from watching him that to do work well, the artist must spend his life in incessant labour, and deny himself everything for that purpose. It is a lesson we actors and actresses cannot learn too early, for the bright and glorious heyday of our success must always be brief at best.

Henry Irving, when he played Petruchio, had been toiling in the provinces for eleven solid years, and not until Rawdon Scudamore in "Hunted Down" had he had any success. Even that was forgotten in his failure as Petruchio. What a trouncing he received from the critics who have since heaped praise on many worse men!

I think this was the peculiar quality in his acting afterwards—a kind of fine temper, like the purest steel, produced by the perpetual fight against difficulties. Socrates, it is said, had every capacity for evil in his face, yet he was good as a naturally good man could never be. Henry Irving at first had everything against him as an actor. He could not speak, he could not walk, he could not *look*. He wanted to do things in a part, and he could not do them. His amazing power was imprisoned, and only after long and weary years did he succeed in setting it free.

A man with a will like that *must* be impressive! To quick-seeing eyes he must, no doubt. But my eyes were not quick, and they were, moreover, fixed on a world outside the theatre. Better than his talent and his will I remember his courtesy. In those days, instead of having our salaries brought to our dressing-rooms, we used to wait in a queue on Treasury Day to receive them. I was always late in coming, and always in a hurry to get away. Very gravely and quietly Henry Irving used to give up his place to me.

I played once more at the Queen's after Katherine and Petruchio. It was in a little piece called "The Household Fairy", and I remember it chiefly through an accident which befell poor Jack Clayton through me. The curtain had fallen on "The Household Fairy", and Clayton, who had acted with me in it, was dancing with me on the stage to the music which was being played during the wait, instead of changing his dress for the next piece. This dancing during the entr'acte was very popular among us. Many a burlesque quadrille I had with Terriss and others in later days. On this occasion Clayton suddenly found he was late in changing, and, rushing upstairs to his dressing-room in a hurry, he missed his footing and fell back on his head. This made me very miserable, as I could not help feeling that I was responsible. Soon afterwards I left the stage for six years, without the slightest idea of ever going back. I left it without regret. And I was very happy, leading a quiet, domestic life in the heart of the country. When my two children were born, I thought of the stage less than ever. They absorbed all my time, all my interest, all my love.

IV

A SIX-YEAR VACATION

1868–1874

MY disappearance from the stage must have been a heavy blow to my father and mother, who had urged me to return in 1866 and were quite certain that I had a great future. For the first time for years they had no child in the theatre. Marion and Floss, who were afterward to adopt the stage as a profession, were still at school; Kate had married; and none of their sons had shown any great aptitude for acting. Fred, who was afterwards to do so well, was at this time hardly out of petticoats.

Perhaps it was because I knew they would oppose me that I left the stage quite quietly and secretly. It seemed to outsiders natural, if regrettable, that I should follow Kate's example. But I was troubling myself little about what people were thinking and saying. "They are saying—what are they saying? Let them be saying!"

Then a dreadful thing happened. A body was found in the river—the dead body of a young woman very fair and slight and tall. Every one thought it was my body.

I had gone away without a word. No one knew where I was. My own father identified the corpse, and Floss and Marion, at their boarding-school, were put into mourning. Then mother went. She kept her head under the shock of the likeness, and bethought her of "a strawberry mark upon my left arm". (*Really* I had one over my left knee.) That settled it, for there was no such mark to be found upon the poor corpse. It was just at this moment that the news came to me in my country retreat that I had been found dead, and I flew up to London to give ocular proof to my poor distracted parents that I was alive. Mother, who had been the only one not to identify the drowned girl, confessed to me that she was so like me that just for a second she, too, was deceived. You see, they knew I had not been very happy since my return to the stage, and when I went away without a word, they were terribly anxious, and prepared to believe the first bad tidings that came to hand. It came in the shape of that most extraordinary likeness between me and that poor soul who threw herself into the river.

I was not twenty-one when I left the stage for the second time, and I haven't made up my mind yet whether it was good or bad for me, as an actress, to cease from practising my craft for six years. Talma, the great French actor, recommends long spells of rest, and says that "perpetual indulgence in the excitement of impersonation dulls the sympathy and impairs the imaginative faculty of the comedian". This is very useful in my defence, yet I could find many examples which prove the contrary. I

48

could never imagine Henry Irving leaving the stage for six months, let alone six years, and I don't think it would have been of the slightest benefit to him. But he had not been on the stage as a child. If I was able to rest so long without rusting, it was, I am sure, because I had been thoroughly trained in the technique of acting long before I reached my twentieth year—an age at which most students are just beginning to wrestle with elementary principles.

Of course I did not argue in this way at the time! As I have said, I had no intention of ever acting again when I left the Queen's Theatre. If it is the mark of the artist to love art before everything, to renounce everything for its sake, to think all the sweet human things of life well lost if only he may attain something, do some good, great work—then I was never an artist. I have been happiest in my work when I was working for some one else. I admire those impersonal people who care for nothing outside their own ambition, yet I detest them at the same time, and I have the simplest faith that absolute devotion to another human being means the greatest *happiness*. That happiness was now mine.

I led a most unconventional life, and experienced exquisite delight from the mere fact of being in the country. No one knows what "the country" means until he or she has lived in it. "Then, if ever, come perfect days."

What a sensation it was, too, to be untrammelled by time! Actors must take care of themselves and their voices, husband their strength for the evening's work, and when it is over they are too tired to do anything! For the first time I was able to put all my energies into living. Charles Lamb says, I think, that when he left the East India House, he felt embarrassed by the vast estates of time at his disposal, and wished that he had a bailiff to manage them for him, but I knew no such embarrassment. I began gardening, "the purest of human pleasures"; I learned to cook, and in time cooked very well, though my first essay in that difficult art was rewarded with dire and complete failure.

It was a chicken! Now, as all the chickens had names—Sultan, Duke, Lord Tom Noddy, Lady Teazle, and so forth—and as I was very proud of them as living birds, it was a great wrench to kill one at all, to start with. It was the murder of Sultan, not the killing of a chicken. However, at last it was done, and Sultan deprived of his feathers, floured, and trussed. I had no idea *how* this was all done, but I tried to make him "sit up" nicely like the chickens in the shops.

He came up to the table looking magnificent—almost turkey-like in his proportions.

"Hasn't this chicken rather an odd smell?" said our visitor.

"How can you!" I answered. "It must be quite fresh—it's Sultan!"

However, when we began to carve, the smell grew more and more potent.

I had cooked Sultan without taking out his in'ards!

There was no dinner that day except bread-sauce, beautifully made, well-cooked vegetables, and pastry like the foam of the sea. I had a wonderful hand for pastry!

My hour of rising at this pleasant place near Mackery End in Hertfordshire was six. Then I washed the babies. I had a perfect mania for *washing* everything and everybody. We had one little servant, and I insisted on washing her head. Her mother came up from the village to protest.

"Never washed her head in my life. Never washed any of my children's heads. And just look at their splendid hair!"

After the washing I fed the animals. There were two hundred ducks and fowls to feed, as well as the children. By the time I had done this, and cooked the dinner, the morning had flown away. After the midday meal I sewed. Sometimes I drove out in the pony-cart. And in the evening I walked across the common to fetch the milk. The babies used to roam where they liked on this common in charge of a bulldog, while I sat and read.

I studied cookery-books instead of parts—Mrs. Beeton instead of Shakespeare!

Of course, I thought my children the most brilliant and beautiful children in the world, and, indeed, "this side idolatry", they were exceptional, and they had an exceptional bringing up. They were allowed no rubbishy picture-books, but from the first Japanese prints and fans lined their nursery walls, and Walter Crane was their classic. If injudicious friends gave the wrong sort of present, it was promptly burned! A mechanical mouse in which Edy, my little daughter, showed keen interest and delight, was taken away as being "realistic and common". Only wooden toys were allowed. This severe training proved so effective that when a doll dressed in a violent pink silk dress was given to Edy, she said it was "vulgar"!

By that time she had found a tongue, but until she was two years old she never spoke a word, though she seemed to notice everything with her grave dark eyes. We were out driving when I heard her voice for the first time:

"There's some more."

She spoke quite distinctly. It was almost uncanny.

"More what?" I asked in a trembling voice, afraid that having delivered herself once, she might lapse into dumbness.

"Birds!"

The nursemaid, Essie, described Edy tersely as "a piece", while Teddy, who was adored by every one because he was fat and fair and angelic-looking, she called "the feather of England".

"The feather of England" was considered by his sister a great coward. She used to hit him on the head with a wooden spoon for crying, and exhort him, when he said, "Master Teddy afraid of the dark," to be a *woman*!

I feel that if I go maundering on much longer about my children, some one will exclaim, with a witty and delightful author when he saw "Peter Pan" for the seventh time: "Oh, for an hour of Herod!" When I think of little Edy bringing me in minute bunches of flowers all the morning, with the reassuring intelligence that "there are lots more", I could cry. But why should any one be interested in that? Is it interesting to any one else that when she dug up a turnip in the garden for the first time, she should have come running in to beg me to come quick: "Miss Edy found a radish. It's as big as—as big as *God*!"

When I took her to her first theatre—it was Sanger's Circus—and the clown pretended to fall from the tightrope, and the drum went bang! she said: "Take me away! take me away! you ought never to have brought me here!" No wonder she was considered a dour child! I immediately and humbly obeyed.

It was truly the simple life we led in Hertfordshire. From scrubbing floors and lighting fires, cooking, gardening, and harnessing the pony, I grew thinner than ever—as thin as a whipping-post, a hurdle, or a haddock! I went to church in blue-and-white cotton, with my servant in silk. "I don't half like it," she said. "They'll take you for the cook, and me for the lady!"

We kept a goat, a dear fellow whom I liked very much until I caught him one day chasing my daughter. I seized him by his horns to inflict severe punishment; but then I saw that his eyes were exactly like mine, and it made me laugh so much that I let him go and never punished him at all.

"Boo" became an institution in these days. She was the wife of a doctor who kept a private asylum in the neighbouring village, and on his death she tried to look after the lunatics herself. But she wasn't at all successful! They kept escaping, and people didn't like it. This was my gain, for "Boo" came to look after me instead, and for the next thirty years I was her only lunatic, and she my most constant companion and dear and loyal friend.

We seldom went to London. When we did, Ted nearly had a fit at seeing so many "we'els go wound". But we went to Normandy, and saw Lisieux, Mantes, Bayeux. Long afterwards, when I was feeling as hard as sandpaper on the stage, I had only to recall some of the divine music I had heard in those great churches abroad to become soft, melted, able to act. I remember in some cathedral we left little Edy sitting down below while we climbed up into the clerestory to look at some beautiful piece of architecture. The choir were practising, and suddenly there rose a boy's voice, pure, effortless, and clear. . . . For years that moment stayed with me. When we came down to fetch Edy, she said:

"Ssh! ssh! Miss Edy has seen the angels!"

Oh, blissful quiet days! How soon they came to an end! Already the shadow of financial trouble fell across my peace. Yet still I never thought of returning to the stage.

One day I was driving in a narrow lane, when the wheel of the pony-cart came off. I was standing there, thinking what I should do next, when a whole crowd of horsemen in "pink" came leaping over the hedge into the lane. One of them stopped and asked if he could do anything. Then he looked hard at me and exclaimed: "Good God! it's Nelly!"

The man was Charles Reade.

"Where have you been all these years?" he said.

"I have been having a very happy time," I answered.

"Well, you've had it long enough. Come back to the stage!"

"No, never!"

"You're a fool! You ought to come back."

Suddenly I remembered the bailiff in the house a few miles away, and I said laughingly: "Well, perhaps I would think of it if some one would give me forty pounds a week!"

"Done!" said Charles Reade. "I'll give you that, and more, if you'll come and play Philippa Chester in 'The Wandering Heir'."

He went on to explain that Mrs. John Wood, who had been playing Philippa at the New Queen's, of which he was the lessee, would have to relinquish the part soon, because she was under contract to appear elsewhere. The piece was a great success, and promised to run a long time if he could find a good Philippa to replace Mrs. Wood. It was a kind of Rosalind part, and Charles Reade only exaggerated pardonably when he said that I should never have any part better suited to me!

In a very short time after that meeting in the lane, it was announced that the new Philippa was to be an actress who was returning to the stage "after a long period of retirement". Only just before the first night did any one guess who it was, and then there was great excitement among those who remembered me. The acclamation with which I was welcomed back on the first night surprised me. The papers were more flattering than they had ever been before. It was a tremendous success for me, and I was all the more pleased because I was following an accomplished actress in the part.

It is curious how often I have "followed" others. I never "created" a part, as theatrical parlance has it, until I played Olivia at the Court, and I had to challenge comparison, in turn, with Miss Marie Wilton, Mrs. John Wood and Mrs. Kendal. Perhaps it was better for me than if I had

had parts specially written for me, and with which no other names were associated.

The hero of "The Wandering Heir", when I first took up the part of Philippa, was played by Edmund Leathes, but afterward by Johnstone Forbes-Robertson. Every one knows how good-looking he is now, but as a boy he was wonderful—a dreamy, poetic-looking creature in a blue smock, far more of an artist than an actor—he promised to paint quite beautifully—and full of aspirations and ideals. In those days began a friendship between us which has lasted unbroken until this moment. His father and mother were delightful people, and very kind to me always.

Every one was kind to me at this time. Friends whom I had thought would be estranged by my long absence rallied round me and welcomed me as if it were six minutes instead of six years since I had dropped out of their ken. I was not yet a "made" woman, but I had a profitable engagement, and a delightful one, too, with Charles Reade, and I felt an enthusiasm for my work which had been wholly absent when I had returned to the stage the first time. My children were left in the country at first, but they came up and joined me when, in the year following "The Wandering Heir", I went to the Bancrofts at the Prince of Wales's. I never had the slightest fear of leaving them to their own devices, for they always knew how to amuse themselves, and were very independent and dependable in spite of their extreme youth. I have often thanked Heaven since that, with all their faults, my boy and girl have never been lazy and never dull. At this time Teddy always had a pencil in his hand, when he wasn't looking for his biscuit—he was a greedy little thing!—and Edy was hammering clothes on to her dolls with tin-tacks! Teddy said poetry beautifully, and when he and his sister were still tiny mites, they used to go through scene after scene of "As You like It", for their own amusement, not for an audience, in the wilderness at Hampton Court. They were by no means prodigies, but it did not surprise me that my son, when he grew up, should be first a good actor, then an artist of some originality, and should finally turn all his brains and industry to new developments in the art of the theatre. My daughter has acted also—not enough to please me, for I have a very firm belief in her talents—and has shown again and again that she can design and make clothes for the stage that are both lovely and effective. In all my most successful stage dresses lately she has had a hand, and if I had anything to do with a national theatre, I should, without prejudice, put her in charge of the wardrobe at once!

I may be a proud parent, but I have always refrained from "pushing" my children. They have had to fight for themselves, and to their mother their actual achievements have mattered very little. So long as they were not lazy, I have always felt that I could forgive them anything!

And now Teddy and Edy—Teddy in a minute white piqué suit, and Edy in a tiny kimono, in which she looked as Japanese as everything which surrounded her—disappear from these pages for quite a long time. But all this time, you must understand, they are educating their mother!

Charles Reade, having brought me back to the stage, and being my manager into the bargain, was deeply concerned about my progress as an actress. During the run of "The Wandering Heir" he used to sit in a private box every night to watch the play, and would send me round notes between the acts, telling me what I had done ill and what well in the preceding act. Dear, kind, unjust, generous, cautious, impulsive, passionate, gentle Charles Reade! Never have I known any one who combined so many qualities, far asunder as the poles, in one single disposition. He was placid and turbulent, yet always majestic. He was inexplicable and entirely lovable—a stupid old dear, and as wise as Solomon! He seemed guileless, and yet had moments of suspicion and craftiness worthy of the wisdom of the serpent. One moment he would call me "dearest child"; the next, with indignant emphasis, *"Madam!"*

When "The Wandering Heir" had at last exhausted its great popularity, I went on a tour with Charles Reade in several of his plays. In spite of his many and varied interests, he had entirely succumbed to the magic of the "irresistible theatre", and it used to strike me as rather pathetic to see a man of his power and originality working the stage sea at nights, in company with a rough lad, in his dramatic version of "Hard Cash". In this play, which was known as "Our Seamen", I had a part which I could not bear to be paid twenty-five pounds a week for acting. I knew that the tour was not a financial success, and I ventured to suggest that it would be good economy to get some one else for Susan Merton. For answer I got a fiery "Madam, you are a rat! You desert a sinking ship!" My dear old companion, Boo, who was with me, resented this very much: "How can you say such things to my Nelly?"

"Your Nelly!" said Charles Reade. "I love her a thousand times better than you do, or any puling woman." Another time he grew white with rage, and his dark eyes blazed, because the same "puling woman" said very lightly and playfully: "Why did poor Nell come home from rehearsal looking so tired yesterday? You work her too hard." He thought this unfair, as the work had to be done, and flamed out at us with such violence that it was almost impossible to identify him with the kind old gentleman of the Colonel Newcome type whom I had seen stand up at the Tom Taylors', on Sunday evenings, and sing "The Girl I Left Behind Me" with such pathos that he himself was moved to tears. But, though it was a painful time for both of us, it was almost worth while to quarrel with him, because when we made it up he was sure to give me some "treat"—a luncheon, a present, or a drive. We both felt we needed some jollification because we had suffered so much from being estranged. He used to say that there should be no such word as "quarrel", and one morning he wrote me a letter with the following postscript written in big letters:

THERE DO EXIST SUCH THINGS AS HONEST MISUNDERSTANDINGS
There, my Eleanora Delicia [this was his name for me, my real, full name being Ellen Alicia], stick that up in some place where you will often see it. Better put it on *your looking-glass*. And if you can once get those words into your noddle, it will save you a world of unhappiness.

I think he was quite right about this. Would that he had been as right in his theories about stage management! He was a rare one for realism. He had *preached* it in all his plays, and when he produced a one-act play, "Rachael the Reaper", in front of "The Wandering Heir", he began to practise what he preached—jumped into reality up to the neck!

He began by buying *real* pigs, *real* sheep, a *real* goat, and a *real* dog. *Real* litter was strewn all over the stage, much to the inconvenience of the unreal farm-labourer, Charles Kelly, who could not compete with it, although he looked as like a farmer as any actor could. They all looked their parts better than the real wall which ran across the stage, piteously naked of *real* shadows, owing to the absence of the *real* sun, and, of course, deficient in the painted shadows which make a painted wall look so like the real thing.

Never, never can I forget Charles Reade's arrival at the theatre in a four-wheeler with a goat and a lot of little pigs. When the cab drew up at the stage-door, the goat seemed to say, as plainly as any goat could: "I'm dashed if I stay in this cab any longer with these pigs!" and while Charles Reade was trying to pacify it, the piggies escaped! Unfortunately, they didn't all go in the same direction, and poor dear Charles Reade had a "divided duty". There was the goat, too, in a nasty mood. Oh, his serious face, as he decided to leave the goat and run for the pigs, with his loose trousers, each one a yard wide at least, flapping in the wind!

"That's a relief, at any rate," said Charles Kelly, who was watching the flight of the pigs. "I sha'n't have those d——d pigs to spoil my acting as well as the d——d dog and the d——d goat!"

How we all laughed when Charles Reade returned from the pig-hunt to rehearsal with the brief direction to the stage manager that the pigs would be "cut out".

The reason for the real wall was made more evident when the real goat was tied up to it. A painted wall would never have stood such a strain.

On the first night, the real dog bit Kelly's real ankles, and in real anger he kicked the real animal by a real mistake into the orchestra's real drum.

So much for realism as practised by Charles Reade! There was still something to remind him of the experiment in Rachael, the circus goat. Rachael—he was no she, but what of that?—was given the free run of the garden of Reade's house at Knightsbridge. He had everything that any normal goat could desire—a rustic stable, a green lawn, the best of food. Yet Rachael pined and grew thinner and thinner. One night when we were all sitting at dinner, with the French windows open on to the lawn because it was a hot night, Rachael came prancing into the room, looking happy, lively, and quite at home. All the time, while Charles Reade had been fashing himself to provide every sort of rural joy for his goat, the ungrateful beast had been longing for the naphtha lights of the circus, for lively conversation and the applause of the crowd.

You can't force a goat any more than you can force a child to live the simple life. "N'Yawk's the place," said the child of a Bowery tenement in New York, on the night of her return from an enforced sojourn in Arcady. She hated picking daisies, and drinking rich new milk made her sick. When the kind teacher who had brought her to the country strove to impress her by taking her to see a cow milked, she remarked witheringly to the man who was milking: "Gee! You put it in!"

Rachael's sentiments were of the same type, I think. "Back to the circus!" was his cry, not "Back to the land!"

I hope, when he felt the sawdust under his feet again (I think Charles Reade sent him back to the ring), he remembered his late master with gratitude. To how many animals, and not only four-footed ones, was not Charles Reade generously kind, and to none of them more kind than to Ellen Terry.

V

THE ACTRESS AND THE PLAYWRIGHT

THE END OF MY APPRENTICESHIP

1874

THE relation between author and actor is a very important element in the life of the stage. It is the way with some dramatists to despise those who interpret their plays, to accuse us of ruining their creations, to suffer disappointment and rage because we do not, or cannot, carry out their ideas.

Other dramatists admit that we players can teach them something; but I have noticed that it is generally in "the other fellow's" play that we can teach them, not in their own!

As they are necessary to us, and we to them, the great thing is to reduce friction by sympathy. The actor should understand that the author can be of use to him; the author, on his side, should believe that the actor can be of service to the author, and sometimes in ways which only a long and severe training in the actor's trade can discover.

The first author with whom I had to deal, at a critical point in my progress as an actress, was Charles Reade, and he helped me enormously. He might, and often did, make twelve suggestions that were wrong; but against them he would make one that was so right that its value was immeasurable and unforgettable.

It is through the dissatisfaction of a man like Charles Reade that an actress *learns*—that is, if she is not conceited. Conceit is an insuperable obstacle to all progress. On the other hand, it is of little use to take criticism in a slavish spirit and to act on it without understanding it. Charles Reade constantly wrote and said things to me which were not absolutely just criticism; but they directed my attention to the true cause of the faults which he found in my performance, and put me on the way to mending them.

A letter which he wrote me during the run of "The Wandering Heir" was such a wonderful lesson to me that I am going to quote it almost in full, in the hope that it may be a lesson to other actresses—"happy in this, they are not yet so old but they can learn"; unhappy in this, that they have never had a Charles Reade to give them a trouncing!

Well, the letter begins with sheer eulogy. Eulogy is nice, but one does not learn anything from it. Had dear Charles Reade stopped after writing "womanly grace, subtlety, delicacy, the variety yet invariable truth-fulness of the facial expression, compared with which the faces beside yours are wooden, uniform dolls," he would have done nothing to advance me in my art; but this was only the jam in which I was to take the powder!

Here followed more jam—with the first taste of the powder:

> I prefer you for my Philippa to any other actress, and shall do so still, even if you will not, or cannot, throw more vigour into the lines that need it. I do not pretend to be as good a writer of plays as you are an actress [*how naughty of him!*], but I do pretend to be a great judge of acting in general. [*He wasn't, although in particular details he was a brilliant critic and adviser.*] And I know how my own lines and business ought to be rendered infinitely better than any one else, except the Omniscient. It is only on this narrow ground I presume to teach a woman of your gifts. If I teach you Philippa, you will teach me Juliet; for I am very sure that when I have seen you act her, I shall know a vast deal more about her than I do at present.
>
> No great quality of an actress is absent from your performance. Very often you have *vigour*. But in other places where it is as much required, or even more, you turn *limp*. You have limp lines, limp business, and in Act III limp exits instead of ardent exits.

Except in the actual word used, he was perfectly right. I was not *limp*, but I was exhausted. By a natural instinct, I had produced my voice scientifically almost from the first, and I had found out for my self many things, which in these days of Delsarte systems and the science of voice-production, are taught. But when, after my six years' absence from the stage, I came back, and played a long and arduous part, I found that my breathing was still not right. This accounted for my exhaustion, or limpness and lack of vigour, as Charles Reade preferred to call it.

As for the "ardent" exits, how right he was! That word set me on the track of learning the value of moving off the stage with a swift rush. I had always had the gift of being rapid in movement, but to *have* a gift, and *to use* it, are two very different things.

I never realised that I was rather quick in movement until one day when I was sitting on a sofa talking to the famous throat specialist, Dr. Morell Mackenzie. In the middle of one of his sentences I said: "Wait a minute while I get a glass of water." I was out of the room and back so soon that he said, "Well, go and get it then!" and was paralysed when he saw that the glass was in my hand and that I was sitting down again!

Consider! That was one of Charles Reade's favourite expressions, and just hearing him say the word used to make me consider, and think, and come to conclusions—perhaps not always the conclusions that he wished, but suggested by him.

In this matter of an "ardent" exit, he wrote:

The swift rush of the words, the personal rush, should carry you off the stage. It is in reality as easy as shelling peas, if you will only go by the right method instead of by the wrong. You have overcome far greater difficulties than this, yet night after night you go on suffering ignoble defeat at this point. Come, courage! You took a leaf out of Reade's dictionary at Manchester, and trampled on two difficulties—impossibilities, you called them. That was on Saturday. Monday you knocked the poor impossibilities down. Tuesday you kicked them where they lay. Wednesday you walked placidly over their prostrate bodies!

The difficulty that he was now urging me to knock down was one of *pace*, and I am afraid that in all my stage life subsequently I never quite succeeded in kicking it or walking over its prostrate body!

Looking backward, I remember many times when I failed in rapidity of utterance, and was "pumped" at moments when swiftness was essential. Pace is the soul of comedy, and to elaborate lines at the expense of pace is disastrous. Curiously enough, I have met and envied this gift of pace in actors who were not conspicuously talented in other respects, and no Rosalind that I have ever seen has had enough of it. Of course, it is not a question of swift utterance only, but of swift thinking. I am able to think more swiftly on the stage now than at the time Charles Reade wrote to me, and I only wish I were young enough to take advantage of it. But youth thinks *slowly*, as a rule.

Vary the pace. Charles Reade was never tired of saying this, and, indeed, it is one of the foundations of all good acting.

You don't seem quite to realise [he writes in the letter before me] that uniformity of pace leads inevitably to languor. You should deliver a pistol-shot or two. Remember Philippa is a fiery girl; she can snap. If only for variety, she should snap James' head off when she says, "Do I *speak* as if I loved them!"

My memories of the part of Philippa are rather vague, but I know that Reade was right in insisting that I needed more "bite" in the passages when I was dressed as a boy. Though he complimented me on my self-denial in making what he called "some sacrifice of beauty" to pass for a boy, "so that the audience can't say, 'Why, James must be a fool not to see she is a girl,'" he scolded me for my want of bluntness.

Fix your mind on the adjective "blunt" and the substantive "pistol-shot"; they will do you good service.

They did! And I recommend them to any one who finds it hard to overcome monotony of pace and languor of diction.

When you come to tell old Surefoot about his daughter's love [the letter goes on], you should fall into a positive imitation of his manner: erect, motionless, and hands in front, and deliver your preambles with a nasal twang. But at the second invitation to speak out, you should cast this to the winds, and go into the other extreme of bluntness and rapidity. [*Quite right!*] When you meet him after the exposure, you should speak as you are coming to him and stop him in mid-career, and *then* attack him. You should also (in Act II) get the pearls back into the tree before you say: "Oh, I hope he did not see me!"

Yes, I remember that in both these places I used to muddle and blur the effect by doing the business and speaking at the same time. By acting on Reade's suggestion I gained confidence in making a pause.

After the beating, wait at least ten seconds longer than you do—to rouse expectation—and when you do come on, make a little more of it. You ought to be very pale indeed—even to enter with a slight totter, done moderately, of course; and before you say a single word, you ought to stand shaking and with your brows knitting, looking almost terrible. Of course, I do not expect or desire to make a melodramatic actress of you, but still I think you capable of any effect, provided *it is not sustained too long*.

A truer word was never spoken. It has never been in my power to *sustain*. In private life, I cannot sustain a hatred or a resentment. On the stage, I can pass swiftly from one effect to another, but I cannot fix *one*, and dwell on it, with that superb concentration which seems to me the special attribute of the tragic actress. To sustain, with me, is to lose the impression that I have created, not to increase its intensity.

The last passage of the third act is just a little too hurried. Break the line. "Now, James—for England and liberty!"

I remember that I never could see that he was right about that, and if I can't see a thing I can't do it. The author's idea must become mine before I can carry it out—at least, with any sincerity, and obedience without sincerity would be of small service to an author. It must be despairing to him, if he wants me to say a line in a certain way, to find that I always say it in another; but I can't help it. I have tried to act passages as I have been told, just *because* I was told and without conviction, and I have failed miserably and have had to go back to my own way.

Climax is reached not only by rush but by increasing pace. Your exit speech is a failure at present, because you do not vary the pace of its delivery. Get by yourself for one half-hour—if you can! Get by the seaside, if you can, since there it was Demosthenes studied eloquence and overcame mountains—not mole-hills like this. Being by the seaside, study those lines by themselves: "And then let them find their young gentleman, and find him quickly, for London shall not hold me long—no, nor England either."

Study to speak these lines with great volubility and fire, and settle the exact syllable to run at.

I remember that Reade, with characteristic generosity, gave me ten pounds and sent me to the seaside in earnest, as he suggests my doing, half in fun, in the letter. "I know you won't go otherwise," he said, "because you want to insure your life or do something of that sort. Here! go to Brighton—go anywhere by the sea for Sunday. Don't thank me! It's all for Philippa."

As I read these notes of his on anti-climax, monotony of pace, and all the other offences against scientific principles of acting which I committed in this one part, I feel more strongly than ever how important it is to master these principles. Until you have learned them and practised them you cannot afford to discard them. There is all the difference in the world between departure from recognised rules by one who has learned to obey them, and neglect of them through want of training or want of skill or want of understanding. Before you can be eccentric you must know where the circle is.

This is accepted, I am told, even in shorthand, where the pupil acquires the knowledge of a number of signs, only for the purpose of discarding them when he is proficient enough to make an individual system. It is also accepted in music, where only the advanced pianist or singer can afford to play tricks with *tempo*. And I am sure it should be accepted in acting.

Nowadays acting is less scientific (except in the matter of voice-production) than it was when I was receiving hints, cautions, and advice from my two dramatist friends, Charles Reade and Tom Taylor; and the leading principles to which they attached importance have come to be regarded as old-fashioned and superfluous. This attitude is comparatively harmless in the interpretation of those modern plays in which parts are made to fit the actors and personality is everything. But those who have been led to believe that they can make their own rules find their mistake when they come to tackle Shakespeare or any of the standard dramatists in which the actors have to fit themselves to the parts. Then, if ever, technique is avenged!

All my life the thing which has struck me as wanting on the stage is *variety*. Some people are "tone-deaf", and they find it physically impossible to observe the law of contrasts. But even a physical deficiency can be overcome by that faculty for taking infinite pains which may not be genius but is certainly a good substitute for it.

When it comes to pointing out an example, Henry Irving is the monument, the great mark set up to show the genius of *will*. For years he worked to overcome the dragging leg, which seemed to attract more attention from some small-minded critics (sharp of eye, yet how dull of vision!) than all the mental splendour of his impersonations. He toiled, and he overcame this defect, just as he overcame his disregard of the vowels and the self-consciousness which in the early stages of his career used to hamper and incommode him. His *self* was to him on a first night what the shell is to a lobster on dry land. In "Hamlet", when we first acted together after that long-ago Katherine and Petruchio period at the Queen's, he used to discuss with me the secret of my freedom from self-consciousness; and I suggested a more swift entrance on to the stage from the dressing-room. I told him that, in spite of the advantage in ease which I had gained through having been on the stage when still a mere child, I should be paralysed with fright from over-acute realisation of the audience if I stood at the wing for ten minutes, as he was in the habit of doing. He did not heed me then, nor during the run of our next play, "The Lady of Lyons"; but when it came to Shylock, a quite new part to him, he tried the experiment, and, as he told me, with great comfort to himself and success with the audience.

Only a great actor finds the difficulties of the actor's art infinite. Even up to the last five years of his life, Henry Irving was striving, striving. He never rested on old triumphs, never found a part in which there was no more to do. Once when I was touring with him in America, at the time when he was at the highest point of his fame, I watched him one day in the train—always a delightful occupation, for his face provided many pictures a minute—and being struck by a curious look, half puzzled, half despairing, asked him what he was thinking about.

"I was thinking," he answered slowly, "how strange it is that I should have made the reputation I have as an actor, with nothing to help me—no equipment. My legs, my voice—everything has been against me. For an actor who can't walk, can't talk, and has no face to speak of, I've done pretty well."

And I, looking at that splendid head, those wonderful hands, the whole strange beauty of him, thought, "Ah, you little know!"

PORTIA

1875

The brilliant story of the Bancroft management of the old Prince of Wales's Theatre was more familiar twenty years back than it is now. I think that few of the youngest playgoers who point out, on the first nights of important productions, a remarkably striking figure of a man with erect carriage, white hair, and flashing dark eyes—a man whose eye-glass, manners, and clothes all suggest Thackeray and Major Pendennis, in spite of his success in keeping abreast of everything modern—few playgoers, I say, who point this man out as Sir Squire Bancroft could give any adequate account of what he did for the English theatre in the 'seventies. Nor do the public who see an elegant little lady starting for a drive from a certain house in Berkeley Square realise that this is Marie Wilton, afterward Mrs. Bancroft, now Lady Bancroft, the comedienne who created the heroines of Tom Robertson, and, with her husband, brought what is called the cup-and-saucer drama to absolute perfection.

We players know quite well and accept with philosophy the fact that when we have done we are forgotten. We are sometimes told that we live too much in the public eye and enjoy too much public favour and attention; but at least we make up for it by leaving no trace of our short and merry reign behind us when it is over!

I have never, even in Paris, seen anything more admirable than the ensemble of the Bancroft productions. Every part in the domestic comedies, the presentation of which, up to 1875, they had made their policy, was played with such point and finish that the more rough, uneven, and emotional acting of the present day has not produced anything so good in the same line. The Prince of Wales's Theatre was the most fashionable in London, and there seemed no reason why the triumph of Robertson should not go on for ever.

But that's the strange thing about theatrical success. However great, it is limited in its force and duration, as we found out at the Lyceum twenty years later. It was not only because the Bancrofts were ambitious that they determined on a Shakespearean revival in 1875: they felt that you can give the public too much even of a good thing, and thought that a complete change might bring their theatre new popularity as well as new honour.

I, however, thought little of this at the time. After my return to the stage in "The Wandering Heir" and my tour with Charles Reade, my interest in the theatre again declined. It has always been my fate or my nature—perhaps they are really the same thing—to be very happy or very miserable. At this time I was very miserable. I was worried to death by domestic troubles and financial difficulties. The house in which I first lived in London, after I left Hertfordshire, had been dismantled of some of its most beautiful treasures by the brokers. Pressure was being put on me by well-meaning friends to leave this house and make a great change in my life. Everything was at its darkest when Mrs. Bancroft came to call on me and offered me the part of Portia in "The Merchant of Venice".

I had, of course, known her before, in the way that all people in the theatre seem to know each other, and I had seen her act; but on this day, when she came to me as a kind of messenger of Fate, the harbinger of the true dawn of my success, she should have had for me some special and extraordinary significance. I could invest that interview now with many dramatic features, but my memory, either because it is bad or because it is good, corrects my imagination.

"May I come in?"

An ordinary remark, truly, to stick in one's head for thirty-odd years! But it was made in such a *very* pretty voice—one of the most silvery voices I have ever heard from any woman except the late Queen Victoria, whose voice was like a silver stream flowing over golden stones.

The smart little figure—Mrs. Bancroft was, above all things, *petite*—dressed in black—elegant Parisian black—came into a room which had been almost completely stripped of furniture. The floor was covered with Japanese matting, and at one end was a cast of the Venus of Milo, almost the same colossal size as the original.

Mrs. Bancroft's wonderful grey eyes examined it curiously. The room, the statue, and I myself must all have seemed very strange to her. I wore a dress of some deep yellow woollen material which my little daughter used to call the "frog dress", because it was speckled with brown like a frog's skin. It was cut like a Viollet-le-Duc tabard, and had not a trace of the fashion of the time. Mrs. Bancroft, however, did not look at me less kindly because I wore aesthetic clothes and was painfully thin. She explained that they were going to put on "The Merchant of Venice" at the Prince of Wales's, that she was to rest for a while for reasons connected with her health; that she and Mr. Bancroft had thought of me for Portia!

Portia! It seemed too good to be true! I was a student when I was young. I knew not only every word of the part, but every detail of that period of Venetian splendour in which the action of the play takes place. I had studied Vecellio. Now I am old, it is impossible for me to work like that, but I never acknowledge that I get on as well without it.

Mrs. Bancroft told me that the production would be as beautiful as money and thought could make it. The artistic side of the venture was to be in the hands of Mr. Godwin, who had designed my dress for Titania at Bristol.

"Well, what do you say?" said Mrs. Bancroft. "Will you put your shoulder to the wheel with us?"

I answered incoherently and joyfully, that of all things I had been wanting most to play in Shakespeare; that in Shakespeare I had always felt I would play for half the salary; that—oh, I don't know what I said! Probably it was all very foolish and unbusinesslike, but the engagement was practically settled before Mrs. Bancroft left the house, although I was charged not to say anything about it yet.

But theatre secrets are generally *secrets de polichinelle*. When I went to Charles Reade's house at Albert Gate on the following Sunday for one of his regular Sunday parties, he came up to me at once with a knowing look and said:

"So you've got an engagement."

"I'm not to say anything about it."

"It's in Shakespeare!"

"I'm not to tell."

"But I know. I've been thinking it out. It's 'The Merchant of Venice'."

"Nothing is settled yet. It's on the cards."

"I know! I know!" said wise old Charles. "Well, you'll never have such a good part as Philippa Chester!"

"No, Nelly, never!" said Mrs. Seymour, who happened to overhear this. "They call Philippa a Rosalind part. Rosalind! Rosalind is not to be compared with it!"

Between Mrs. Seymour and Charles Reade existed a friendship of that rare sort about which it is easy for people who are not at all rare, unfortunately to say ill-natured things. Charles Reade worshipped Laura Seymour, and she understood him and sympathised with his work and his whims. She died before he did, and he never got over it. The great success of one of his last plays, "Drink", an adaptation from the French, in which Charles Warner is still thrilling audiences to this day, meant nothing to him because she was not alive to share it. The "In Memoriam" which he had inscribed over her grave is characteristic of the man, the woman, and their friendship:

HERE LIES THE GREAT HEART OF
LAURA SEYMOUR

I liked Mrs. Seymour so much that I was hurt when I found that she had instructed Charles Reade to tell Nelly Terry "not to paint her face" in the daytime, and I was young enough to enjoy revenging myself in my own way. We used to play childish games at Charles Reade's house sometimes, and with "Follow my leader" came my opportunity. I asked for a basin of water and a towel and scrubbed my face with a significant thoroughness. The rules of the game meant that every one had to follow my example! When I had dried my face I powdered it, and then darkened my eyebrows. I wished to be quite frank about the harmless little bit of artifice which Mrs. Seymour had exaggerated into a crime. She was now hoist with her own petard, for, being heavily made up, she could not and would not follow the leader. After this Charles Reade acquitted me of the use of "pigments red", but he still kept up a campaign against "Chalky", as he humorously christened my powder-puff. "Don't be pig-headed,

65

love," he wrote to me once; "it is because Chalky does not improve you that I forbid it. Trust unprejudiced and friendly eyes and drop it altogether."

Although Mrs. Seymour was naturally prejudiced where Charles Reade's work was concerned, she only spoke the truth, pardonably exaggerated, about the part of Philippa Chester. I know no part which is a patch on it for effectiveness; yet there is little in it of the stuff which endures. The play itself was too unbusinesslike ever to become a classic.

Not for years afterwards did I find out that I was not the "first choice" for Portia. The Bancrofts had tried the Kendals first, with the idea of making a double engagement; but the negotiations failed. Perhaps the rivalry between Mrs. Kendal and me might have become of more significance had she appeared as Portia at the Prince of Wales's and preferred Shakespeare to domestic comedy. In after years she played Rosalind—I never did, alas!—and quite recently acted with me in "The Merry Wives of Windsor"; but the best of her fame will always be associated with such plays as "The Squire", "The Ironmaster", "Lady Clancarty", and many more plays of that type. When she played with me in Shakespeare she laughingly challenged me to come and play with her in a modern piece, a domestic play, and I said, "Done!" but it has not been done yet, although in Mrs. Clifford's "The Likeness of the Night" there was a good medium for the experiment. I found Mrs. Kendal wonderful to act with. No other English actress has such extraordinary skill. Of course, people have said we are jealous of each other. "Ellen Terry Acts with Lifelong Enemy", proclaimed an American newspaper in five-inch type, when we played together as Mistress Page and Mistress Ford in Mr. Tree's Coronation production of "The Merry Wives of Windsor". But the enmity did not seem to worry us as much as the newspaper men over the Atlantic had represented.

It was during this engagement in 1902 that a young actor who was watching us coming in at the stage-door at His Majesty's one day is reported to have said: "Look at Mr. Tree between his two 'stars'!"

"You mean Ancient Lights!" answered the witty actress to whom the remark was made.

However, "e'en in our ashes burn our wonted fires," or, to descend from the sublime to the ridiculous, and from the poetry of Gray to the pantomime gag of Drury Lane and Herbert Campbell, "Better to be a good old has-been than a never-was-er!"

But it was long before the "has-been" days that Mrs. Kendal decided not to bring her consummately dexterous and humorous workmanship to the task of playing Portia, and left the field open for me. My fires were only just beginning to burn. Success I had had of a kind, and I had tasted the delight of knowing that audiences liked me, and had liked them back again. But never until I appeared as Portia at the Prince of Wales's had I experienced that awe-struck feeling which comes, I suppose, to no actress more than once in a life-time—the feeling of the conqueror. In homely parlance, I knew that I had "got them" at the moment when I spoke the speech beginning, "You see me, Lord Bassanio, where I stand".

"What can this be?" I thought. "*Quite* this thing has never come to me before! *This is different!* It has never been quite the same before."

It was never to be quite the same again.

Elation, triumph, being lifted on high by a single stroke of the mighty wing of glory—call it by any name, think of it as you like—it was as Portia that I had my first and last sense of it. And, while it made me happy, it made me miserable because I foresaw, as plainly as my own success, another's failure.

Charles Coghlan, an actor whose previous record was fine enough to justify his engagement as Shylock, showed that night the fatal quality of *indecision*.

A worse performance than his, carried through with decision and attack, might have succeeded, but Coghlan's Shylock was not even bad. It was *nothing*.

You could hardly hear a word he said. He spoke as though he had a sponge in his mouth, and moved as if paralysed. The perspiration poured down his face; yet what he was doing no one could guess. It was a case of moral cowardice rather than incompetency. At rehearsals no one had entirely believed in him, and this, instead of stinging him into a resolution to triumph, had made him take fright and run away.

People felt that they were witnessing a great play with a great part cut out, and "The Merchant of Venice" ran for three weeks!

It was a pity, if only because a more gorgeous and complete little spectacle had never been seen on the English stage. Veronese's "Marriage in Cana" had inspired many of the stage pictures, and the expenditure in carrying them out had been lavish.

In the casket scene I wore a dress like almond-blossom. I was very thin, but Portia and all the ideal *young* heroines of Shakespeare ought to be thin. Fat is fatal to ideality!

I played the part more stiffly and more slowly at the Prince of Wales's than I did in later years. I moved and spoke slowly. The clothes seemed to demand it, and the setting of the play developed the Italian feeling in it, and let the English Elizabethan side take care of itself. The silver casket scene with the Prince of Aragon was preserved, and so was the last act, which had hitherto been cut out in nearly all stage versions.

I have tried five or six different ways of treating Portia, but the way I think best is not the one which finds the heartiest response from my audiences. Has there ever been a dramatist, I wonder, whose parts admit of as many different interpretations as do Shakespeare's? There lies his immortality as an acting force. For times change, and parts have to be acted differently for different generations. Some parts are not sufficiently universal for this to be possible, but every ten years an actor can reconsider a Shakespeare part and find new life in it for his new purpose and new audiences.

The aesthetic craze, with all its faults, was responsible for a great deal of true enthusiasm for anything beautiful. It made people welcome the Bancrofts' production of "The Merchant of Venice" with an appreciation which took the practical form of an offer to keep the performances going by subscription, as the general public was not supporting them. Sir Frederick and Lady Pollock, James Spedding, Edwin Arnold, Sir Frederick Leighton and others made the proposal to the Bancrofts, but nothing came of it.

Short as the run of the play was, it was a wonderful time for me. Everyone seemed to be in love with me! I had sweethearts by the dozen, known and unknown. Most of the letters written to me I destroyed long ago, but the feeling of sweetness and light with which some of them filled me can never be destroyed. The task of reading and answering letters has been at heavy one all my life, but it would be ungrateful to complain of it. To some people expression is life itself. Half my letters begin: "I cannot help writing to tell you," and I believe that this is the simple truth. I, for one, should have been poorer, though my eyes might have been stronger, if they *had* been able to help it.

There turns up today, out of a long-neglected box, a charming note about "The Merchant of Venice" from some unknown friend.

"Playing to such houses," he wrote, "is not an encouraging pursuit; but to give to human beings the greatest pleasure that they are capable of receiving must always be worth doing. You have given me that pleasure, and I write to offer you my poor thanks. Portia has always been my favourite heroine, and I saw her last night as sweet and lovely as I had always hoped she might be. I hope that I shall see you again in other Shakespearean characters, and that nothing will tempt you to withhold your talents from their proper sphere."

The audiences may have been scanty, but they were wonderful. O'Shaughnessy, Watts-Dunton, Oscar Wilde, Alfred Gilbert, and, I think Swinburne were there. A poetic and artistic atmosphere pervaded the front of the house as well as the stage itself.

TOM TAYLOR AND LAVENDER SWEEP

I have read in some of the biographies of me that have been published from time to time, that I was chagrined at Coghlan's fiasco because it brought my success as Portia so soon to an end. As a matter of fact, I never thought about it. I was just sorry for clever Coghlan, who was deeply hurt and took his defeat hardly and moodily. He wiped out the public recollection of it to a great extent by his Evelyn in "Money", Sir Charles Pomander in "Masks and Faces", and Claude Melnotte in "The Lady of Lyons", which he played with me at the Princess's Theatre for one night only in the August following the withdrawal of "The Merchant of Venice".

I have been credited with great generosity for appearing in that single performance of "The Lady of Lyons". It was said that I wanted to help Coghlan reinstate himself, and so on. Very likely there was some such feeling in the matter, but there was also a good part and good remuneration! I remember that I played Lytton's proud heroine better than I did at the Lyceum five years later, and Coghlan was more successful as Melnotte than Henry Irving. But I was never really *good*. I tried in vain to have sympathy with a lady who was addressed as "haughty cousin", yet whose very pride had so much inconsistency. How could any woman fall in love with a cad like Melnotte? I used to ask myself despairingly. The very fact that I tried to understand Pauline was against me. There is only one way to play her, and to be bothered by questions of sincerity and consistency means that you will miss that way for a certainty!

I missed it, and fell between two stools. Finding that it was useless to depend upon feeling, I groped after the definite rules which had always governed the delivery of Pauline's fustian, and the fate that commonly overtakes those who try to put old wine into new bottles overtook me.

I knew for instance, exactly how the following speech ought to be done, but I never could do it. It occurs in the fourth act, where Beauseant, after Pauline has been disillusioned, thinks it will be an easy matter to induce the proud beauty to fly with him:

> Go! (*White to the lips.*) Sir, leave this house! It is humble; but a husband's roof, however lowly, is, in the eyes of God and man, the temple of a wife's honour. (*Tumultuous applause.*) Know that I would rather starve—aye, *starve*—with him who has betrayed me than accept *your* lawful hand, even were you the prince whose name he bore. (*Hurrying on quickly to prevent applause before the finish.*) Go!

It is easy to laugh at Lytton's rhetoric, but very few dramatists have had a more complete mastery of theatrical situations, and that is a good thing to be master of. Why the word "theatrical" should have come to be used in a contemptuous sense I cannot understand. "Musical" is a word of praise in music; why not "theatrical" in a theatre? A play in any age which holds the boards so continuously as "The Lady of Lyons" deserves more consideration than the ridicule of those who think that the world has moved on because our playwrights write more naturally than Lytton did. The merit of the play lay, not in its bombast, but in its situation.

Before Pauline I had played Clara Douglas in a revival of "Money", and I found her far more interesting and possible. To act the *balance* of the girl was keen enjoyment; it foreshadowed some of that greater enjoyment I was to have in after years when playing Hermione— another well-judged, well-balanced mind, a woman who is not passion's slave, who never answers on the spur of the moment, but from the depths of reason and divine comprehension. I didn't agree with Clara Douglas's sentiments, but I saw her point of view, and that was everything.

Tom Taylor, like Charles Reade, never hesitated to speak plainly to me about my acting, and, after the first night of "Money", wrote me a letter full of hints and caution and advice:

As I expected, you put feeling into every situation which gave you the opportunity, and the truth of your intention and expression seemed to bring a note of nature into the horribly sophisticated atmosphere of that hollow and most claptrappy of all Bulwerian stage offences. Nothing could be better than the appeal to Evelyn in the last act. It was sweet, womanly and earnest, and rang true in every note.

But you were nervous and uncomfortable in many parts for want of sufficient rehearsal. These passages you will, no doubt, improve in nightly. I would only urge on you the great importance of studying to be quiet and composed, and not fidgetting. There was especially a trick of constantly twiddling with and looking at your fingers which you should, above all, be on your guard against . . . I think, too, you showed too evident feeling in the earlier scene with Evelyn. A blind man must have read what you felt—your sentiment should be more masked.

Laura (Mrs. Taylor) absolutely hates the play. We both thought —— detestable in his part, false in emphasis, violent and coarse. Generally the fault of the performance was, strange to say for that theatre, overacting, want of repose, point, and finish. With you in essentials I was quite satisfied, but *quiet*—not so much movement of arms and hands. Bear this in mind for improvement, and go over your part to yourself with a view to it.

The Allinghams have been here today. They saw you twice as Portia, and were charmed. Mrs. Allingham wants to paint you. Allingham tells me that Spedding is going to write an article on your Portia, and will include Clara Douglas. I am going to see Salvini in "Hamlet" tomorrow morning, but I would call in Charlotte Street between one and two, on the chance of seeing you and talking it over, and amplifying what I have said.

Ever your true old friend,
TOM TAYLOR.

A true old friend indeed he was! I have already tried to convey how much I owed to him—how he stood by me and helped me in difficulties, and said generously and unequivocally, at the time of my separation from my first husband, that "the poor child was not to blame".

I was very fond of my own father, but in many ways Tom Taylor was more of a father to me than my father in blood. Father was charming, but Irish and irresponsible. I think he loved my sister Floss and me most because we were the lawless ones of the family! It was not in his temperament to give wise advice and counsel. Having bequeathed to me light-heartedness and a sanguine disposition, and trained me splendidly for my profession in childhood, he became in after years a very cormorant for adulation of me!

"Duchess, you might have been anything!" was his favourite comment, when I was not living up to his ideas of my position and attainments. And I used to answer: "I've played my cards for what I want."

Years afterwards, when he and mother used to come to first nights at the Lyceum, the grossest flattery of me after the performance was not good enough for them.

"How proud you must be of her!" some one would say. "How well this part suits her!"

"Yes," father would answer, in a sort of "is-that-all-you-have-to-say" tone. "But she ought to play Rosalind!"

To him I owe the gaiety of temperament which has enabled me to dance through the most harsh and desert passages of my life, just as he used to make Kate and me dance along the sordid London streets as we walked home from the Princess's Theatre. He would make us come under his cloak, partly for warmth, partly to hide from us the stages of the journey home. From the comfortable darkness one of us would cry out:

"Oh, I'm so tired! Aren't we nearly home? Where are we, father?"

"You know Schwab, the baker?"

"Yes, yes."

"Well, we're *not* there yet!"

As I grew up, this teasing, jolly, insouciant Irish father of mine was relieved of some of his paternal duties by Tom Taylor. It was not Nelly alone whom Tom Taylor fathered. He adopted the whole family.

At Lavender Sweep, with the horse-chestnut blossoms strewing the drive and making it look like a tessellated pavement, all of us were always welcome, and Tom Taylor would often come to our house and ask mother to grill him a bone! Such intimate friendships are seldom possible in our busy profession, and there was never another Tom Taylor in my life.

When we were not in London and could not go to Lavender Sweep to see him, he wrote almost daily to us. He was angry when other people criticised me, but he did not spare criticism himself.

"Don't be a Nelly Know-all," I remember his saying once. "*I* saw you floundering out of your depth tonight on the subject of butterflies! The man to whom you were talking is one of the greatest entomologists in Europe, and must have seen through you at once."

When William Black's "Madcap Violet" was published, common report said that the heroine had been drawn from Ellen Terry, and some of the reviews made Taylor furious.

"It's disgraceful! I shall deny it. Never will I let it be said of you that you could conceive any vulgarity. I shall write and contradict it. Indiscreet, high-spirited, full of surprises, you may be, but vulgar—never! I shall write at once."

"Don't do that," I said. "Can't you see that the author hasn't described me, but only me in 'New Men and Old Acres'?" As this was Tom Taylor's own play, his rage against "Madcap Violet" was very funny! "There am I, just as you wrote it. My actions, manners, and clothes in the play are all reproduced. You ought to feel pleased, not angry."

When his play "Victims" was being rehearsed at the Court Theatre, an old woman and old actress who had, I think, been in the preceding play was not wanted. The day the management gave her her dismissal, she met Taylor outside the theatre, and poured out a long story of distress. She had not a stocking to her foot, she owed her rent, she was starving. Wouldn't Mr. Taylor tell the management what dismissal meant to her? Wouldn't he get her taken back? Mr. Taylor would try, and Mr. Taylor gave her fifteen pounds in the street then and there! Mrs. Taylor wasn't surprised. She only wondered it wasn't thirty!

"Tom the Adapter" was the Terry dramatist for many years. Kate played in many of the pieces which, some openly, some deviously, he brought to the English stage from the French. When Kate married, my turn came, and the interest that he had taken in my sister's talent he transferred in part to me, although I don't think he ever thought me her equal. Floss made her first appearance in the child's part in Taylor's play "A Sheep in Wolf's Clothing", and Marion her first appearance as Ophelia in his version of "Hamlet"—perhaps "perversion" would be an honester description! Taylor introduced a "fool" who went about whacking people, including the Prince, by way of brightening up the tragedy.

I never saw my sister's Ophelia, but I know it was a fine send-off for her and that she must have looked lovely. Oh, what a pretty young girl she was! Her golden-brown eyes exactly matched her hair, and she was the winsomest thing imaginable! From the first she showed talent.

From Taylor's letters I find—and, indeed, without them I could not have forgotten—that the good, kind friend never ceased to work in our interests. "I have recommended Flossy to play Lady Betty in the country." "I have written to the Bancrofts in favour of Forbes-Robertson for Bassanio." (Evidently this was in answer to a request from me. Naturally, the Bancrofts wanted some one of higher standing, but was I wrong about J. Forbes-Robertson? I think not!) "The mother came to see me the other day. I was extremely sorry to hear the bad news of Tom." (Tom was the black sheep of our family, but a fascinating wretch, all the same.) "I rejoice to think of your coming back," he writes another time, "to show the stage what an actress should be." "A thousand thanks for the photographs. I like the profile best. It is most Paolo Veronesish and gives the right notion of your Portia, although the colour hardly suggests the golden gorgeousness of your dress and the blonde glory of the hair and complexion. . . . I hope you have seen the quiet little boxes at ——'s foolish article." (This refers to an article which attacked my Portia in *Blackwood's Magazine*.) "Of course, if —— found his ideal in —— he must dislike you in Portia, or in anything where it is a case of grace and spontaneity and Nature against affectation, over-emphasis, stilt, and false idealism—in short, utter lack of Nature. How *can* the same critic admire both? However, the public is with you, happily, as it is not always when the struggle is between good art and bad."

I quote these dear letters from my friend, not in my praise, but in his. Until his death in 1880, he never ceased to write to me sympathetically and encouragingly; he rejoiced in my success the more because he had felt himself in part responsible for my marriage and its unhappy ending, and had perhaps feared that my life would suffer. Every little detail about me and my children, or about any of my family, was of interest to him. He was never too busy to give an attentive ear to my difficulties. " 'Think of you lovingly if I can'!" he writes to me at a time when I had taken a course for which all blamed me, perhaps because they did not know enough to pardon enough—*savoir tout c'est tout pardonner*. "Can I think of you otherwise than lovingly? *Never*, if I know you and myself!"

Tom Taylor got through an enormous amount of work. Dramatic critic and art critic for *The Times*, he was also editor of *Punch* and a busy playwright. Every one who wanted an address written or a play altered came to him, and his house was a kind of Mecca for pilgrims from America and from all parts of the world. Yet he all the time occupied a position in a Government office—the Home Office, I think it was—and often walked from Whitehall to Lavender Sweep when his day's work was done. He was an enthusiastic amateur actor, his favourite part being Adam in "As You Like It", perhaps because tradition says this was a part that Shakespeare played; at any rate, he was very good in it.

Gilbert and Sullivan, in very far-off days, used to be concerned in these amateur theatricals. Their names were not associated then, but Kate and I established a prophetic link by carrying on a mild flirtation, I with Arthur Sullivan, Kate with Mr. Gilbert!

Taylor never wasted a moment. He pottered, but thought deeply all the time; and when I used to watch him plucking at his grey beard, I realised that he was just as busy as if his pen had been plucking at his paper. Many would-be writers complain that the necessity of earning a living in some other and more secure profession hinders them from achieving anything. What about Taylor at the Home Office, Charles Lamb at East India House, and Rousseau copying music for bread? It all depends on the point of view. A young lady in Chicago, who has written some charming short stories, told me how eagerly she was looking forward to the time when she would be able to give up teaching and devote herself entirely to a literary career. I wondered, and said I was never sure whether absolute freedom in such a matter *was* desirable. Perhaps Charles Lamb was all the better for being a slave to the desk for so many years.

"Ah, but then, Charles Lamb wrote so little!" was the remarkable answer.

Taylor did not write "so little". He wrote perhaps too much, and I think his heart was too strong for his brain. He was far too simple and lovable a being to be great. The atmosphere of gaiety which pervaded Lavender Sweep arose from his generous, kindly nature, which insisted that it was possible for every one to have a good time.

Once, when we were rushing to catch a train with him, Kate hanging on to one arm and I on to the other, we all three fell down the station steps. "Now, then, none of your jokes!" said a cross man behind us, who seemed to attribute our descent to rowdyism. Taylor stood up with his soft felt hat bashed over one eye, his spectacles broken, and laughed, and laughed, and laughed!

Lavender Sweep was a sort of house of call for everyone of note. Mazzini stayed there some time, and Steele Mackaye, the American actor who played that odd version of "Hamlet" at the Crystal Palace with Polly as Ophelia. Perhaps a man with more acute literary conscience than Taylor would not have condescended to "write up" Shakespeare; perhaps a man of more independence and ambition would not have wasted his really fine accomplishment as a playwright for ever on adaptations. That was his weakness—if it was a weakness. He lived entirely for his age, and so was more prominent in it than Charles Reade, for instance, whose name, no doubt, will live longer.

He put himself at the mercy of Whistler, once, in some Velasquez controversy of which I forget the details, but they are all set out, for those who like mordant ridicule, in "The Gentle Art of Making Enemies".

When Tom Taylor criticised acting he wrote as an expert, and he often said illuminating things to me about actors and actresses which I could apply over again to some of the players with whom I have been associated since. "She is a curious example," he said once of an actress of great conscientiousness, "of how far seriousness, sincerity, and weight will supply the place of almost all the other qualities of an actress." When a famous classic actress reappeared as Rosalind, he described her performance as "all minute-guns and *minauderies*, . . . a foot between every word, and the intensity of the emphasis entirely destroying all the spontaneity and flow of spirits which alone excuse and explain; . . . as unlike Shakespeare's Rosalind, I will stake my head, as human personation could be!"

There was some talk at that time (the early 'seventies) of my playing Rosalind at Manchester for Mr. Charles Calvert, and Tom Taylor urged me to do it. "Then," he said charmingly, "I can sing my stage Nunc Dimittis." The whole plan fell through, including a project for me to star as Juliet to the Romeo of a lady!

I have already said that the Taylors' home was one of the most softening and culturing influences of my early life. Would that I could give an impression of the dear host at the head of his dinner-table, dressed in black silk knee-breeches and velvet cutaway coat—a survival of a politer time, not an affectation of it—beaming on his guests with his *very* brown eyes!

Lavender is still associated in my mind with everything that is lovely and refined. My mother nearly always wore the colour, and the Taylors lived at Lavender Sweep! This may not be an excellent reason for my feelings on the subject, but it is reason good enough.

"Nature repairs her ravages," it is said, but not all. New things come into one's life—new loves, new joys, new interests, new friends—but they cannot replace the old. When Tom Taylor died, I lost a friend the like of whom I never had again.

VI

A YEAR WITH THE BANCROFTS

MY engagement with the Bancrofts lasted a little over a year. After Portia there was nothing momentous about it. I found Clara Douglas difficult, but I enjoyed playing her. I found Mabel Vane easy, and I enjoyed playing her, too, although there was less to be proud of in my success here. Almost any one could have "walked in" to victory on such very simple womanly emotion as the part demanded. At this time friends who had fallen in love with Portia used to gather at the Prince of Wales's and applaud me in a manner more vigorous than judicious. It was their fault that it got about that I had hired a claque to clap me! Now, it seems funny, but at the time I was deeply hurt at the insinuation, and it cast a shadow over what would otherwise have been a very happy time.

It is the way of the public sometimes, to keep all their enthusiasm for an actress who is doing well in a minor part, and to withhold it from the actress who is playing the leading part. I don't say for a minute that Mrs. Bancroft's Peg Woffington in "Masks and Faces" was not appreciated and applauded, but I know that my Mabel Vane was received with a warmth out of all proportion to the merits of my performance, and that this angered some of Mrs. Bancroft's admirers, and made them the bearers of ill-natured stories. Any unpleasantness that it caused between us personally was of the briefest duration. It would have been odd indeed if I had been jealous of her, or she of me. Apart from all else, I had met with my little bit of success in such a different field, and she was almost another Madame Vestris in popular esteem.

When I was playing Blanche Hayes in "Ours", I nearly killed Mrs. Bancroft with the bayonet which it was part of the business of the play for me to "fool" with. I charged as usual; either she made a mistake and moved to the right instead of to the left, or *I* made a mistake. Anyhow, I wounded her in the arm. She had to wear it in a sling, and I felt very badly about it, all the more because of the ill-natured stories of its being no accident.

Miss Marie Tempest is perhaps the actress of the present day who reminds me a little of what Mrs. Bancroft was at the Prince of Wales's, but neither nature nor art succeed in producing two actresses exactly alike. At her best Mrs. Bancroft was unapproachable. I think that the best thing that I ever saw her do was the farewell to the boy in "Sweethearts". It was exquisite!

In "Masks and Faces" Taylor and Reade had collaborated, and the exact share of each in the result was left to one's own discernment. I

76

remember saying to Taylor one night at dinner when Reade was sitting opposite me, that I wished he (Taylor) would write me a part like that. "If only I could have an original part like Peg!"

Charles Reade, after fixing me with his amused and *very* glittering eye, said across the table: "I have something for your private ear, Madam, after this repast!" And he came up *with* the ladies, sat by me, and, calling me "an artful toad"—a favourite expression of his for me!—told me that *he*, Charles Reade and no other, had written every line of Peg, and that I ought to have known it. I *didn't* know, as a matter of fact, but perhaps it was stupid of me. There was more of Tom Taylor in Mabel Vane.

I played five parts in all at the Prince of Wales's, and I think I may claim that the Bancrofts found me a *useful* actress—ever the dull height of my ambition! They wanted Byron—the author of "Our Boys"—to write me a part in the new play, which they had ordered from him, but when "Wrinkles" turned up there was no part which they felt they could offer me, and I think Coghlan was also not included in the cast. At any rate, he was free to take me to see Henry Irving act. Coghlan was always raving about Irving at this time. He said that one evening spent in watching him act was the best education an actor could have. Seeing other people act, even if they are not Irvings, is always an education to us. I have never been to a theatre yet without learning something. It must have been in the spring of 1876 that I received this note:

Will you come in our box on Tuesday for Queen Mary?
Ever yours,   CHARLES T. COGHLAN.
   P.S.—I am afraid that they will soon have to smooth their wrinkled front of the P. of W. Alas! Hélas! Ah, me!

This postscript, I think, must have referred to the approaching withdrawal of "Wrinkles" from the Prince of Wales's, and the return of Coghlan and myself to the cast.

Meanwhile, we went to see Irving's King Philip.

Well, I can only say that he never did anything better to the day of his death. Never shall I forget his expression and manner when Miss Bateman, as Queen Mary (she was *very* good, by the way), was pouring out her heart to him. The horrid, dead look, the cruel unresponsiveness, the indifference of the creature! While the poor woman protested and wept, he went on polishing up his ring! Then the tone in which he asked:

"Is dinner ready?"

It was the perfection of quiet malignity and cruelty.

The extraordinary advance that he had made since the days when we had acted together at the Queen's Theatre did not occur to me. I was just spellbound by a study in cruelty, which seemed to me a triumphant assertion of the power of the actor to create as well as to interpret, for Tennyson never suggested half what Henry Irving did.

We talk of progress, improvement, and advance; but when I think of Henry Irving's Philip, I begin to wonder if Oscar Wilde was not profound as well as witty when he said that a great artist moves in a cycle of masterpieces, of which the last is no more perfect than the first. Only Irving's Petruchio stops me. But, then, he had not found himself. He was not an artist.

"Why did Whistler paint him as Philip?" some one once asked me. How dangerous to "ask why" about any one so freakish as Jimmy Whistler. But I answered then, and would answer now, that it was because, as Philip, Henry, in his dress without much colour (from the common point of view), his long, grey legs, and Velasquez-like attitudes, looked like the kind of thing which Whistler loved to paint. Velasquez had painted a real Philip of the same race. Whistler would paint the actor who had created Philip of the stage.

I have a note from Whistler written to Henry at a later date which refers to the picture, and suggests portraying him in all his characters. It is common knowledge that the sitter never cared much about the portrait. Henry had a strange affection for the wrong pictures of himself. He disliked the Bastien Lepage, the Whistler, and the Sargent, which never even saw the light. He adored the weak, handsome picture by Millais, which I must admit, all the same, held the mirror up to one of the characteristics of Henry's face—its extreme refinement. Whistler's Philip probably seemed to him not nearly showy enough.

Whistler I knew long before he painted the Philip. He gave me the most lovely dinner-set of blue and white Nanking that any woman ever possessed and a set of Venetian glass, too good for a world where glass is broken. He sent my little girl a tiny Japanese kimono when Liberty was hardly a name. Many of his friends were my friends. He was with the dearest of those friends when he died.

The most remarkable men I have known were, without a doubt, Whistler and Oscar Wilde. This does not imply that I liked them better or admired them more than the others, but there was something about both of them more instantaneously individual and audacious than it is possible to describe.

When I went with Coghlan to see Henry Irving's Philip I was no stranger to his acting. I had been present with Tom Taylor, then dramatic critic of *The Times*, at the famous first night at the Lyceum in 1874, when Henry Irving put his fortune, counted not in gold, but in years of scorned delights and laborious days—years of constant study and reflection, of Spartan self-denial, and deep melancholy—I was present when he put it all to the touch "to win or lose it all". This is no exaggeration. Hamlet was by far the greatest part that he had ever played, or was ever to play. If he had failed—but why pursue it? He could not fail.

Yet the success on the first night at the Lyceum in 1874 was not of that electrical, almost hysterical splendour which has greeted the momentous achievements of some actors. The first two acts were received with indifference. The people could not see how packed they were with superb acting—perhaps because the new Hamlet was so simple, so quiet, so free from the exhibition of actors' artifices, which used to bring down the house in "Louis XI" and in "Richelieu", but which were really the *easy* things in acting, and in "Richelieu" (in my opinion) not especially well done. In "Hamlet" Henry Irving did not go to the audience. He made them come to him. Slowly but surely attention gave place to admiration, admiration to enthusiasm, enthusiasm to triumphant acclaim.

I have seen many Hamlets—Fechter, Charles Kean, Rossi, Frederick Haas, Forbes Robertson, and my own son, Gordon Craig, among them, but they were not in the same hemisphere! I refuse to go and see Hamlets now. I want to keep Henry Irving's fresh and clear in my memory until I die.

When he engaged me to play Ophelia in 1878 he asked me to go down to Birmingham to see the play, and that night I saw what I shall always consider the *perfection* of acting. It had been wonderful in 1874. In 1878 it was far more wonderful. It has been said that when he had the "advantage" of my Ophelia, his Hamlet "improved". I don't think so. He was always quite independent of the people with whom he acted.

The Birmingham night he knew I was there. He played—I say it without vanity—for me. We players are not above that weakness, if it be a weakness. If ever anything inspires us to do our best it is the presence in the audience of some fellow-artist who must in the nature of things know more completely than any one what we intend, what we do, what we feel. The response from such a member of the audience flies across the footlights to us like a flame. I felt it once when I played Olivia before Eleonora Duse. I felt that she felt it once when she played Marguerite Gauthier for me.

When I read "Hamlet" now, everything that Henry did in it seems to me more absolutely right, even than I thought at the time. I would give much to be able to record it all in detail, but—it may be my fault—writing is not the medium in which this can be done. Sometimes I have thought of giving readings of "Hamlet", for I can remember every tone of Henry's voice, every emphasis, every shade of meaning that he saw in the lines and made manifest to the discerning. Yes, I think I could give some pale idea of what his Hamlet was if I read the play.

"Words! words! words!" What is it to say, for instance, that the cardinal qualities of his Prince of Denmark were strength, delicacy, distinction? There was never a touch of commonness. Whatever he did or said, blood and breeding pervaded him.

His "make-up" was very pale, and this made his face beautiful when one was close to him, but at a distance it gave him a haggard look. Some said he looked twice his age.

He kept three things going at the same time—the antic madness, the sanity, the sense of the theatre. The last was to all that he imagined and thought, what charity is said by St. Paul to be to all other virtues.

He was never cross or moody—only melancholy. His melancholy was as simple as it was profound. It was touching, too, rather than defiant. You never thought that he was wantonly sad and enjoying his own misery.

He neglected no *coup de théâtre* to assist him, but who notices the servants when the host is present?

For instance, his first entrance as Hamlet was, what we call in the theatre, very much "worked up". He was always a tremendous believer in processions, and rightly. It is through such means that Royalty keeps its hold on the feeling of the public, and makes its mark as a Figure and a Symbol. Henry Irving understood this. Therefore, to music so apt that it was not remarkable in itself, but merely a contribution to the general excited anticipation, the Prince of Denmark came on to the stage. I understood later on at the Lyceum what days of patient work had gone to the making of that procession.

At its tail, when the excitement was at fever heat, came the solitary figure of Hamlet, looking extraordinarily tall and thin. The lights were turned down—another stage trick—to help the effect that the figure was spirit rather than man.

He was weary—his cloak trailed on the ground. He did *not* wear the miniature of his father obtrusively round his neck! His attitude was one which I have seen in a common little illustration to the "Reciter", compiled by Dr. Pinches (Henry Irving's old schoolmaster). Yet how right to have taken it, to have been indifferent to its humble origin! Nothing could have been better when translated into life by Irving's genius.

The hair looked blue-black, like the plumage of a crow, the eyes burning—two fires veiled as yet by melancholy. But the appearance of the man was not single, straight or obvious, as it is when I describe it—any more than his passions throughout the play were. I only remember one moment when his intensity concentrated itself in a straightforward, unmistakable emotion, without side-current or back-water. It was when he said:

80

> The play's the thing
> With which to catch the conscience of the King.

and, as the curtain came down, was seen to be writing madly on his tablets against one of the pillars.

"Oh, God, that I were a writer!" I paraphrase Beatrice with all my heart. Surely a *writer* could not string words together about Henry Irving's Hamlet and say *nothing, nothing*.

"We must start this play a living thing," he used to say at rehearsals, and he worked until the skin grew tight over his face, until he became livid with fatigue, yet still beautiful, to get the opening lines said with individuality, suggestiveness, speed, and power.

Bernardo: Who's there?
Francisco: Nay, answer me; stand, and unfold yourself.
Bernardo: Long live the King!
Francisco: Bernardo?
Bernardo: He.
Francisco: You come most carefully upon your hour.
Bernardo: 'Tis now struck twelve; get thee to bed, Francisco.
Francisco: For this relief much thanks; 'tis bitter cold. . . .

And all that he tried to make others do with these lines, he himself did with every line of his own part. Every word lived.

Some said: "Oh, Irving only makes Hamlet a love poem!" They said that, I suppose, because in the Nunnery scene with Ophelia he was the lover above the prince and the poet. With what passionate longing his hands hovered over Ophelia at her words:

Rich gifts wax poor when givers prove unkind.

His advice to the players was not advice. He did not speak it as an actor. Nearly all Hamlets in that scene give away the fact that they are actors, and not dilettanti of royal blood. Irving defined the way he would have the players speak as an *order*, an instruction of the merit of which he was regally sure. There was no patronising flavour in his acting here, not a touch of "I'll teach you how to do it". He was swift—swift and simple—pausing for the right word now and again, as in the phrase "to hold as 'twere the mirror up to nature". His slight pause and eloquent gesture as the all-embracing word "Nature" came in answer to his call, were exactly repeated unconsciously years later by the Queen of Roumania (Carmen Sylva). She was telling us the story of a play that she had written. The words rushed out swiftly, but occasionally she would wait for the one that expressed her meaning most comprehensively and exactly, and as she got it, up went her hand in triumph over her head. "Like yours in 'Hamlet'," I told Henry at the time.

I knew this Hamlet both ways—as an actress from the stage, and as an actress putting away her profession for the time as one of the audience—and both ways it was superb to me. Tennyson, I know, said it was not a perfect Hamlet. I wonder, then, where he hoped to find perfection!

James Spedding, considered a fine critic in his day, said Irving was "simply hideous . . . a monster!" Another of these fine critics declared that he never could believe in Irving's Hamlet after having seen "*part* (sic) of his performance as a murderer in a commonplace melodrama". Would one believe that any one could seriously write so stupidly as that about the earnest effort of an earnest actor, if it were not quoted by some of Irving's biographers?

Some criticism, however severe, however misguided, remains within the bounds of justice, but what is one to think of the *Quarterly* Reviewer who declared that "the enormous pains taken with the scenery had ensured Mr. Irving's success"? The scenery was of the simplest—no money was spent on it even when the play was revived at the Lyceum after Colonel Bateman's death. Henry's dress probably cost him about £2!

My Ophelia dress was made of material which could not have cost more than 2*s.* a yard, and not many yards were wanted, as I was at the time thin to vanishing point! I have the dress still, and, looking at it the other day, I wondered what leading lady now would consent to wear it.

At all its best points, Henry's Hamlet was susceptible of absurd imitation. Think of this well, young actors, who are content to play for safety, to avoid ridicule at all costs, to be "natural"—oh, word most vilely abused! What sort of *naturalness* is this of Hamlet's?

O, villain, villain, smiling damned villain!

Henry Irving's imitators could make people burst with laughter when they took off his delivery of that line. And, indeed, the original, too, was almost provocative of laughter—rightly so, for such emotional indignation has its funny as well as its terrible aspect. The mad, and all are mad who have, as Socrates put it, "a divine release from the common ways of men," may speak ludicrously, even when they speak the truth.

All great acting has a certain strain of extravagance which the imitators catch hold of and give us the eccentric body without the sublime soul.

From the first I saw this extravagance, this bizarrerie in Henry

Irving's acting. I noticed, too, its infinite variety. In "Hamlet", during the first scene with Horatio, Marcellus and Bernardo, he began by being very absent and distant. He exchanged greetings sweetly and gently, but he was the visionary. His feet might be on the ground, but his head was towards the stars "where the eternal are". Years later he said to me of another actor in "Hamlet": "*He* would never have seen the ghost." Well, there was never any doubt that Henry Irving saw it, and it was through his acting in the Horatio scene that he made us sure.

As a bad actor befogs Shakespeare's meaning, so a good actor illuminates it. Bit by bit as Horatio talks, Hamlet comes back into the world. He is still out of it when he says:

My father! Methinks I see my father.

But the dreamer becomes attentive, sharp as a needle, with the words:

For God's love, let me hear.

Irving's face, as he listened to Horatio's tale, blazed with intelligence. He cross-examined the men with keenness and authority. His mental deductions as they answered were clearly shown. With "I would I had been there" the cloud of unseen witnesses with whom he had before been communing again descended. For a second or two Horatio and the rest did not exist for him . . . So onward to the crowning couplet:

. . . foul deeds will rise,
Though all the earth o'erwhelm them to men's eyes.

After having been very quiet and rapid, very discreet, he pronounced these lines in a loud, clear voice, dragged out every syllable as if there never could be an end to his horror and his rage.

I had been familiar with the scene from my childhood—I had studied it; I had heard from my father how Macready acted in it, and now I found that I had had a *fool* of an idea of it! That's the advantage of study, good people, who go to see Shakespeare acted. It makes you know sometimes what is being done, and what you never dreamed would be done when you read the scene at home.

As one of the audience I was much struck by Irving's treatment of interjections and exclamations in "Hamlet". He breathed the line: "O, that this too, too solid flesh would melt," as one long yearning, and, "O horrible, O horrible! most horrible!" as a groan. When we first went to America his address at Harvard touched on this very subject, and it may be interesting to know that what he preached in 1885 he had practised as far back as 1874.

On the question of pronunciation, there is something to be said which I think in ordinary teaching is not sufficiently considered. Pronunciation should be simple and unaffected, but not always fashioned rigidly according to a dictionary standard. No less an authority than Cicero points out that pronunciation must vary widely according to the emotions to be expressed; that it may be broken or cut with a varying or direct sound, and that it serves for the actor the purpose of colour to the painter, from which to draw variations. Take the simplest illustration. The formal pronunciation of A-h is 'Ah', of O-h, 'Oh', but you cannot stereotype the expression of emotion like this. These exclamations are words of one syllable, but the speaker who is sounding the gamut of human feeling will not be restricted in his pronunciation by dictionary rule. It is said of Edmund Kean that he never spoke such ejaculations, but always sighed or groaned them. Fancy an actor saying:

"My Desdemona! Oh! oh! oh!"

Words are intended to express feelings and ideas, not to bind them in rigid fetters; the accents of pleasure are different from the accents of pain, and if a feeling is more accurately expressed as in nature by a variation of sound not provided by the laws of pronunciation, then such imperfect laws must be disregarded and nature vindicated!

It was of the address in which these words occur that a Boston hearer said that it was felt by every one present that "the truth had been spoken by a man who had learned it through living and not through theory".

I leave his Hamlet for the present with one further reflection. It was in *courtesy* and *humour* that it differed most widely from other Hamlets that I have seen and heard of. This Hamlet was never rude to Polonius. His attitude towards the old Bromide (I thank you, Mr. Gelett Burgess, for teaching me that word which so lightly and charmingly describes the child of darkness and of platitude) was that of one who should say: "You dear, funny old simpleton, whom I have had to bear with all my life—how terribly in the way you seem now." With what slightly amused and cynical playfulness this Hamlet said: "I had thought some of Nature's journeymen had made men and not made them well; they imitated humanity so abominably."

Hamlet was by far his greatest triumph, although he would not admit it himself—preferring in some moods to declare that his finest work was done in Macbeth, which was almost universally disliked.

When I went with Coghlan to see Irving's Philip, this "Hamlet" digression may have suggested that I was not in the least surprised at what I saw. Being a person little given to dreaming, and always living wholly in the present, it did not occur to me to wonder if I should ever act with this marvellous man. He was not at this time lessee of the Lyceum—Colonel Bateman was still alive—and I looked no further than my engagement at the Prince of Wales's, although in a few months it was to come to an end.

Although I was now earning a good salary, I still lived in lodgings at Camden Town, took an omnibus to and from the theatre, and denied myself all luxuries. I did not take a house until I went to the Court Theatre. It was then, too, that I had my first cottage—a wee place at Hampton Court where my children were very happy. They used to give performances of "As You Like It" for the benefit of the Palace custodians—old Crimean veterans, most of them—and when the children had grown up these old men would still ask affectionately after "little Miss Edy" and "Master Teddy", forgetting the passing of time.

My little daughter was a very severe critic! I think if I had listened to her, I should have left the stage in despair. She saw me act for the first time as Mabel Vane, but no compliments were to be extracted from her.

"You *did* look long and thin in your grey dress."

"When you fainted I thought you was going to fall into the orchestra—you was so *long*."

In "New Men and Old Acres" I had to play the piano while I conducted a conversation consisting on my side chiefly of haughty remarks to the effect that "blood would tell," to talk naturally and play at the same time. I "shied" at the lines, became self-conscious, and either sang the words or altered the rhythm of the tune to suit the pace of the speech. I grew anxious about it, and was always practising it at home. After much hard work Edy used to wither me with:

"*That's* not right!"

Teddy was of a more flattering disposition, but very obstinate when he chose. I remember "wrestling" with him for hours over a little Blake poem which he had learned by heart, to say to his mother:

> When the voices of children are heard on the green,
> And laughing is heard on the hill,
> My heart is at rest within my breast,
> And everything else is still.
> Then come home, my children, the sun is gone down,
> And the dews of the night arise.
> Come, come, leave off play, and let us away,
> Till morning appears in the skies.

No, no, let us play, for yet it is day,
And we cannot go to sleep.
Besides, in the sky the little birds fly,
And the hills are all covered with sheep. . . .

All went well until the last line. Then he came to a stop.
Nothing would make him say sheep!
With a face beaming with anxiety to please, looking adorable, he
would offer any word but the right one.
"And the hills are all covered with ——"
"With what, Teddy?"
"Master Teddy don't know."
"Something white, Teddy."
"Snow?"
"No, no—does snow rhyme with 'sleep'?"
"Paper?"
"No, no. Now, I am not going to the theatre until you say the right
word. What are the hills covered with?"
"People."
"Teddy, you're a very naughty boy."
At this point he was put in the corner. His first suggestion when he
came out was:
"Grass? Trees?"
"Are grass or trees white?" said the despairing mother with her eye on
the clock, which warned her that, after all, she would have to go to the
theatre without winning.
Meanwhile, Edy was murmuring: "*Sheep*, Teddy," in a loud aside,
but Teddy would *not* say it, not even when both he and I burst into tears!
At Hampton Court the two children, dressed in blue and white check
pinafores, their hair closely cropped—the little boy fat and fair (at this
time he bore a remarkable resemblance to Laurence's portrait of the
youthful King of Rome), the little girl thin and dark—ran as wild as
though the desert had been their playground instead of the gardens of
this old palace of kings! They were always ready to show visitors (not so
numerous then as now) the sights; prattled freely to them of "my
mamma," who was acting in London, and showed them the new trees
which they had assisted the gardeners to plant in the wild garden, and
christened after my parts. A silver birch was Iolanthe, a maple Portia, an
oak Mabel Vane. Through their kind offices many a stranger found it
easy to follow the intricacies of the famous Maze. It was a fine life for
them, surely, this unrestricted running to and fro in the gardens, with
the great Palace as a civilising influence!
It was for their sake that I was most glad of my increasing prosperity in
my profession. My engagement with the Bancrofts was exchanged at the

close of the summer season of 1876 for an even more popular one with Mr. John Hare at the Court Theatre, Sloane Square.

I had learned a great deal at the Prince of Wales's, notably that the art of playing in modern plays in a tiny theatre was quite different from the art of playing in the classics in a big theatre. The methods for big and little theatres are alike, yet quite unlike. I had learned breadth in Shakespeare at the Princess's, and had had to employ it again in romantic plays for Charles Reade. The pit and gallery were the audience which we had to reach. At the Prince of Wales's I had to adopt a more delicate, more subtle, more intimate style. But the breadth had to be there just the same—as seen through the wrong end of the microscope. In acting one must possess great strength before one can be delicate in the right way. Too often weakness is mistaken for delicacy.

Mr. Hare was one of the best stage managers that I have met during the whole of my long experience in the theatre. He was snappy in manner, extremely irritable if anything went wrong, but he knew what he wanted, and he got it. No one has ever surpassed him in the securing of a perfect *ensemble*. He was the Meissonier among the theatre artists. Very likely he would have failed if he had been called upon to produce "King John", but what better witness to his talent than that he knew his line and stuck to it?

The members of his company were his, body and soul, while they were rehearsing. He gave them fifteen minutes for lunch, and any actor or actress who was foolish or unlucky enough to be a minute late, was sorry afterwards. Mr. Hare was peppery and irascible, and lost his temper easily.

Personally, I always got on well with my new manager, and I ought to be grateful to him, if only because he gave me the second great opportunity of my career—the part of Olivia in Wills's play from "The Vicar of Wakefield". During this engagement at the Court I married again. I had met Charles Wardell, whose stage name was Kelly, when he was acting in "Rachael the Reaper" for Charles Reade. At the Court we played together in several pieces. He had not been bred an actor, but a soldier. He was in the 66th Regiment, and had fought in the Crimean War; been wounded, too—no carpet knight. His father was a clergyman, vicar of Winlaton, Northumberland—a charming type of the old-fashioned parson, a friendship with Sir Walter Scott in the background, and many little possessions of the great Sir Walter's in the foreground to remind one of what had been.

Charlie Kelly, owing to his lack of training, had to be very carefully suited with a part before he shone as an actor. But when he was suited— his line was the bluff, hearty, kindly, soldier-like Englishman—he was better than many people who had twenty years' start of him in experience. This is absurdly faint praise. In such parts as Mr. Brown in "New

87

Men and Old Acres", the farmer father in "Dora", Diogenes in "Iris", no one could have bettered him. His most ambitious attempt was Benedick, which he played with me when I first appeared as Beatrice at Leeds. It was in many respects a splendid performance, and perhaps better for the play than the more polished, thoughtful, and deliberate Benedick of Henry Irving.

Physically a manly, bulldog sort of a man, Charles Kelly possessed as an actor great tenderness and humour. It was foolish of him to refuse the part of Burchell in "Olivia", in which he would have made a success equal to that achieved by Terriss as the Squire. But he was piqued at not being cast for the Vicar, which he could not have played well, and stubbornly refused to play Burchell.

Alas! many actors are just as blind to their true interests.

We were married in 1876, and after I left the Court Theatre for the Lyceum, we continued to tour together in the provinces during the vacation time when the Lyceum was closed. These tours were very successful, but I never worked harder in my life! When we played "Dora" at Liverpool, Charles Reade, who had adapted the play from Tennyson's poem, wrote:

> Nincompoop!
> What have you to fear from me for such a masterly performance! Be assured nobody can appreciate your value and Mr. Kelly's as I do. It is well played all round.

VII

EARLY DAYS AT THE LYCEUM

I<small>T</small> is humiliating to me to confess that I have not the faintest recollection of "Brothers", the play by Coghlan, in which I see by the evidence of an old play-bill that I made my first appearance under Mr. Hare's management. I remember another play by Coghlan, in which Henry Kemble made one of his early appearances in the part of a butler, and how funny he was, even in those days, in a struggle to get rid of a pet monkey—a "property" monkey made of brown wool with no "devil" in it, except that supplied by the comedian's imagination. We trusted to our acting, not to real monkeys and real dogs to bring us through, and when the acting was Henry Kemble's, it was good enough to rely upon!

Charles Coghlan seems to have been consistently unlucky. Yet he was a good actor and a brilliant man. I always enjoyed his companionship; found him a pleasant, natural fellow, absorbed in his work, and not at all the "dangerous" man that some people represented him.

Within less than a month from the date of the production of "Brothers", "New Men and Old Acres" was put into the Court bill. It was not a new play, but the public at once began to crowd to see it, and I have heard that it brought Mr. Hare £30,000. My part, Lilian Vavasour, had been played in the original production by Mrs. Kendal, but it had been written for me by Tom Taylor when I was at the Haymarket, and it suited me very well. The revival was well acted all round. Charles Kelly was splendid as Mr. Brown, and Mr. Hare played a small part perfectly.

H. B. Conway, a young actor whose good looks were talked of everywhere, was also in the cast. He was a descendant of Lord Byron's, and had a look of the *handsomest* portraits of the poet. With his bright hair curling tightly all over his well-shaped head, his beautiful figure, and charming presence, Conway created a sensation in the 'eighties almost equal to that made by the more famous beauty, Lillie Langtry.

As an actor he belonged to the Terriss type, but he was not nearly as good as Terriss. Of his extraordinary failure in the Lyceum "Faust" I shall say something when I come to the Lyceum productions.

After "New Men and Old Acres", Mr. Hare tried a posthumous play by Lord Lytton—"The House of Darnley". It was *not* a good play, and I was *not* good in it, although the pleasant adulation of some of my friends has made me out so. The play met with some success, and during its run Mr. Hare commissioned Wills to write "Olivia".

I had known Wills before this through the Forbes-Robertsons. He was at one time engaged to one of the girls, but it was a good thing it ended in smoke. With all his charm, Wills was not cut out for a husband. He was

Irish all over—the strangest mixture of the aristocrat and the sloven. He could eat a large raw onion every night like any peasant, yet his ideas were magnificent and instinct with refinement.

A true Bohemian in money matters, he made a great deal out of his plays—and never had a farthing to bless himself with!

In the theatre he was charming—from an actor's point of view. He interfered very little with the stage management, and did not care to sit in the stalls and criticise. But he would come quietly to me and tell me things which were most illuminating, and he paid me the compliment of weeping at the wing while I rehearsed "Olivia".

I was generally weeping, too, for Olivia, more than any part, touched me to the heart. I cried too much in it, just as I cried too much later on in the Nunnery scene in "Hamlet", and in the last act of "Charles I". My real tears on the stage have astonished some people, and have been the envy of others, but they have often been a hindrance to me. I have had to *work* to restrain them.

Oddly enough, although "Olivia" was such a great success at the Court, it has never made much money since. The play could pack a tiny theatre; it could never appeal in a big way to the masses. In itself it had a sure message—the love story of an injured woman is one of the cards in the stage pack which it is always safe to play—but against this there was a bad last act, one of the worst I have ever acted in. It was always being tinkered with, but patching and alteration only seems to weaken it.

Mr. Hare produced "Olivia" perfectly. Marcus Stone designed the clothes, and I found my dresses—both faithful and charming as reproductions of the eighteenth-century spirit—stood the advance of time and the progress of ideas when I played the part later at the Lyceum. I had not to alter anything. Henry Irving discovered the same thing about the scenery and stage management. They could not be improved upon. There was very little scenery at the Court, but a great deal of taste and care in selection.

Every one was "Olivia" mad. The Olivia cap shared public favour with the Langtry bonnet. That most lovely and exquisite creature, Mrs. Langtry, could not go out anywhere, at the dawn of the 'eighties, without a crowd collecting to look at her! It was no rare thing to see the crowd, to ask its cause, to receive the answer, "Mrs. Langtry!" and to look in vain for the object of the crowd's admiring curiosity.

This was all the more remarkable, and honourable to public taste, too, because Mrs. Langtry's was not a showy beauty. Her hair was the colour that it had pleased God to make it; her complexion was her own; in evening dress she did not display nearly as much of her neck and arms as was the vogue, yet they outshone all other necks and arms through their own perfection.

"No worker has a right to criticise *publicly* the work of another in the same field," Henry Irving once said to me, and Heaven forbid that I should disregard advice so wise! I am aware that the professional critics and the public did not transfer to Mrs. Langtry the actress the homage that they had paid to Mrs. Langtry the beauty, but I can only speak of the simplicity with which she approached her work, of her industry, and utter lack of vanity about her powers. When she played Rosalind (which my daughter, the best critic of acting *I* know, tells me was in many respects admirable), she wrote to me:

> DEAR NELLIE, I bundled through my part somehow last night, a disgraceful performance, and *no* waist-padding! Oh, what an impudent wretch you must think me to attempt such a part! I pinched my arm once or twice last night to see if it was really me. It was so sweet of you to write me such a nice letter, and then a telegram, too!
>
> Yours ever, dear Nell,
> LILLIE.
>
> P.S.—I am rehearsing, all day—"The Honeymoon" next week. I love the hard work, and the thinking and study.

Just at this time there was a great dearth on the stage of people with lovely diction, and Lillie Langtry had it. I can imagine that she spoke Rosalind's lines beautifully, and that her clear grey eyes and frank manner, too well-bred to be hoydenish, must have been of great value.

To go back to "Olivia". Like all Hare's plays, it was perfectly cast. Where all were good, it will be admitted, I think, by every one who saw the production, that Terriss was the best. "As you stand there, whipping your boot, you look the very picture of vain indifference," Olivia says to Squire Thornhill in the first act, and never did I say it without thinking how absolutely *to the life* Terriss realised that description.

As I look back, I remember no figure in the theatre more remarkable than Terriss. He was one of those heaven-born actors who, like kings by divine right, can, up to a certain point, do no wrong. Very often, like Dr. Johnson's "inspired idiot", Mrs. Pritchard, he did not know what he was talking about. Yet he "got there", while many cleverer men stayed behind. He had unbounded impudence, yet so much charm that no one could ever be angry with him. Sometimes he reminded me of a butcher-boy flashing past, whistling, on the high seat of his cart, or of Phaethon driving the chariot of the sun—pretty much the same thing, I imagine! When he was "dressed up" Terriss was spoiled by fine feathers; when he was in rough clothes, he looked a prince.

He always commanded the love of his intimates as well as that of the outside public. To the end he was "Sailor Bill"—a sort of grown-up midshipmite, whose weaknesses provoked no more condemnation than

91

the weaknesses of a child. In the theatre he had the tidy habits of a sailor. He folded up his clothes and kept them in beautiful condition; and of a young man who had proposed for his daughter's hand he said: "The man's a blackguard! Why, he throws his things all over the room! The most untidy chap I ever saw!"

Terriss had had every sort of adventure by land and sea before I acted with him at the Court. He had been midshipman, tea-planter, engineer, sheep-farmer, and horse-breeder. He had, to use his own words, "hob-nobbed with every kind of queer folk, and found myself in extremely queer predicaments". The adventurous, dare-devil spirit of the roamer, the incarnate gipsy, always looked out of his insolent eyes. Yet, audacious as he seemed, no man was ever more nervous on the stage. On a first night he was shaking all over with fright, in spite of his confident and dashing appearance.

His bluff was colossal. Once when he was a little boy and wanted money, he said to his mother: "Give me £5 or I'll jump out of the window." And she at once believed he meant it, and cried out: "Come back, come back! and I'll give you anything."

He showed the same sort of "attack" with audiences. He made them believe in him the moment he stepped on to the stage.

His conversation was extremely entertaining—and, let me add, ingenuous. One of his favourite reflections was: "Tempus fugit! So make the most of it. While you're alive, gather roses; for when you're dead, you're dead a d——d long time."

He was a perfect rider, and loved to do cowboy "stunts" in Richmond Park while riding to the "Star and Garter".

When he had presents from the front, which happened every night, he gave them at once to the call-boy or the gas-man. To the women-folk, especially the plainer ones, he was always delightful. Never was any man more adored by the theatre staff. And children, my own Edy included, were simply *daft* about him. A little American girl, daughter of William Winter, the famous critic, when staying with me in England, announced gravely when we were out driving:

"I've gone a mash on Terriss."

There was much laughter. When it had subsided, the child said gravely:

"Oh, you can laugh, but it's true. I wish I was hammered to him!"

Perhaps if he had lived longer, Terriss would have lost his throne. He died as a beautiful youth, a kind of Adonis, although he was fifty years old when he was stabbed at the stage-door of the Adelphi Theatre.

Terriss had a beautiful mouth. That predisposed me in his favour at once! I have always been "cracked" on pretty mouths! I remember that I used to say "Naughty Teddy!" to my own little boy just for the pleasure of seeing him put out his under-lip, when his mouth looked lovely!

At the Court Terriss was still under thirty, but doing the best work of his life. He *never* did anything finer that Squire Thornhill, although he was clever as Henry VIII. His gravity as Flutter in "The Belle's Stratagem" was very fetching; as Bucklaw in "Ravenswood" he looked magnificent, and, of course, as the sailor hero in Adelphi melodrama he was as good as could be. But it is as Thornhill that I like best to remember him. He was precisely the handsome, reckless, unworthy creature that good women are fools enough to love.

In the Court production of "Olivia", both my children walked on to the stage for the first time. Teddy had such red cheeks that they made all the *rouged* cheeks look quite pale! Little Edy gave me a bunch of real flowers that she had picked in the country the day before.

Young Norman Forbes-Robertson was the Moses of the original cast. He played the part again at the Lyceum. How charming he was! And how very, very young! He at once gave promise of being a good actor and of having done the right thing in following his brother on to the stage. At the present day I consider him the only actor on the stage who can play Shakespeare's fools as they should be played.

Among the girls "walking on" was Kate Rorke. This made me take a special interest in watching what she did later on. No one who saw her fine performance in "The Profligate" could easily forget it, and I shall never understand why the London public ever let her go.

It was during the run of "Olivia" that Henry Irving became sole lessee of the Lyceum Theatre. For a long time he had been contemplating the step, but it was one of such magnitude that it could not be done in a hurry. I daresay he found it difficult to separate from Mrs. Bateman and from her daughter, who had for such a long time been his "leading lady". He had to be a little cruel, not for the last time, in a career devoted unremittingly and unrelentingly to his art and his ambition.

It was said by an idle tongue in later years that rich ladies financed Henry Irving's ventures. The only shadow of foundation for this statement is that at the beginning of his tenancy of the Lyceum, the Baroness Burdett-Coutts lent him a certain sum of money, every farthing of which was repaid during the first few months of his management.

The first letter that I ever received from Henry Irving was written on July 20, 1878, from 15A, Grafton Street, the house in which he lived during the entire period of his Lyceum management.

DEAR MISS TERRY,   I look forward to the pleasure of calling upon you on Tuesday next at two o'clock.

With every good wish, believe me, sincerely,

HENRY IRVING.

The call was in reference to my engagement as Ophelia. Strangely characteristic I see it now to have been of Henry that he was content to take my powers as an actress more or less on trust. A mutual friend, Lady Pollock, had told him that I was the very person for him; that "all London" was talking of my Olivia; that I had acted well in Shakespeare with the Bancrofts; that I should bring to the Lyceum Theatre what players call "a personal following". Henry chose his friends as carefully as he chose his company and his staff. He believed in Lady Pollock implicitly, and he did not—it is possible that he could not—come and see my Olivia for himself.

I was living in Longridge Road when Henry Irving first came to see me.

Not a word of our conversation about the engagement can I remember. I did notice, however, the great change that had taken place in the man since I had last met him in 1867. Then he was really almost ordinary looking—with a moustache, an unwrinkled face, and a sloping forehead. The only wonderful thing about him was his melancholy. When I was playing the piano once in the greenroom at the Queen's Theatre, he came in and listened. I remember being made aware of his presence by his sigh—the deepest, profoundest, sincerest sigh I ever heard from any human being. He asked me if I would not play the piece again.

The incident impressed itself on my mind, inseparably associated with a picture of him as he looked at thirty—a picture by no means pleasing. He looked conceited, and almost savagely proud of the isolation in which he lived. There was a touch of exaggeration in his appearance—a dash of Werther, with a few flourishes of Jingle! Nervously sensitive to ridicule, self-conscious, suffering deeply from his inability to express himself through his art, Henry Irving, in 1867, was a very different person from the Henry Irving who called on me at Longridge Road in 1878.

In ten years he had found himself, and so lost himself—lost, I mean, much of that stiff, ugly, self-consciousness which had encased him as the shell encases the lobster. His forehead had become more massive, and the very outline of his features had altered. He was a man of the world, whose strenuous fighting now was to be done as a general—not, as hitherto, in the ranks. His manner was very quiet and gentle. "In quietness and confidence shall be your strength," says the Psalmist. That was always like Henry Irving.

And here, perhaps, is the place to say that I, of all people, can perhaps appreciate Henry Irving least justly, although I was his associate on the stage for a quarter of a century, and was on the terms of the closest friendship with him for almost as long a time. He had precisely the qualities that I never find likeable.

He was an egotist—an egotist of the great type, *never* "a mean egotist", as he was once slanderously described—and all his faults sprang from egotism, which is in one sense, after all, only another name for greatness.

So much absorbed was he in his own achievements that he was unable or unwilling to appreciate the achievements of others. I never heard him speak in high terms of the great foreign actors and actresses who from time to time visited England. It would be easy to attribute this to jealousy, but the easy explanation is not the true one. He simply would not give himself up to appreciation. Perhaps appreciation is a *wasting* though a generous quality of the mind and heart, and best left to lookers-on, who have plenty of time to develop it.

I was with him when he saw Sarah Bernhardt act for the first time. The play was "Ruy Blas", and it was one of Sarah's bad days. She was walking through the part listlessly, and I was angry that there should be any ground for Henry's indifference. The same thing happened years later, when I took him to see Eleonora Duse. The play was "La Locandiera", in which to my mind she is not at her very best. He was surprised at my enthusiasm. There was an element of justice in his attitude towards the performance which infuriated me, but I doubt if he would have shown more enthusiasm if he had seen her at her very best.

As the years went on he grew very much attached to Sarah Bernhardt, and admired her as a colleague whose managerial work in the theatre was as dignified as his own, but of her superb powers as an actress, I don't believe he ever had a glimmering notion!

Perhaps it is not true, but, as I believe it to be true, I may as well state it: *It was never any pleasure to him to see the acting of the other actors and actresses*. All the same, Salvini's Othello I know he thought magnificent, but he would not speak of it.

How dangerous it is to write things that may not be understood! What I have written I have written merely to indicate the qualities in Henry Irving's nature, which were unintelligible to me, perhaps because I have always been more woman than artist. He always put the theatre first. He lived in it, he died in it. He had none of what I may call my *bourgeois* qualities—the love of being in love, the love of a home, the dislike of solitude. I have always thought it hard to find my inferiors. He was sure of his high place. He was far simpler than I in some ways. He would talk, for instance, in such an ingenuous way to painters and musicians that I blushed for him. But I know now that my blush was far more unworthy than his freedom from all pretentiousness in matters of art.

He never pretended. One of his biographers has said that he posed as being a French scholar. Such a thing, and all things like it, were impossible to his nature. If it were necessary in one of his plays to say a few French words, he took infinite pains to learn them and said them beautifully.

Henry once told me that in the early part of his career, before I knew him, he had been hooted because of his thin legs. The first service I did him was to tell him they were beautiful, and to make him give up padding them.

"What do you want with fat, podgy, prize-fighter legs!" I expostulated.

Praise to some people at certain stages of their career is more developing than blame. I admired the very things in Henry for which other people criticised him. I hope this helped him a little.

I brought help, too, in pictorial matters. Henry Irving had had little training in such matters—I had had a great deal. Judgment about colours, clothes, and lighting must be *trained*. I had learned from Mr. Watts, from Mr. Godwin, and from other artists, until a sense of decorative effect had become second nature to me.

Before the rehearsals of "Hamlet" began at the Lyceum I went on a provincial tour with Charles Kelly, and played for the first time in "Dora", and "Iris", besides doing a steady round of old parts. In Birmingham I went to see Henry's Hamlet. (I have tried already, most inadequately, to say what it was to me.) I had also appeared for the first time as Lady Teazle—a part which I wish I was not too old to play now, for I could play it better. My performance in 1877 was not finished enough, not light enough. I think I did the screen scene well. When the screen was knocked over I did not stand still and rigid with eyes cast down. That seemed to me an attitude of guilt. Only a *guilty* woman, surely, in such a situation would assume an air of conscious virtue. I shrank back, and tried to hide my face—a natural movement, so it seemed to me, for a woman who had been craning forward, listening in increasing agitation to the conversation between Charles and Joseph Surface.

I shall always regret that we never did "The School for Scandal", or any of the other classic comedies, at the Lyceum. There came a time when Henry was anxious for me to play Lady Teazle, but I opposed him, as I thought that I was too old. It should have been one of my best parts.

"Star" performances, for the benefit of veteran actors retiring from the stage, were as common in my youth as now. About this time I played in "Money" for the benefit of Henry Compton, a fine comedian who had delighted audiences at the Haymarket for many years. On this occasion I did not play Clara Douglas as I had done during the revival at the Prince of Wales's, but the comedy part, Georgina Vesey. John Hare, Mr. and Mrs. Kendal, Henry Neville, Mr. and Mrs. Bancroft, and, last but not least, Benjamin Webster, who came out of his retirement to play Graves—"his original part"—were in the cast.

I don't think that Webster ever appeared on the stage again, although he lived on for many years in an old-fashioned house near Kennington

Church, and died at a great age. He has a descendant on the stage in Mr. Ben Webster, who acted with us at the Lyceum, and is now well known both in England and America.

Henry Compton's son, Edward, was in this performance of "Money". He was engaged to the beautiful Adelaide Neilson, an actress whose brilliant career was cut off suddenly when she was riding in the Bois. She drank a glass of milk when she was overheated, was taken ill, and died. I am told that she commanded £700 a week in America, and in England people went wild over her Juliet. She looked like a child of the warm South, although she was born, I think, in Manchester, and her looks were much in her favour as Juliet. She belonged to the ripe, luscious, pomegranate type of woman. The only living actress with the same kind of beauty is Maxine Elliott.

Adelaide Neilson had a short reign, but a most triumphant one. It was easy to understand it when one saw her. She was so gracious, so feminine, so lovely. She did things well, but more from instinct than anything else. She had no science. Edward Compton now takes his own company round the provinces in an excellent repertoire of old comedies. He has done as much to make country audiences familiar with them as Mr. Benson has done to make them familiar with Shakespeare.

I come now to the Lyceum rehearsals of November 1878. Although Henry Irving had played Hamlet for over two hundred nights in London, and for I don't know how many nights in the provinces, he always rehearsed in cloak and rapier. This careful attention to detail came back to my mind years afterwards, when he gave readings of Macbeth. He never gave a public reading without first going through the entire play at home—at home, that is to say, in a miserably uncomfortable hotel.

During the first rehearsal he read every one's part except mine, which he skipped, and the power that he put into each part was extraordinary. He threw himself so thoroughly into it that his skin contracted and his eyes shone. His lips grew whiter and whiter, and his skin more and more drawn as the time went on, until he looked like a livid thing, but beautiful.

He never got at anything *easily*, and often I felt angry that he would waste so much of his strength in trying to teach people to do things in the right way. Very often it only ended in his producing actors who gave colourless, feeble, and unintelligent imitations of him. There were exceptions, of course.

When it came to the last ten days before the date named for the production of "Hamlet", and my scenes with him were still unrehearsed, I grew very anxious and miserable. I was still a stranger in the theatre, and in awe of Henry Irving personally; but I plucked up courage, and said:

97

"I am very nervous about my first appearance with you. Couldn't we rehearse *our* scenes?"

"*We* shall be all right!" he answered, "but we are not going to run the risk of being bottled up by a gas-man or a fiddler."

When I spoke, I think he was conducting a band rehearsal. Although he did not understand a note of music, he felt, through intuition, what the music ought to be, and would pull it about and have alterations made. No one was cleverer than Hamilton Clarke, Henry's first musical director, and a most gifted composer, at carrying out his instructions. Hamilton Clarke often grew angry and flung out of the theatre, saying that it was quite impossible to do what Mr. Irving required.

"Patch it together, indeed!" he used to say to me indignantly, when I was told off to smooth him down. "Mr. Irving knows nothing about music, or he couldn't ask me to do such a thing."

But the next day he would return with the score altered on the lines suggested by Henry, and would confess that the music was improved. "Upon my soul, it's better! The 'Guv'nor' was perfectly right."

His Danish march in "Hamlet", his Brocken music in "Faust", and his music for "The Merchant of Venice" were all, to my mind, exactly *right*. The brilliant gifts of Clarke, before many years had passed, "o'er-leaped" themselves, and he ended his days in a lunatic asylum.

The only person who did not profit by Henry's ceaseless labours was poor Ophelia. When the first night came, I did not play the part well, although the critics and the public were pleased. To myself I *failed*. I had not rehearsed enough. I can remember one occasion when I played Ophelia really well. It was in Chicago some ten years later. At Drury Lane, in 1896, when I played the mad scene for Nelly Farren's benefit, and took farewell of the part for ever, I was just *damnable*!

Ophelia only *pervades* the scenes in which she is concerned until the mad scene. This was a tremendous thing for me, who am not capable of *sustained* effort, but can perhaps manage a *cumulative* effort better than most actresses. I have been told that Ophelia has "nothing to do" at first. I found so much to do! Little bits of business which, slight in themselves, contributed to a definite result, and kept me always in the picture.

Like all Ophelias before (and after) me, I went to the madhouse to study wits astray. I was disheartened at first. There was no beauty, no nature, no pity in most of the lunatics. Strange as it may sound, they were too *theatrical* to teach me anything. Then, just as I was going away, I noticed a young girl gazing at the wall. I went between her and the wall to see her face. It was quite vacant, but the body expressed that she was waiting, waiting. Suddenly she threw up her hands and sped across the room like a swallow. I never forgot it. She was very thin, very pathetic, very young, and the movement was as poignant as it was beautiful.

I saw another woman laugh with a face that had no gleam of laughter anywhere—a face of pathetic and resigned grief.

My experiences convinced me that the actor must imagine first and observe afterwards. It is no good observing life and bringing the result to the stage without selection, without a definite idea. The idea must come first, the realism afterwards.

Perhaps because I was nervous and irritable about my own part from insufficient rehearsal, perhaps because his responsibility as lessee weighed upon him, Henry Irving's Hamlet on the first night at the Lyceum seemed to me less wonderful than it had been at Birmingham. At rehearsals he had been the perfection of grace. On the night itself, he dragged his leg and seemed stiff from self-consciousness. He asked me later on if I thought the ill-natured criticism of his walk was in any way justified, and if he really said "Gud" for "God", and the rest of it. I said straight out that he *did* say his vowels in a peculiar way, and that he *did* drag his leg.

I begged him to give up that dreadful, paralysing waiting at the side for his cue, and after a time he took my advice. He was never obstinate in such matters. His one object was to *find out*, to *test* suggestion, and follow it if it stood his test.

He was very diplomatic when he meant to have his own way. He never blustered or enforced or threatened. My first acquaintance with this side of him was made over my dresses for Ophelia. He had heard that I intended to wear black in the mad scene, and he intended me to wear white. When he first mentioned the subject, I had no idea that there would be any opposition. He spoke of my dresses, and I told him that as I was very anxious not to be worried about them at the last minute, they had been got on with early and were now finished.

"Finished! That's very interesting! Very interesting. And what—er—what colours are they?"

"In the first scene I wear a pinkish dress. It's all rose-coloured with her. Her father and brother love her. The Prince loves her—and so she wears pink."

"Pink," repeated Henry thoughtfully.

"In the nunnery scene I have a pale, gold, amber dress—the most beautiful colour. The material is a church brocade. It will 'tone down' the colour of my hair. In the last scene I wear a transparent, black dress."

Henry did not wag an eyelid.

"I see. In mourning for her father."

"No, not exactly that. I think *red* was the mourning colour of the period. But black seems to me *right*—like the character, like the situation."

"Would you put the dress on?" said Henry gravely.

At that minute Walter Lacy came up, that very Walter Lacy who had been with Charles Kean when I was a child, and who now acted as adviser to Henry Irving in his Shakespearean productions.

"Ah, here's Lacy. Would you mind, Miss Terry, telling Mr. Lacy what you are going to wear?"

Rather surprised, but still unsuspecting, I told Lacy all over again. Pink in the first scene, yellow in the second, black——

You should have seen Lacy's face at the word "black". He was going to burst out, but Henry stopped him. He was more diplomatic than that!

"They generally wear *white*, don't they?"

"I believe so," I answered, "but black is more interesting."

"I should have thought you would look much better in white."

"Oh, no!" I said.

And then they dropped the subject for that day. It *was* clever of him! The next day Lacy came up to me:

"You didn't really mean that you are going to wear black in the mad scene?"

"Yes, I did. Why not?"

"*Why not!* My God! Madam, there must be only one black figure in this play, and that's Hamlet!"

I did feel a fool. What a blundering donkey I had been not to see it before! I was very thrifty in those days, and the thought of having been the cause of needless expense worried me. So instead of the *crêpe de Chine* and miniver, which had been used for the black dress, I had for the white dress Bolton sheeting and rabbit, and I believe it looked better.

The incident, whether Henry was right or not, led me to see that, although I knew more of art and archaeology in dress than he did, he had a finer sense of what was right for the *scene*. After this he always consulted me about the costumes, but if he said: "I want such and such a scene to be kept dark and mysterious," I knew better than to try and introduce pale-coloured dresses into it.

Henry always had a fondness for "the old actor", and would engage him in preference to the tyro any day. "I can trust them," he explained briefly.

In the cast of "Hamlet" Mr. Forrester, Mr. Chippendale, and Tom Mead worthily repaid the trust. Mead, in spite of a terrible excellence in "Meadisms"—he substituted the most excruciatingly funny words for Shakespeare's when his memory of the text failed—was a remarkable actor. His voice as the Ghost was beautiful, and his appearance splendid. With his deep-set eyes, hawk-like nose, and clear brow, he reminded me of the Rameses head in the British Museum.

We had young men in the cast, too. There was one very studious youth who could never be caught loafing. He was always reading, or busy in the greenroom studying by turns the pictures of past actor-humanity with which the walls were peopled, or the present realities of actors who came in and out of the room. Although he was so much younger then, Mr. Pinero looked much as he does now. He played Rosencrantz very neatly. Consummate care, precision, and brains characterised his work as an actor always, but his chief ambition lay another way. Rosencrantz and the rest were his school of stage-craft.

Kyrle Bellew, the Osric of the production, was another man of the future, though we did not know it. He was very handsome, a tremendous lady-killer! He wore his hair rather long, had a graceful figure, and a good voice, as became the son of a preacher who had the reputation of saying the Lord's Prayer so dramatically that his congregation sobbed.

Frank Cooper, a descendant of the Kembles, another actor who has risen to eminence since, played Laertes. It was he who first led me on to the Lyceum stage. Twenty years later he became my leading man on the first tour I took independently of Henry Irving since my tours with my husband, Charles Kelly.

VIII

WORK AT THE LYCEUM

WHEN I am asked what I remember about the first ten years at the Lyceum, I can answer in one word: *Work*. I was hardly ever out of the theatre. What with acting, rehearsing, and studying—twenty-five reference books were a "simple coming-in" for one part—I sometimes thought I should go blind and mad. It was not only for my parts at the Lyceum that I had to rehearse. From August to October I was still touring in the provinces on my own account. My brother George acted as my business manager. His enthusiasm was not greater than his loyalty and industry. When we were playing in small towns he used to rush into my dressing-room after the curtain was up and say excitedly:

"We've got twenty-five more people in our gallery than the Blank Theatre opposite!"

Although he was very delicate, he worked for me like a slave. When my tours with Mr. Kelly ended in 1880 and I promised Henry Irving that in future I would go to the provincial towns with him, my brother was given a position at the Lyceum, where, I fear, his scrupulous and uncompromising honesty often got him into trouble. "Perks", as they are called in domestic service, are one of the heaviest additions to a manager's working expenses, and George tried to fight the system. He hurt no one so much as himself.

One of my productions in the provinces was an English version of "Frou-Frou", made for me by my dear friend Mrs. Comyns Carr, who for many years designed the dresses that I wore in different Lyceum plays. "Butterfly", as "Frou-Frou" was called when it was produced in English, went well; indeed, the Scots of Edinburgh received it with overwhelming favour, and it served my purpose at the time, but when I saw Sarah Bernhardt play the part I wondered that I had had the presumption to meddle with it. It was not a case of my having a different view of the character and playing it according to my imagination, as it was, for instance, when Duse played "La Dame aux Camélias", and gave a performance that one could not say was *inferior* to Bernhardt's, although it was so utterly *different*. No people in their right senses could have accepted my "Frou-Frou" instead of Sarah's. What I lacked technically in it was *pace*.

Of course, it is partly the language. English cannot be phrased as rapidly as French. But I have heard foreign actors, playing in the English tongue, show us this rapidity, this warmth, this fury—call it what you will—and have just wondered why we are, most of us, so deficient in it.

Fechter had it, so had Edwin Forrest. When strongly moved, their passions and their fervour made them swift. The more Henry Irving felt, the more deliberate he became. I said to him once: "You seem to be hampered in the vehemence of passion." "I *am*," he answered. This is what crippled his Othello, and made his scene with Tubal in "The Merchant of Venice" the least successful *to him*. What it was to the audience is another matter. But he had to take refuge in speechless rage when he would have liked to pour out his words like a torrent.

In the company which Charles Kelly and I took round the provinces in 1880 were Henry Kemble and Charles Brookfield. Young Brookfield was just beginning life as an actor, and he was so brilliantly funny off the stage that he was always a little disappointing *on* it. My old manageress, Mrs. Wigan, first brought him to my notice, writing in a charming little note that she knew him "to have a power of *personation* very rare in an unpractised actor," and that if we could give him varied practice, she would feel it a courtesy to her.

I had reason to admire Mr. Brookfield's "powers of personation" when I was acting at Buxton. He and Kemble had no parts in one of our plays, so they amused themselves during their "off" night by hiring bath-chairs and pretending to be paralytics! We were acting in a hall, and the most infirm of the invalids visiting the place to take the waters were wheeled in at the back, and up the centre aisle. In the middle of a very pathetic scene I caught sight of Kemble and Brookfield in their bath-chairs, and could not *speak* for several minutes.

Mr. Brookfield does not tell this little story in his "Random Reminiscences". It is about the only one that he has left out! To my mind he is the prince of story-tellers. All the cleverness that he should have put into his acting and his play-writing (of which since those early days he has done a great deal) he seems to have put into his life. I remember him more clearly as a delightful companion than an actor, and he won my heart at once by his kindness to my little daughter Edy, who accompanied me on this tour. He has too great a sense of humour to resent my inadequate recollection of him. Did he not in his own book quote gleefully from an obituary notice published on a false report of his death, the summary: "Never a great actor, he was invaluable in small parts. But after all it is at his club that he will be most missed!"

In the last act of "Butterfly", as we called the English version of "Frou-Frou", where the poor woman is dying, her husband shows her a locket with a picture of her child in it. Night after night we used a "property" locket, but on my birthday, when we happened to be playing the piece, Charles Kelly bought a silver locket of Indian work and put inside it two little coloured photographs of my children, Edy and Teddy, and gave it to me on the stage instead of the "property" one. When I opened it, I burst into very real tears! I have often wondered since if the audience that night knew that they were seeing *real* instead of assumed emotion! Probably the difference did not tell at all.

At Leeds we produced "Much Ado About Nothing". I never played Beatrice as well again. When I began to "take soundings" from life for my idea of her, I found in my friend Anne Codrington (now Lady Winchilsea) what I wanted. There was before me a Beatrice—as fine a lady as ever lived, a great-hearted woman—beautiful, accomplished, merry, tender. When Nan Codrington came into a room it was as if the sun came out. She was the daughter of an admiral, and always tried to make her room look as like a cabin as she could. "An excellent musician," as Benedick hints Beatrice was, Nan composed the little song that I sang at the Lyceum in "The Cup", and very good it was, too.

When Henry Irving put on "Much Ado About Nothing"—a play which he may be said to have done for me, as he never really liked the part of Benedick—I was not the same Beatrice at all. A great actor can do nothing badly, and there was so very much to admire in Henry Irving's Benedick. But he gave me little help. Beatrice must be swift, swift, swift! Owing to Henry's rather finicking, deliberate method as Benedick, I could never put the right pace into my part. I was also feeling unhappy about it, because I had been compelled to give way about a traditional "gag" in the church scene, with which we ended the fourth act. In my own production we had scorned this gag, and let the curtain come down on Benedick's line: "Go, comfort your cousin; I must say she is dead, and so farewell." When I was told that we were to descend to the buffoonery of:

Beatrice: Benedick, kill him—kill him if you can.
Benedick: As sure as I'm alive, I will!

I protested, and implored Henry not to do it. He said that it was necessary: otherwise the "curtain" would be received in dead silence. I assured him that we had often had seven and eight calls without it. I used every argument, artistic and otherwise. Henry, according to his custom, was gentle, would not discuss it much, but remained obdurate. After holding out for a week, I gave in. "It's my duty to obey your orders, and do it," I said, "but I do it under protest." Then I burst into tears. It was really for his sake just as much as for mine. I thought it must bring such disgrace on him! Looking back on the incident, I find that the most humorous thing in connection with it was that the critics, never reluctant to accuse Henry of "monkeying" with Shakespeare if they could find cause, never noticed the gag at all!

Such disagreements occurred very seldom. In "The Merchant of Venice" I found that Henry Irving's Shylock necessitated an entire revision of my conception of Portia, especially in the trial scene, but here there was no point of honour involved. I had considered, and still am of the same mind, that Portia in the trial scene ought to be very *quiet*. I saw an extraordinary effect in this quietness. But as Henry's Shylock was quiet, I had to give it up. His heroic saint was splendid, but it wasn't good for Portia.

Of course, there were always injudicious friends to say that I had not "chances" enough at the Lyceum. Even my father said to me after "Othello":

"We must have no more of these Ophelias and Desdemonas!"

"*Father!*" I cried out, really shocked.

"They're second fiddle parts—not the parts for you, Duchess."

"Father!" I gasped out again, for really I thought Ophelia a pretty good part, and was delighted at my success with it.

But granting these *were* "second fiddle" parts, I want to make quite clear that I had my turn of "first fiddle" ones. "Romeo and Juliet", "Much Ado About Nothing", "Olivia", and "The Cup" all gave me finer opportunities than they gave Henry. In "The Merchant of Venice" and "Charles I" they were at least equal to his.

I have sometimes wondered what I should have accomplished without Henry Irving. I might have had "bigger" parts, but it doesn't follow that they would have been better ones, and if they had been written by contemporary dramatists my success would have been less durable. "No actor or actress who doesn't play in the 'classics'—in Shakespeare or old comedy—will be heard of long," was one of Henry Irving's sayings, by the way, and he was right.

It was a long time before we had much talk with each other. In the "Hamlet" days, Henry Irving's melancholy was appalling. I remember feeling as if I had laughed in church when he came to the foot of the stairs leading to my dressing-room, and caught me sliding down the banisters! He smiled at me, but didn't seem able to get over it.

"Lacy," he said some days later, "what do you think! I found her the other day sliding down the banisters!"

Some one says—I think it is Keats, in a letter—that the poet lives not in one, but in a thousand worlds, and the actor has not one, but a hundred natures. What was the real Henry Irving? I used to speculate!

His religious upbringing always left its mark on him, though no one could be more "raffiish" and mischievous than he when entertaining friends at supper in the Beefsteak-room, or chaffing his valued adjutants, Bram Stoker and Loveday. H. J. Loveday, our dear stage manager, was, I think, as absolutely devoted to Henry as any one except his fox-terrier, Fussy. Loveday's loyalty made him agree with everything that Henry said, however preposterous, and didn't Henry trade on it sometimes!

Once while he was talking to me, when he was making-up, he absently took a white lily out of a bowl on the table and began to stripe and dot the petals with the stick of grease-paint in his hand. He pulled off one or two of the petals, and held it out to me.

"Pretty flower, isn't it?"

"Oh, don't be ridiculous, Henry!" I said.

"You wait!" he said mischievously. "We'll show it to Loveday."

Loveday was sent for on some business connected with the evening's performance. Henry held out the flower obtrusively, but Loveday wouldn't notice it.

"Pretty, isn't it?" said Henry carelessly.

"Very," said Loveday. "I always like those lilies. A friend of mine has his garden full of them, and he says they're not so difficult to grow if only you give 'em enough water."

Henry's delight at having "taken in" Loveday was childish. But sometimes I think Loveday must have seen through these innocent jokes, only he wouldn't have spoiled "the Guv'nor's" bit of fun for the world.

When Henry first met him he was conducting an orchestra. I forget the precise details, but I know that he gave up this position to follow Henry, that he was with him during the Bateman régime at the Lyceum, and that when the Lyceum became a thing of the past, he still kept the post of stage manager. He was literally "faithful unto death", for it was only at Henry's death that his service ended.

Bram Stoker, whose recently published "Reminiscences of Irving" have told, as well as it ever *can* be told, the history of the Lyceum Theatre under Irving's direction, was as good a servant in the front of the theatre as Loveday was on the stage. Like a true Irishman, he has given me some lovely blarney in his book. He has also told *all* the stories that I might have told, and described every one connected with the Lyceum except himself. I can fill *that* deficiency to a certain extent by saying that he is one of the most kind and tender-hearted of men. He filled a difficult position with great tact, and was not so universally abused as most business managers, because he was always straight with the company, and never took a mean advantage of them.

Stoker and Loveday were daily, nay, hourly, associated for many years with Henry Irving; but, after all, did they or any one else *really* know him? And what was Henry Irving's attitude. I believe myself that he never wholly trusted his friends, and never admitted them to his intimacy, although they thought he did, which was the same thing to *them*.

From his childhood up, Henry was lonely. His chief companions in youth were the Bible and Shakespeare. He used to study "Hamlet" in the Cornish fields, when he was sent out by his aunt, Mrs. Penberthy, to call in the cows. One day, when he was in one of the deep, narrow lanes common in that part of England, he looked up and saw the face of a sweet little lamb gazing at him from the top of the bank. The symbol of the lamb in the Bible had always attracted him, and his heart went out to the dear little creature. With some difficulty he scrambled up the bank, slipping often in the damp, red earth, threw his arms round the lamb's neck and kissed it.

The lamb bit him!

Did this set-back in early childhood influence him? I wonder! He had another such set-back when he first went on the stage, and for some six weeks in Dublin was subjected every night to groans, hoots, hisses, and cat-calls from audiences who resented him because he had taken the place of a dismissed favourite. In such a situation an actor is not likely to take stock of *reasons*. Henry Irving only knew that the Dublin people made him the object of violent personal antipathy. "I played my parts not badly for me," he said simply, "in spite of the howls of execration with which I was received."

The bitterness of this Dublin episode was never quite forgotten. It coloured Henry Irving's attitude towards the public. When he made his humble little speeches of thanks to them before the curtain, there was always a touch of pride in the humility. Perhaps he would not have received adulation in quite the same dignified way if he had never known what it was to wear the martyr's "shirt of flame".

This is the worst of my trying to give a consecutive narrative of my first years at the Lyceum. Henry Irving looms across them, reducing all events, all feelings, all that happened, and all that was suggested, to pigmy size.

Let me speak *generally* of his method of procedure in producing a play.

First he studied it for three months himself, and nothing in that play would escape him. Some one once asked him a question about "Titus Andronicus". "God bless my soul!" he said. "I never read it, so how should I know!" The Shakespearean scholar who had questioned him was a little shocked—a fact which Henry Irving, the closest observer of men, did not fail to notice.

"When I am going to do 'Titus Andronicus', or any other play," he said to me afterwards, "I shall know more about it than A—— or any other student."

There was no conceit in this. It was just a statement of fact. And it may not have been an admirable quality of Henry Irving's, but all his life he only took an interest in the things which concerned the work that he had in hand. When there was a question of his playing Napoleon, his room at Grafton Street was filled with Napoleonic literature. Busts of Napoleon, pictures of Napoleon, relics of Napoleon were everywhere. Then, when another play was being prepared, the busts, however fine, would probably go down to the cellar. It was not *Napoleon* who interested Henry Irving, but *Napoleon for his purpose*—two very different things.

His concentration during his three months' study of the play which he had in view was marvellous. When, at the end of the three months, he called the first rehearsal, he read the play exactly as it was going to be done on the first night. He knew exactly by that time what he personally was going to do on the first night, and the company did well to notice how he read his own part, for never again until the first night, though he rehearsed with them, would he show his conception so fully and completely.

These readings, which took place sometimes in the greenroom or Beefsteak-room at the Lyceum, sometimes at his house in Grafton Street, were wonderful. Never were the names of the characters said by the reader, but never was there the slightest doubt as to which was speaking. Henry Irving swiftly, surely, acted every part in the piece as he read. While he read, he made notes as to the position of the characters and the order of the crowds and processions. At the end of the first reading he gave out the parts.

The next day there was the "comparing" of the parts. It generally took place on the stage, and we sat down for it. Each person took his own character, and took up the cues to make sure that no blunder had been made in writing them out. Parts at the Lyceum were written, or printed, not typed.

These first two rehearsals—the one devoted to the reading of the play, and the other to the comparing of the parts, were generally arranged for Thursday and Friday. Then there was two days' grace. On Monday came the first stand-up rehearsal on the stage.

We then did one act straight through, and, after that, straight through again, even if it took all day. There was no luncheon interval. People took a bite when they could, or went without. Henry himself generally went without. The second day exactly the same method was pursued with the second act. All the time Henry gave the stage his personal direction, gave it keenly, and gave it whole. He was the sole superintendent of his rehearsals, with Mr. Loveday as his working assistant, and Mr. Allen as his prompter. This despotism meant much less wasted time than when actor-manager, "producer", literary adviser, stage manager, and any one who likes to offer a suggestion are all competing in giving orders and advice to a company.

Henry Irving never spent much time on the women in the company, except in regard to position. Sometimes he would ask me to suggest things to them, to do for them what he did for the men. The men were as much like him when they tried to carry out his instructions as brass is like gold; but he never grew weary of "coaching" them, down to the most minute detail. Once during the rehearsals of "Hamlet" I saw him growing more and more fatigued with his efforts to get the actors who opened the play to perceive his meaning. He wanted the first voice to ring out like a pistol shot.

"Who's there?"

"Do give it up," I said. "It's no better!"

"Yes, it's a little better," he answered quietly, "and so it's worth doing."

From the first the scenery or substitute scenery was put upon the stage for rehearsal, and the properties or substitute properties were to hand.

After each act had been gone through twice each day, it came to half an act once in a whole day, because of the development of detail. There was no detail too small for Henry Irving's notice. He never missed anything that was cumulative—that would contribute something to the whole effect.

The messenger who came in to announce something always needed a great deal of rehearsal. There were processions, and half processions, quiet bits when no word was spoken. There was *timing*. Nothing was left to chance.

In the master carpenter, Arnott, we had a splendid man. He inspired confidence at once through his strong, able personality, and, as time went on, deserved it through all the knowledge he acquired and through his excellence in never making a difficulty.

"You shall have it," was no bluff from Arnott. You *did* "have it".

We could not find precisely the right material for one of my dresses in "The Cup". At last, poking about myself in quest of it, I came across the very thing at Liberty's—a saffron silk with a design woven into it by hand with many-coloured threads and little jewels. I brought a yard to rehearsal. It was declared perfect, but I declared the price prohibitive.

"It's twelve guineas a yard, and I shall want yards and yards!"

In these days I am afraid they would not only put such material on to the leading lady, but on to the supers too! At the Lyceum *wanton* extravagance was unknown.

"Where can I get anything at all like it?"

"You leave it to me," said Arnott. "I'll get it for you. That'll be all right."

"But, Arnott, it's a hand-woven Indian material. How *can* you get it?"

"You leave it to me," Arnott repeated in his slow, quiet, confident way. "Do you mind letting me have this yard as a pattern?"

He went off with it, and before the dress rehearsal had produced about twenty yards of silk, which on the stage looked better than the twelve-guinea original.

"There's plenty more if you want it," he said drily.

He had had some raw silk dyed the exact saffron. He had had two blocks made, one red and the other black, and the design had been printed, and a few cheap spangles had been added to replace the real jewels. My toga looked beautiful.

This was but one of the many emergencies to which Arnott rose with talent and promptitude.

With the staff of the theatre he was a bit of a bully—one of those men not easily roused, but being vexed, "nasty in the extreme!" As a craftsman he had wonderful taste, and could copy antique furniture so that one could not tell the copy from the original.

The great aim at the Lyceum was to get everything "rotten perfect", as the theatrical slang has it, before the dress rehearsal. Father's test of being rotten perfect was not a bad one. "If you can get out of bed in the middle of the night and do your part, you're perfect. If you can't, you don't really know it!"

Henry Irving applied some such test to every one concerned in the production. I cannot remember any play at the Lyceum which did not begin punctually and end at the advertised time, except "Olivia", when some unwise changes in the last act led to delay.

He never hesitated to discard scenery if it did not suit his purpose. There was enough scenery rejected in "Faust" to have furnished three productions, and what was finally used for the famous Brocken scene cost next to nothing.

Even the best scene-painters sometimes think more of their pictures than of scenic effects. Henry would never accept anything that was not right *theatrically* as well as pictorially beautiful. His instinct in this was unerring and incomparable.

I remember that at one scene-rehearsal every one was fatuously pleased with the scenery. Henry sat in the stalls talking about everything *but* the scenery. It was hard to tell what he thought.

"Well, are you ready?" he asked at last.

"Yes, sir."

"My God! Is that what you think I am going to give the public?"

Never shall I forget the astonishment of stage manager, scene-painter, and staff! It was never safe to indulge in too much self-satisfaction beforehand with Henry. He was always liable to drop such bombs!

He believed very much in "front" scenes, seeing how necessary they were to the swift progress of Shakespeare's diverging plots. These cloths were sometimes so wonderfully painted and lighted that they constituted scenes of remarkable beauty. The best of all were the Apothecary scene in "Romeo and Juliet" and the exterior of Aufidius's house in "Coriolanus".

We never had electricity installed at the Lyceum until Daly took the theatre. When I saw the effect on the faces of the electric footlights, I entreated Henry to have the gas restored, and he did. We used gas footlights and gas limes there until we left the theatre for good in 1902.

To this I attribute much of the beauty of our lighting. I say "our" because this was a branch of Henry's work in which I was always his chief helper. Until electricity has been greatly improved and developed, it can never be to the stage what gas was. The thick softness of gaslight, with the lovely specks and motes in it, so like *natural* light, gave illusion to many a scene which is now revealed in all its naked trashness by electricity.

The artificial is always noticed and recognised as art by the superficial critic. I think this is what made some people think Irving was at his best in such parts as Louis XI, Dubosc, and Richard III. He could have played Louis XI three times a day "on his head", as the saying is. In "The Lyons Mail", Dubosc the wicked man was easy enough—strange that the unprofessional looker-on always admires the actor's art when it is employed on easy things!—but Lesurques, the *good* man in the same play ("The Lyons Mail"), was difficult. Any actor, skilful in the tricks of the business, can play the drunkard; but to play a good man sincerely, as he did here, to show that double thing, the look of guilt which an innocent man wears when accused of crime, requires great acting, for "*the look*" is the outward and visible sign of the inward and spiritual emotion—and this delicate emotion can only be perfectly expressed when the actor's heart and mind and soul and skill are in absolute accord.

In dual parts Irving depended little on make-up. Make-up was, indeed, always his servant, not his master. He knew its uselessness when not informed by the *spirit*. "The letter" (and in characterisation grease-paint is the letter) "killeth—the spirit giveth life." His Lesurques was different from his Dubosc because of the way he held his shoulders, because of his expression. He always took a deep interest in crime (an interest which his sons have inherited), and often went to the police-court to study the faces of the accused. He told me that the innocent man generally looked guilty and hesitated when asked a question, but that the round, wide-open eyes corrected the bad impression. The result of this careful watching was seen in his expression as Lesurques. He opened his eyes wide. As Dubosc he kept them half closed.

Our plays from 1878 to 1887 were "Hamlet", "The Lady of Lyons", "Eugene Aram", "Charles I", "The Merchant of Venice", "Iolanthe", "The Cup", "The Belle's Stratagem", "Othello", "Romeo and Juliet", "Much Ado About Nothing", "Twelfth Night", "Olivia" "Faust", "Raising the Wind", and "The Amber Heart". I give this list to keep myself straight. My mental division of the years at the Lyceum is *before* "Macbeth", and *after*. I divide it up like this, perhaps, because "Macbeth" was the most important of all our productions, if I judge it by the amount of preparation and thought that it cost us and by the discussion which it provoked.

Of the characters played by Henry Irving in the plays of the first division—before "Macbeth", that is to say—I think every one knows that I considered Hamlet to be his greatest triumph. Sometimes I think that was so because it was the only part that was big enough for him. It was more difficult, and he had more scope in it than in any other. If there had been a finer part than Hamlet, that particular part would have been his finest.

When one praises an actor in this way, one is always open to accusations of prejudice, hyperbole, uncritical gush, unreasoned eulogy, and the rest. Must a careful and deliberate opinion *always* deny a great man genius? If so, no careful and deliberate opinions from me!

I have no doubt in the world of Irving's genius—no doubt that he is with David Garrick and Edmund Kean, rather than with other actors of great talents and great achievements—actors who rightly won high opinions from the multitude of their day, but who have not left behind them an impression of that inexplicable thing which we call genius.

Since my great comrade died I have read many biographies of him, and nearly all of them denied what I assert. "Now, who shall arbitrate?" I find no contradiction of my testimony in the fact that he was not appreciated for a long time, that some found him like olives, an acquired taste, that others mocked and derided him.

My father, who worshipped Macready, put Irving above him because of Irving's *originality*. The old school were not usually so generous. Fanny Kemble thought it necessary to write as follows of one who had had his share of misfortune and failure before he came into his kingdom and made her jealous, I suppose, for the dead kings among her kindred:

> I have seen some of the accounts and critiques of Mr. Irving's acting, and rather elaborate ones of his Hamlet, which, however, give me no very distinct idea of his performance, and a very hazy one indeed of the part itself as seen from the point of view of his critics. Edward Fitzgerald wrote me word that he looked like my people, and sent me a photograph to prove it, which I thought much more like Young than my father or uncle. *I have not seen a play of Shakespeare's acted I do not know when. I think I should find such an exhibition extremely curious as well as entertaining.*

Now, shall I put on record what Henry Irving thought of Fanny Kemble! If there is a touch of malice in my doing so, surely the passage that I have quoted gives me leave.

Having lived with Hamlet nearly all his life, studied the part when he was a clerk, dreamed of a day when he might play it, the young Henry Irving saw that Mrs. Butler, the famous Fanny Kemble, was going to give a reading of the play. His heart throbbed high with anticipation, for in those days TRADITION was everything—the name of Kemble a beacon and a star.

The studious young clerk went to the reading.

An attendant came on to the platform, first, and made trivial and apparently unnecessary alterations in the position of the reading desk. A glass of water and a book were placed on it.

After a portentous wait, on swept a lady with an extraordinarily flashing eye, a masculine and muscular outside. Pounding the book with terrific energy, as if she wished to knock the stuffing out of it, she announced in thrilling tones:

" 'HAM—A—LETTE.'
By
Will—y—am Shak—es—peare."

"I suppose this is all right," thought the young clerk, a little dismayed at the fierce and sectional enunciation.

Then the reader came to Act 1, Sc.2, which the old actor (to leave the Kemble reading for a minute), with but a hazy notion of the text, used to begin:

Although of Hamlet, our dear brother's death,
The memory be—memory be—(What *is* the —— colour?) *green* . . .

When Fanny Kemble came to this scene the future Hamlet began to listen more intently.

Gertrude: Let not thy mother lose *her* prayers, Ham—a—lette.
Hamlet: I shall in all respects obey *you*, madam (obviously with a fiery flashing eye of hate upon the King).

When he heard this and more like it, Henry Irving exercised his independence of opinion and refused to accept Fanny Kemble's view of the gentle, melancholy, and well-bred Prince of Denmark.

He was a stickler for tradition, and always studied it, followed it, sometimes to his own detriment, but he was not influenced by the Kemble Hamlet, except that for some time he wore the absurd John Philip feather, which he would have been much better without!

Let me pray that I, representing the old school, may never look on the new school with the patronising airs of "Old Fitz"[1] and Fanny Kemble. I wish that I could *see* the new school of acting in Shakespeare. Shakespeare must be kept up, or we shall become a third-rate nation!

Henry told me this story of Fanny Kemble's reading without a spark of ill-nature, but with many a gleam of humour. He told me at the same

[1]Edward FitzGerald.

time of the wonderful effect that Adelaide Kemble (Mrs. Sartoris) used to make when she recited Shelley's lines, beginning:

> Good-night—Ah, no, the hour is ill,
> Which severs those it should unite.
> Let us remain together still—
> Then it will be *good-night!*

I have already said that I never could cope with Pauline Deschapelles, and why Henry wanted to play Melnotte was a mystery. Claude Melnotte after Hamlet! Oddly enough, Henry was always attracted by fustian. He simply revelled in the big speeches. The play was beautifully staged; the garden scene alone probably cost as much as the whole of "Hamlet". The march past the window of the apparently unending army—that good old trick which sends the supers flying round the back-cloth to cross the stage again and again—created a superb effect. The curtain used to go up and down as often as we liked and chose to keep the army marching! The play ran some time, I suppose because even at our worst the public found *something* in our acting to like.

As Ruth Meadowes I had very little to do, but what there was, was worth doing. The last act of "Eugene Aram", like the last act of "Ravenswood", gave me opportunity. It was staged with a great appreciation of grim and poetic effect. Henry always thought that the dark, overhanging branch of the cedar was like the cruel outstretched hand of Fate. He called it the Fate Tree, and used it in "Hamlet", in "Eugene Aram", and in "Romeo and Juliet".

In "Eugene Aram", the Fate Tree drooped low over the graves in the churchyard. On one of them Henry used to be lying in a black cloak as the curtain went up on the last act. Not until a moonbeam struck the dark mass did you see that it was a man.

He played all such parts well. Melancholy and the horrors had a peculiar fascination for him—especially in these early days. But his recitation of the poem "Eugene Aram" was finer than anything in the play—especially when he did it in a frock-coat. No one ever looked so well in a frock-coat! He was always ready to recite it—used to do it after supper anywhere. We had a talk about it once, and I told him that it was *too much* for a room. No man was ever more willing to listen to suggestion or less obstinate about taking advice. He immediately moderated his methods when reciting in *a room*, making it all less theatrical. The play was a good répertoire play, and we did it later on in America with success. There the part of Houseman was played by Terriss, who was quite splendid in it, and at Chicago my little boy Teddy made his second appearance on any stage as Joey, a gardener's boy. He had, when still a mere baby, come on to the stage at the Court in "Olivia", and this must

114

be counted his *first* appearance, although the chroniclers, ignoring both that and Joey in "Eugene Aram" *say* he never appeared at all until he played an important part in "The Dead Heart".

It is because of Teddy that "Eugene Aram" is associated in my mind with one of the most beautiful sights upon the stage that I ever saw in my life. He was about ten or eleven at the time, and as he tied up the stage roses, his cheeks, untouched by rouge, put the reddest of them to shame! He was so graceful and natural; he spoke his lines with ease, and smiled all over his face! "A born actor!" I said, although Joey was my son. Whenever I think of him in that stage garden, I weep for pride, and for sorrow, too, because before he was thirty my son had left the stage—he who had it all in him. I have good reason to be proud of what he has done since, but I regret the lost actor *always*.

Henry Irving could not at first keep away from melancholy pieces. Henrietta Maria was another sad part for me—but I used to play it well, except when I cried too much in the last act. The play had been one of the Bateman productions, and I had seen Miss Isabel Bateman as Henrietta Maria and liked her, although I could not find it possible to follow her example and play the part with a French accent! I constantly catch myself saying of Henry Irving, "That is by far the best thing that he ever did." I could say it of some things in "Charles I"—of the way he gave up his sword to Cromwell, of the way he came into the room in the last act and shut the door behind him. It was not a man coming on to a stage to meet some one. It was a king going to the scaffold, quietly, unobtrusively, and courageously. However often I played that scene with him, I knew that when he first came on he was not aware of my presence nor of any *earthly* presence: he seemed to be already in heaven.

Much has been said of his "make-up" as Charles I. Edwin Long painted him a triptych of Vandyck heads, which he always had in his dressing-room, and which is now in my possession. He used to come on to the stage looking precisely like the Vandyck portraits, but not because he had been busy building up his face with wig-paste and similar atrocities. His make-up in this, as in other parts, was the process of *assisting subtly and surely the expression from within.* It was elastic, and never hampered him. It changed with the expression. As Charles, he was assisted by Nature, who had given him the most beautiful Stuart hands, but his clothes most actors would have consigned to the dust-bin! Before we had done with Charles I—we played it together for the last time in 1902—these clothes were really threadbare. Yet he looked in them every inch a king.

His care of detail may be judged from the fact that in the last act his wig was not only greyer, but had far less hair in it. I should hardly think it necessary to mention this if I had not noticed how many actors seem to think that age may be procured by the simple expedient of dipping their heads, covered with mats of flourishing hair, into a flour-barrel!

Unlike most stage kings, he never seemed to be *assuming* dignity. He was very, very simple.

Wills has been much blamed for making Cromwell out to be such a wretch—a mean blackguard, not even a great bad man. But in plays the villain must not compete for sympathy with the hero, or both fall to the ground! I think that Wills showed himself a true poet in his play, and in the last act a great playwright. He gave us both wonderful opportunities, yet very few words were spoken.

Some people thought me best in the camp scene in the third act, where I had even fewer lines to speak. I was proud of it myself when I found that it had inspired Oscar Wilde to write me this lovely sonnet:

> In the lone tent, waiting for victory,
> She stands with eyes marred by the mists of pain
> Like some wan lily overdrenched with rain;
> The clamorous clang of arms, the ensanguined sky,
> War's ruin, and the wreck of chivalry
> To her proud soul no common fear can bring;
> Bravely she tarrieth for her Lord, the King,
> Her soul aflame with passionate ecstasy.
> O, hair of gold! O, crimson lips! O, face
> Made for the luring and the love of man!
> With thee I do forget the toil and stress,
> The loveless road that knows no resting place,
> Time's straitened pulse, the soul's dread weariness,
> My freedom, and my life republican!

That phrase "wan lily" represented perfectly what I had tried to convey, not only in this part but in Ophelia. I hope I thanked Oscar enough at the time. Now he is dead, and I cannot thank him any more. . . . I had so much *bad* poetry written to me that these lovely sonnets from a real poet should have given me the greater pleasure. "He often has the poet's heart, who never felt the poet's fire." There is more good *heart* and kind feeling in most of the verses written to me than real poetry.

"One must discriminate," even if it sounds unkind. At the time that Whistler was having one of his most undignified "rows" with a sitter over a portrait and wrangling over the price, another artist was painting frescoes in a cathedral for nothing. "It is sad that it should be so," a friend said to me, "but *one must discriminate*. The man haggling over the sixpence is the great artist!"

How splendid it is that *in time* this is recognised. The immortal soul of the artist is in his work, the transient and mortal one is in his conduct.

Another sonnet from Oscar Wilde—to Portia this time—is the first document that I find in connection with "The Merchant", as the play was always called by the theatre staff.

> I marvel not Bassanio was so bold
> To peril all he had upon the lead,
> Or that proud Aragon bent low his head,
> Or that Morocco's fiery heart grew cold:
> For in that gorgeous dress of beaten gold,
> Which is more golden than the golden sun,
> No woman Veronese looked upon
> Was half so fair as thou whom I behold.
> Yet fairer when with wisdom as your shield
> The sober-suited lawyer's gown you donned,
> And would not let the laws of Venice yield
> Antonio's heart to that accursed Jew—
> O, Portia! take my heart; it is thy due:
> I think I will not quarrel with the Bond.

Henry Irving's Shylock dress was designed by Sir John Gilbert. It was never replaced, and only once cleaned by Henry's dresser and valet, Walter Collinson. Walter, I think, replaced "Doody", Henry's first dresser at the Lyceum, during the run of "The Merchant of Venice". Walter was a wig-maker by trade—assistant to Clarkson the elder. It was Doody who, on being asked his opinion of a production, said that it was fine—"not a *join*[1] to be seen anywhere!" It was Walter who was asked by Henry to say which he thought his master's best part. Walter could not be "drawn" for a long time. At last he said Macbeth.

This pleased Henry immensely, for, as I hope to show later on, he fancied himself in Macbeth more than in any other part.

"It is generally conceded to be Hamlet," said Henry.

"Oh, no, sir," said Walter, "*Macbeth*. You sweat twice as much in that."

In appearance Walter was very like Shakespeare's bust in Stratford Church. He was a most faithful and devoted servant, and was the only person with Henry Irving when he died. Quiet in his ways, discreet, gentle, and very quick, he was the ideal dresser.

The Lyceum production of "The Merchant of Venice" was not so strictly archaeological as the Bancrofts' had been, but it was very gravely beautiful and effective. If less attention was paid to details of costume and scenery, the play itself was arranged and acted very attractively and always went with a swing. To the end of my partnership with Henry

---

[1] A "join" in theatrical wig-makers' parlance is the point where the front-piece of the wig ends and the actor's forehead begins.

Irving it was a safe "draw" both in England and America. By this time I must have played Portia over a thousand times. During the first run of it the severe attack made on my acting of the part in *Blackwood's Magazine* is worth alluding to. The suggestion that I showed too much of a "coming-on" disposition in the Casket Scene affected me for years, and made me self-conscious and uncomfortable. At last I lived it down. Any suggestion of *indelicacy* in my treatment of a part always blighted me. Mr. Dodgson (Lewis Carroll, of the immortal "Alice in Wonderland") once brought a little girl to see me in "Faust". He wrote and told me that she had said (where Margaret begins to undress): "Where is it going to stop?" and that perhaps in consideration of the fact that it could affect a mere child disagreeably, I ought to alter my business!

I had known dear Mr. Dodgson for years and years. He was as fond of me as he could be of any one over the age of ten, but I was *furious*. "I thought you only knew *nice* children" was all the answer I gave him. "It would have seemed to me awful for a *child* to see harm where harm is; how much more when she sees it where harm is not."

But I felt ashamed and shy whenever I played that scene. It was the Casket Scene over again.

The unkind *Blackwood* article also blamed me for showing too plainly that Portia loves Bassanio before he has actually won her. This seemed to me unjust, if only because Shakespeare makes Portia say *before* Bassanio chooses the right casket:

> One half of me is yours—the other half yours——
> *All yours!*

Surely this suggests that she was not concealing her fondness like a Victorian maiden, and that Bassanio had most surely won her love, though not yet the right to be her husband.

"There is a soul of goodness in things evil," and the criticism made me alter the setting of the scene, and so contrive it that Portia was behind and out of sight of the men who made hazard for her love.

Dr. Furnivall, a great Shakespearean scholar, was so kind as to write me the following letter about Portia:

Being founder and director of the New Shakespeare Society, I venture to thank you most heartily for your most charming and admirable impersonation of our poet's Portia, which I witnessed tonight with a real delight. You have given me a new light on the character, and by your so pretty by-play in the Casket Scene have made bright in my memory for ever the spot which almost all critics have felt dull, and I hope to say this in a new edition of "Shakespeare".

(He did say it, in "The Leopold" edition.)

Again those touches of the wife's love in the advocate when Bassanio says he'd give up his wife for Antonio, and when you kist your hand to him behind his back in the Ring bit—how pretty and natural they were! Your whole conception and acting of the character are so true to Shakespeare's lines that one longs he could be here to see you. A lady gracious and graceful, handsome, witty, loving and wise, you are his Portia to the life.

That's the best of Shakespeare, *I* say. His characters can be interpreted in at least eight different ways, and of each way some one will say: "That is Shakespeare!" The German actress plays Portia as a low comedy part. She wears an eighteenth-century law wig, horn spectacles, a cravat (this last anachronism is not confined to Germans), and often a moustache! There is something to be said for it all, though I should not like to play the part that way myself.

Lady Pollock, who first brought me to Henry Irving's notice as a possible leading lady, thought my Portia better at the Lyceum than it had been at the Prince of Wales's.

Thanks, my dear Valentine and enchanting Portia [she writes to me in response to a photograph that I had sent her], but the photographers don't see you as you are, and have not the poetry in them to do you justice. . . . You were especially admirable in the Casket Scene. You kept your by-play quieter, and it gained in effect from the addition of repose—and I rejoiced that you did not kneel to Bassanio at "My Lord, my governor, my King". I used to feel that too much like worship from any girl to her affianced, and Portia's position being one of command, I should doubt the possibility of such an action. . . .

I think I received more letters about my Portia than about all my other parts put together. Many of them came from university men. One old playgoer wrote to tell me that he liked me better than my former instructress, Mrs. Charles Kean. "She mouthed it as she did most things. . . . She was not real—a staid, sentimental 'Anglaise', and more than a little stiffly pokerish."

Henry Irving's Shylock was generally conceded to be full of talent and reality, but some of his critics could not resist saying that this was *not* the Jew that Shakespeare drew! Now, who is in a position to say what *is* the Jew that Shakespeare drew? I think Henry Irving knew as well as most! Nay, I am sure that in his age he was the only person able to decide.

Some said his Shylock was intellectual, and appealed more to the intellect of his audiences than to their emotions. Surely this is talking for the sake of talking. I recall so many things that touched people to the heart! For absolute pathos, achieved by absolute simplicity of means, I never saw anything in the theatre to compare with his Shylock's return home over the bridge to his deserted house after Jessica's flight.

A younger actor, producing "The Merchant of Venice" in recent years, asked Irving if he might borrow this bit of business. "By all means," said Henry. "With great pleasure."

"Then, why didn't you do it?" inquired my daughter bluntly when the actor was telling us how kind and courteous Henry had been in allowing him to use his stroke of invention.

"What do you mean?" asked the astonished actor.

My daughter told him that Henry had dropped the curtain on a stage full of noise, and lights, and revelry. When it went up again the stage was empty, desolate, with no light but a pale moon, and all sounds of life at a great distance—and then over the bridge came the wearied figure of the Jew. This marked the passing of time between Jessica's elopement and Shylock's return home. It created an atmosphere of silence, and the middle of the night.

"*You* came back without dropping the curtain," said my daughter, "and so it wasn't a bit the same."

"I couldn't risk dropping the curtain for the business," answered the actor, "*because it needed applause to take it up again!*"

Henry Irving never grew tired of a part, never ceased to work at it, just as he never gave up the fight against his limitations. His diction, as the years went on, grew far clearer when he was depicting rage and passion. His dragging leg dragged no more. To this heroic perseverance he added an almost childlike eagerness in hearing any suggestion for the improvement of his interpretations which commended itself to his imagination and his judgment. From a blind man came the most illuminating criticism of his Shylock. The sensitive ear of the sightless hearer detected a fault in Henry Irving's method of delivering the opening line of his part:

"Three thousand ducats—well!"

"I hear no sound of the usurer in that," the blind man said at the end of the performance. "It is said with the reflective air of a man to whom money means very little."

The justice of the criticism appealed strongly to Henry. He revised his reading not only of the first line, but of many other lines in which he saw now that he had not been enough of the money-lender.

In more recent years he made one change in his dress. He asked my daughter—whose cleverness in such things he fully recognised—to put some stage jewels on to the scarf that he wore round his head when he supped with the Christians.

"I have an idea that, when he went to that supper, he'd like to flaunt his wealth in the Christian dogs' faces. It will look well, too—'like the toad, ugly and venomous,' wearing precious jewels on his head!"

The scarf, witnessing to that untiring love of throwing new light on his impersonations which distinguished Henry to the last, is now in my daughter's possession. She values no relic of him more unless it be the wreath of oak-leaves that she made him for "Coriolanus".

We had a beautiful scene for this play—a garden with a dark pine forest in the distance. Henry was *not* good in it. He had a Romeo part which had not been written by Shakespeare. We played it instead of the last act of "The Merchant of Venice". I never liked it being left out, but people used to say, like parrots, that "the interest of the play ended with the Trial Scene," and Henry believed them—for a time. I never did. Shakespeare *never* gives up in the last act like most dramatists.

Twice in "Iolanthe" I forgot that I was blind! The first time was when I saw old Tom Mead and Henry Irving groping for the amulet, which they had to put on my breast to heal me of my infirmity. It had slipped on to the floor, and both of them were too short-sighted to see it! Here was a predicament! I had to stoop and pick it up for them.

The second time I put out my hand and cried: "Look out for my lilies," when Henry nearly stepped on the bunch with which a litle girl friend of mine supplied me every night I played the part.

Iolanthe was one of Helen Faucit's great successes. I never saw this distinguished actress when she was in her prime. Her Rosalind, when she came out of her retirement to play a few performances, appeared to me more like a *lecture* on Rosalind, than like Rosalind herself: a lecture all young actresses would have greatly benefited by hearing, for it was of great beauty. I remember being particularly struck by her treatment of the lines in the scene where Celia conducts the mock marriage between Orlando and Ganymede. Another actress, whom I saw as Rosalind, said the words, "And I do take thee, Orlando, to be my husband," with a comical grimace to the audience. Helen Faucit flushed up and said the line with deep and true emotion, suggesting that she was, indeed, giving herself to Orlando. There was a world of poetry in the way she drooped over his hand.

Mead distinguished himself in "Iolanthe" by speaking of "that immortal land where God has His—His—er—room?—no—lodging?—no—where God hath His apartments!"

The word he could not hit was, I think, "dwelling". He used often to try five or six words before he got the right one *or* the wrong one—it was generally the wrong one—in full hearing of the audience.

LYCEUM PRODUCTIONS

"THE MERCHANT OF VENICE" TO "ROMEO AND JULIET"

"THE Merchant of Venice" was acted two hundred and fifty consecutive nights on the occasion of the first production. On the hundredth night every member of the audience was presented with Henry Irving's acting edition of the play bound in white vellum—a solid permanent souvenir, paper, print and binding all being of the best. The famous Chiswick Press did all his work of this kind. On the title page was printed:

> I count myself in nothing else so happy
> As in a soul remembering my good friends.

At the close of the performance which took place on Saturday, February 14, 1880, Henry entertained a party of 350 to supper on the stage. This was the first of those enormous gatherings which afterwards became an institution at the Lyceum.

It was at this supper that Lord Houghton surprised us all by making a very sarcastic speech about the stage and actors generally. It was no doubt more interesting than the "butter" which is usually applied to the profession at such functions, but every one felt that it was rather rude to abuse long runs when the company were met to celebrate a hundredth performance!

Henry Irving's answer was delightful. He spoke with good sense, good humour and good breeding, and it was all spontaneous. I wish that a phonograph had been in existence that night, and that a record had been taken of the speech. It would be so good for the people who have asserted that Henry Irving always employed journalists (when he could not get Poets Laureate!) to write his speeches for him! The voice was always the voice of Irving, if the hands were sometimes the hands of the professional writer. When Henry was thrown on his debating resources he really spoke better than when he prepared a speech, and his letters prove, if proof were needed, how finely he could write! Those who represent him as dependent in such matters on the help of literary hacks are just ignorant of the facts.

During the many years that I played Portia I seldom had a Bassanio to my mind. It seems to be a most difficult part, to judge by the colourless and disappointing renderings that are given of it. George Alexander was far the best of my Bassanio bunch! Mr. Barnes, "handsome Jack Barnes", as we called him, was a good actor, is a good actor still, as everyone knows, but his gentility as Bassanio was overwhelming. It was said of him that he thought more of the rounding of his legs than the charms of his affianced wife, and that in the love-scenes he appeared to be taking orders for furniture! This was putting it unkindly, but there was some truth in it.

He was so very dignified! My sister Floss (Floss was the first Lyceum Nerissa) and I once tried to make him laugh by substituting two "almond rings" for the real rings. "Handsome Jack" lost his temper, which made us laugh the more. He was quite right to be angry. Such fooling on the stage is very silly. I think it is one of the evils of long runs! When we had seen "handsome Jack Barnes" imperturbably pompous for two hundred nights in succession, it became too much for us, and the almond rings were the result.

Mr. Tyars was the Prince of Morocco. Actors might come, and actors might go in the Lyceum company, but Tyars went on for ever. He never left Henry Irving's management, and was with him in that last performance of "Becket" at Bradford on October 13, 1905—the last performance ever given by Henry Irving, who died the same night.

Tyars was the most useful actor that we ever had in the company. I should think that the number of parts he has played in the same piece would constitute a theatrical record.

I don't remember when Tom Mead first played the Duke, but I remember what happened!

Shylock, the world thinks, and I think so too.

He began the speech in the Trial Scene very slowly.

Between every word Henry was whispering: "Get on—get on!" Old Mead, whose memory was never good, became flustered, and at the end of the line came to a dead stop.

"Get on, get on," said Henry.

Mead looked round with dignity, opened his mouth and shut it, opened it again, and in his anxiety to oblige Henry, did get on indeed!— to the last line of the long speech.

We all expect a gentle answer, Jew.

The first line and the last line were all that we heard of the Duke's speech that night. It must have been the shortest version of it on record.

The Lyceum reopened in the autumn of 1880 with "The Corsican Brothers". I was on the last of my provincial tours with Charles Kelly at the time, but I must have come up to see the revival, for I remember Henry Irving in it very distinctly. He had not played the dual rôle of Louis and Fabien del Franchi before, and he had to compete with old playgoers' memories of Charles Kean and Fechter. Wisely enough he made of it a "period" play, emphasising its old-fashioned atmosphere. In 1891, when the play was revived, the D'Orsay costumes were noticed and considered piquant and charming. In 1880 I am afraid they were regarded with indifference as merely antiquated.

The grace and elegance of Henry as the civilised brother I shall never forget. There was something in *him* to which the perfect style of the D'Orsay period appealed, and he spoke the stilted language with as much truth as he wore the cravat and the tight-waisted full-breasted coats. Such lines as—

'Tis she! Her footstep beats upon my heart!

were not absurd from his lips.

The sincerity of the period, he felt, lay in its elegance. A rough movement, a too undeliberate speech, and the absurdity of the thing might be given away. It was in fact given away by Terriss as Château-Renaud, who was not the smooth, graceful, courteous villain that Alfred Wigan had been and that Henry wanted. He told me that he paid Miss Fowler, an actress who in other respects was not very remarkable, an enormous salary because she could look the high-bred lady of elegant manners.

It was in "The Corsican Brothers" that tableau curtains were first used at the Lyceum. They were made of red plush, which suited the old decoration of the theatre. Those who only saw the Lyceum after its renovation in 1881 do not realise perhaps that before that date it was decorated in dull gold and dark crimson, and had funny boxes with high fronts like old-fashioned church pews. One of these boxes was rented annually by the Baroness Burdett-Coutts. It was rather like the toy cardboard theatre which children used to be able to buy for sixpence. The effect was sombre, but I think I liked it better than the cold, light, shallow, bastard Pompeian decoration of later days.

In Hallam Tennyson's life of his father, I find that I described "The Cup" as a "great little play". After thirty years (nearly) I stick to that. Its chief fault was that it was not long enough, for it involved a tremendous production, tremendous acting, had all the heroic size of tragedy, and yet was all over so quickly that we could play a long play like "The Corsican Brothers" with it in a single evening.

Tennyson read the play to us at Eaton Place. There were present Henry Irving, Ellen Terry, William Terriss, Mr. Knowles, who had arranged the reading, my daughter Edy, who was then about nine, Hallam Tennyson, *and* a dog—I think Charlie, for the days of Fussy were not yet.

Tennyson, like most poets, read in a monotone, rumbling on a low note in much the same way that Shelley is said to have screamed in a high one. For the women's parts he changed his voice suddenly, climbed up into a key which he could not sustain. In spite of this I was beginning to think how impressive it all was, when I looked up and saw Edy, who was sitting on Henry's knee, looking over his shoulder at young Hallam and laughing, and Henry, instead of reproaching her, on the broad grin. There was much discussion as to what the play should be called, and as to whether the names "Synorix" and "Sinnatus" would be confused.

"I don't think they will," I said, for I thought this was a very small matter for the poet to worry about.

"I do!" said Edy in a loud clear voice, "I haven't known one from the other all the time!"

"Edy, be good!" I whispered.

Henry, mischievous as usual, was delighted at Edy's independence, but her mother was unutterably ashamed.

"Leave her alone," said Henry, "she's all right."

Tennyson at first wanted to call the play "The Senator's Wife", then thought of "Sinnatus and Synorix", and finally agreed with us that "The Cup" was the best as it was the simplest title.

The production was one of the most beautiful things that Henry Irving ever accomplished. It has been described again and again, but none of the descriptions are very successful. There was a vastness, a spaciousness of proportion about the scene in the Temple of Artemis which I never saw again upon the stage until my own son attempted something like it in the Church Scene that he designed for my production of "Much Ado About Nothing" in 1903.

A great deal of the effect was due to the lighting. The gigantic figure of the many-breasted Artemis, placed far back in the scene-dock, loomed through a blue mist, while the foreground of the picture was in yellow light. The thrilling effect always to be gained on the stage by the simple expedient of a great number of people doing the same thing in the same way at the same moment, was seen in "The Cup", when the stage was covered with a crowd of women who raised their arms above their heads with a large, rhythmic, sweeping movement and then bowed to the goddess with the regularity of a regiment saluting.

At rehearsals there was one girl who did this movement with peculiar grace. She wore a black velveteen dress, although it was very hot weather, and I called her "Hamlet". I used to chaff her about wearing such a grand dress at rehearsals, but she was never to be seen in any other. The girls at the theatre told me that she was very poor, and that underneath her black velveteen dress, which she wore summer and winter, she had nothing but a pair of stockings and a chemise. Not long after the first night of "The Cup" she disappeared. I made inquiries about her, and found that she was dying in hospital. I went several times to see her. She looked so beautiful in the little white bed. Her great eyes, black, with weary white lids, used to follow me as I left the hospital ward, and I could not always tear myself away from their dumb beseeching-ness, but would turn back and sit down again by the bed. Once she asked me if I would leave something belonging to me that she might look at until I came again. I took off the amber and coral beads that I was wearing at the time and gave them to her. Two days later I had a letter from the nurse telling me that poor Hamlet was dead—that just before she died, with closed eyes, and gasping for breath, she sent her love to her "dear Miss Terry", and wanted me to know that the tall lilies I had brought her on my last visit were to be buried with her, but that she had wiped the coral and amber beads and put them in cotton-wool, to be returned to me when she was dead. Poor "Hamlet"!

Quite as wonderful as the Temple Scene was the setting of the first act, which represented the rocky side of a mountain with a glimpse of a fertile table-land and a pergola with vines growing over it at the top. The acting in this scene all took place on different levels. The hunt swept past on one level; the entrance to the temple was on another. A goatherd played upon a pipe. Scenically speaking, it was not Greece, but Greece in Sicily, Capri, or some such hilly region.

Henry Irving was not able to look like the full-lipped, full-blooded Romans such as we see in long lines in marble at the British Museum, so he conceived his own type of the blend of Roman intellect and sensuality with barbarian cruelty and lust. Tennyson was not pleased with him as Synorix! *How* he failed to delight in it as a picture I can't conceive. With a pale, pale face, bright red hair, gold armour and a tiger-skin, a diabolical expression and very thin crimson lips, Henry looked handsome and sickening at the same time. *Lechery* was written across his forehead.

The first act was well within my means; the second was beyond them, but it was very good for me to try and do it. I had a long apostrophe to the goddess with my back turned to the audience, and I never tackled anything more difficult. My dresses, designed by Mr. Godwin, one of them with the toga made of that wonderful material which Arnott had printed, were simple, fine and free.

I wrote to Tennyson's son Hallam after the first night that I knew his father would be delighted with Henry's splendid performance, but was afraid he would be disappointed in me.

DEAR CAMMA,   [he answered], I have given your messages to my father, but believe me, who am not "common report", that he will thoroughly appreciate your noble, *most* beautiful and imaginative rendering of "Camma". My father and myself hope to see you soon, but not while this detestable cold weather lasts. We trust that you are not now really the worse for that night of nights.

With all our best wishes,
Yours ever sincerely,
HALLAM TENNYSON.

I quite agree with you as to H. I.'s Synorix.

The music of "The Cup" was not up to the level of the rest. Lady Winchilsea's setting of "Moon on the field and the foam", written within the compass of eight notes, for my poor singing voice, which will not go up high nor down low, was effective enough, but the music as a whole was too "chatty" for a severe tragedy. One night when I was singing my very best:

> Moon, bring him home, bring him home,
> Safe from the dark and the cold,

some one in the audience *sneezed*. Every one burst out laughing, and I had to laugh too. I did not even attempt the next line.

"The Cup" was called a failure, but it ran 125 nights, and every night the house was crowded! On the hundredth night I sent Tennyson the Cup itself. I had it made in silver from Mr. Godwin's design—a three-handled cup, pipkin-shaped, standing on three legs.

"The Cup" and "The Corsican Brothers" together made the bill too heavy and too long, even at a time when we still "rang up" at 7.30; and in the April following the production of Tennyson's beautiful tragedy—which I think in sheer poetic intensity surpasses "Becket", although it is not nearly so good a play—"The Belle's Stratagem" was substituted for "The Corsican Brothers". This was the first real rollicking comedy that a Lyceum audience had ever seen, and the way they laughed did my heart good. I had had enough of tragedy and the horrors by this time, and I could have cried with joy at that rare and welcome sight—an audience rocking with laughter. On the first night the play opened propitiously enough with a loud laugh due to the only accident of the kind that ever happened at the Lyceum. The curtain went up before the staff had "cleared", and Arnott, Jimmy and the rest were seen running for their lives out of the centre entrance!

People said that it was so clever of me to play Camma and Letitia Hardy (the comedy part in "The Belle's Stratagem") on the same evening. They used to say the same kind of thing, "only more so", when Henry played Jingle and Matthias in "The Bells". But I never liked doing it. A *tour de force* is always more interesting to the looker-on than to the person who is taking part in it. One feels no pride in such an achievement, which ought to be possible to any one calling himself an

127

actor. Personally, I never play comedy and tragedy on the same night without a sense that one is spoiling the other. Harmonies are more beautiful than contrasts in acting as in other things—and more difficult, too.

Henry Irving was immensely funny as Doricourt. We had sort of Beatrice and Benedick scenes together, and I began to notice what a lot his *face* did for him. There have only been two faces on the stage in my time—his and Duse's.

My face has never been of much use to me, but my *pace* has filled the deficiency sometimes, in comedy at any rate. In "The Belle's Stratagem" the public had face and pace together, and they seemed to like it.

There was one scene in which I sang "Where are you going to, my pretty maid?" I used to act it all the way through and give imitations of Doricourt—ending up by chucking him under the chin. The house rose at it!

I was often asked at this time when I went out to a party if I would not sing that dear little song from "The Cup". When I said I didn't think it would sound very nice without the harp, as it was only a chant on two or three notes, some one would be sure to say:

"Well then, the song in 'The Belle's Stratagem'! *That* has no accompaniment!"

"No," I used to answer, "but it isn't a song. It's a look here, a gesture there, a laugh anywhere, *and* Henry Irving's face everywhere!"

Miss Winifred Emery came to us for "The Belle's Stratagem" and played the part that I had played years before at the Haymarket. She was bewitching, and in her white wig in the ball-room, beautiful as well. She knew how to bear herself on the stage instinctively, and could dance a minuet to perfection. The daughter of Sam Emery, a great comedian in a day of comedians, and the granddaughter of *the* Emery, it was not surprising that she should show aptitude for the stage.

Mr. Howe was another new arrival in the Lyceum company. He was at his funniest as Mr. Hardy in "The Belle's Stratagem". It was not the first time that he had played my father in a piece (we had acted father and daughter in "The Little Treasure"), and I always called him "Daddy". The dear old man was much liked by every one. He had a tremendous pair of legs, was bluff and bustling in manner, though courtly too, and cared more about gardening than acting. He had a little farm at Isleworth, and he was one of those actors who do not allow the longest theatrical season to interfere with domesticity and horticulture! Because of his stout gaitered legs and his Isleworth estate, Henry called him "the agricultural actor". He was a good old port and whisky drinker, but he could carry his liquor like a Regency man.

He was a walking history of the stage. "Yes, my dear," he used to say to me, "I was in the original cast of the first performance of 'The Lady of Lyons', which Lord Lytton gave Macready as a present, and I was the original François when 'Richelieu' was produced. Lord Lytton wrote this part for a lady, but at rehearsal it was found that there was a good deal of movement awkward for a lady to do, and so I was put into it."

"What year was it, Daddy?"

"God bless me, I must think . . . It must have been about a year after Her Majesty took the throne."

For forty years and nine months old Mr. Howe had acted at the Haymarket Theatre! When he was first there, the theatre was lighted with oil lamps, and when a lamp smoked or went out, one of the servants of the theatre came on and lighted it up again during the action of the play.

It was the acting of Edmund Kean in "Richard III" which first filled Daddy Howe with the desire to go on the stage. He saw the great actor again when he was living in retirement at Richmond—in those last sad days when the Baroness Burdett-Coutts (then the rich young heiress, Miss Angela Burdett-Coutts), driving up the hill, saw him sitting huddled up on one of the public seats and asked if she could do anything for him.

"Nothing, I think," he answered sadly. "Ah yes, there is one thing. You were kind enough the other day to send me some very excellent brandy. *Send me some more.*"[1]

Of Henry Irving as an actor Mr. Howe once said to me that at first he was prejudiced against him because he was so different from the other great actors that he had known.

" 'This isn't a bit like Iago,' I said to myself when I first saw him in 'Othello'. That was at the end of the first act. But he had commanded my attention to his innovations. In the second act I found myself deeply interested in watching and studying the development of his conception. In the third act I was fascinated by his originality. By the end of the play I wondered that I could ever have thought that the part ought to be played differently."

Daddy Howe was the first member of the Lyceum company who got a reception from the audience on his entrance as a public favourite. He remained with us until his death, which took place on our fourth American tour in 1893.

Every one has commended Henry Irving's kindly courtesy in inviting Edwin Booth to come and play with him at the Lyceum Theatre. Booth was having a wretched season at the Princess's, which was when he went there a theatre on the down-grade, and under a thoroughly

---

[1] This was a favourite story of Henry Irving's, and for that reason alone I think it worth telling, although Sir Squire Bancroft assures me that stubborn dates make it impossible that the tale should be true.

commercial management. The great American actor, through much domestic trouble and bereavement, had more or less "given up" things. At any rate he had not the spirit which can combat such treatment as he received at the Princess's, where the pieces in which he appeared were "thrown" on to the stage with every mark of assumption that he was not going to be a success.

Yet, although he accepted with gratitude Henry Irving's suggestion that he should migrate from them Princess's to the Lyceum and appear there three times a week as Othello with the Lyceum company and its manager to support him, I cannot be sure that Booth's pride was not more hurt by this magnificent hospitality than it ever could have been by disaster. It is always more difficult to *receive* than to *give*.

Few people thought of this, I suppose. I did, because I could imagine Henry Irving in America in the same situation—accepting the hospitality of Booth. Would not he too have been melancholy, quiet, unassertive, *almost* as uninteresting as Booth was?

I saw him first at a benefit performance at Drury Lane. I came to the door of the room where Henry was dressing, and Booth was sitting there with his back to me.

"Here's Miss Terry," said Henry as I came round the door. Booth looked up at me swiftly. I have never in any face, in any country, seen such wonderful eyes. There was a mystery about his appearance and his manner—a sort of pride which seemed to say: "Don't try to know me, for I am not what I have been." He seemed broken, and devoid of ambition.

At rehearsal he was very gentle and apathetic. Accustomed to playing Othello with stock companies, he had few suggestions to make about the stage-management. The part was to him more or less of a monologue.

"I shall never make you black," he said one morning. "When I take your hand I shall have a corner of my drapery in my hand. That will protect you."

I am bound to say I thought of Mr. Booth's "protection" with some yearning the next week when I played Desdemona to *Henry's* Othello. Before he had done with me I was nearly as black as he.

Booth was a melancholy, dignified Othello, but not great as Salvini was great. Salvini's Hamlet made me scream with mirth, but his Othello was the grandest, biggest, most glorious thing. We often prate of "reserved force". Salvini had it, for the simple reason that he was the gigantic force which may be restrained because of its immensity. Men have no need to dam up a little purling brook. If they do it in acting, it is tame, absurd and pretentious. But Salvini held himself in, and still his groan was like a tempest, his passion huge.

The fact is that, apart from Salvini's personal genius, the foreign temperament is better fitted to deal with Othello than the English. Shakespeare's French and Italians, Greeks and Latins, medievals and barbarians, fancifuls and reals, all have a dash of Elizabethan English men in them, but not Othello.

Booth's Othello was very helpful to my Desdemona. It is difficult to preserve the simple, heroic blindness of Desdemona to the fact that her lord mistrusts her, if her lord is raving and stamping under her nose! Booth was gentle in the scenes with Desdemona until *the* scene where Othello overwhelms her with the foul word and destroys her fool's paradise. Love *does* make fools of us all, surely, but I wanted to make Desdemona out the fool who is the victim of love and faith; not the simpleton, whose want of tact in continually pleading Cassio's cause is sometimes irritating to the audience.

My greatest triumph as Desdemona was not gained with the audience but with Henry Irving! He found my endeavours to accept comfort from Iago so pathetic that they brought the tears to his eyes. It was the oddest sensation when I said "Oh, good Iago, what shall I do to win my lord again?" to look up—my own eyes dry, for Desdemona is past crying then—and see Henry's eyes at their biggest, luminous, soft and full of tears! He was, in spite of Iago and in spite of his power of identifying himself with the part, very deeply moved by my acting. But he knew how to turn it to his purpose: he obtrusively took the tears with his fingers and blew his nose with much feeling, softly and long (so much expression there is, by the way, in blowing the nose on the stage), so that the audience might think his emotion a fresh stroke of hypocrisy.

Every one liked Henry's Iago. For the first time in his life he knew what it was to win unanimous praise. Nothing could be better, I think, than Mr. Walkley's[1] description: "Daringly Italian, a true compatriot of the Borgias, or rather, better than Italians, that devil incarnate, an Englishman Italianate."

One adored him, devil though he was. He was so full of charm, so sincerely the "honest" Iago, peculiarly sympathetic with Othello, Desdemona, Roderigo, *all* of them—except his wife. It was only in the soliloquies and in the scenes with his wife that he revealed his devil's nature. Could one ever forget those grapes which he plucked in the first act, and slowly ate, spitting out the seeds, as if each one represented a worthy virtue to be put out of his mouth, as God, according to the evangelist, puts out the lukewarm virtues. His Iago and his Romeo in different ways proved his power to portray *Italian* passions—the passions of lovely, treacherous people, who will either sing you a love sonnet or stab you in the back—you are not sure which!

We played "Othello" for six weeks, three performances a week, to

[1] Mr. A. B. Walkley, the gifted dramatic critic of *The Times*.

guinea stalls, and could have played it longer. Each week Henry and Booth changed parts. For both of them it was a change *for the worse*.

Booth's Iago seemed deadly commonplace after Henry's. He was always the snake in the grass; he showed the villain in all the scenes. He could not resist the temptation of making polished and ornate effects.

Henry Irving's Othello was condemned almost as universally as his Iago was praised. For once I find myself with the majority. He screamed and ranted and raved—lost his voice, was slow where he should have been swift, incoherent where he should have been strong. I could not bear to see him in the part. It was painful to me. Yet night after night he achieved in the speech to the Senate one of the most superb and beautiful bits of acting of his life. It was *wonderful*. He spoke the speech, beaming on Desdemona all the time. The gallantry of the thing is indescribable.

I think his failure as Othello was one of the unspoken bitternesses of Henry's life. When I say "failure" I am of course judging him by his own standard, and using the word to describe what he was to himself, not what he was to the public. On the last night, he rolled up the clothes that he had worn as the Moor one by one, carefully laying one garment on top of the other, and then, half-humorously and very deliberately said, *"Never again!"* Then he stretched himself with his arms above his head and gave a great sigh of relief.

Mr. Pinero was excellent as Roderigo in this production. He was always good in the "silly ass" type of part, and no one could say of him that he was playing himself!

Desdemona is not counted a big part by actresses, but I loved playing it. Some nights I played it beautifully. My appearance was right—I was such a poor wraith of a thing. But let there be no mistake—it took strength to act this weakness and passiveness of Desdemona's. I soon found that, like Cordelia, she has plenty of character.

Reading the play the other day, I studied the opening scene. It is the finest opening to a play I know.

How many times Shakespeare draws fathers and daughters, and how little stock he seems to take of *mothers*! Portia and Desdemona, Cordelia, Rosalind and Miranda, Lady Macbeth, Queen Katherine and Hermione, Ophelia, Jessica, Hero, and many more are daughters of *fathers*, but of their mothers we hear nothing. My own daughter called my attention to this fact quite recently, and it is really a singular fact. Of mothers of sons there are plenty of examples: Constance, Volumnia, the Countess Rousillon, Gertrude; but if there are mothers of daughters at all, they are poor examples, like Juliet's mother and Mrs. Page. I wonder if in all the many hundreds of books written on Shakespeare and his plays this point has been taken up? I once wrote a paper on the "Letters in Shakespeare's Plays", and congratulated myself that they had never been made a separate study. The very day after I first read my paper before the British Empire Shakespeare League, a lady wrote to me from Oxford and said I was mistaken in thinking that there was no other contribution to the subject. She enclosed an essay of her own which had either been published or read before some society. Probably some one else has dealt with Shakespeare's patronage of fathers and neglect of mothers! I often wonder what the mothers of Goneril, Regan, and Cordelia were like. I think Lear must have married twice.

This was the first of Henry Irving's great Shakespearean productions. "Hamlet" and "Othello" had been mounted with care, but, in spite of statements that I have seen to the contrary, they were not true reflections of Irving as a producer. In beauty I do not think that "Romeo and Juliet" surpassed "The Cup", but it was very sumptuous, impressive and Italian. It was the most *elaborate* of all the Lyceum productions. In it Henry first displayed his mastery of crowds. The brawling of the rival houses in the streets, the procession of girls to wake Juliet on her wedding morning, the musicians, the magnificent reconciliation of the two houses which closed the play, every one on the stage holding a torch, were all treated with a marvellous sense of pictorial effect.

Henry once said to me: " 'Hamlet' could be played anywhere on its acting merits. It marches from situation to situation. But 'Romeo and Juliet' proceeds from picture to picture. Every line suggests a picture. It is a dramatic poem rather than a drama, and I mean to treat it from that point of view."

While he was preparing the production he revived "The Two Roses", a comedy in which as Digby Grant he had made a great success years before. I rehearsed the part of Lottie two or three times, but Henry released me because I was studying Juliet; and as he said, "You've got to do all you know with it".

Perhaps the sense of this responsibility weighed on me. Perhaps I was neither young enough nor old enough to play Juliet. I read everything that had ever been written about her before I had myself decided what she was. It was a dreadful mistake. That was the first thing wrong with my Juliet—lack of original impulse.

As for the second and the third and the fourth—well, I am not more than common vain, I trust, but I see no occasion to write them *all* down.

It was perhaps the greatest opportunity that I had yet had at the Lyceum. I studied the part at my cottage at Hampton Court in a bedroom looking out over the park. There was nothing wrong with *that*. By the way, how important it is to be careful about environment and everything else when one is studying. One ought to be in the country, but not all the time. . . . It is good to go about and see pictures, hear music, and watch everything. One should be very much alone, and should study early and late—all night, if need be, even at the cost of sleep. Everything that one does or thinks or sees will have an effect upon the part, precisely as on an unborn child.

I wish now that instead of reading how this and that actress had played Juliet, and cracking my brain over the different readings of her lines and making myself familiar with the different opinions of philosophers and critics, I had gone to Verona, and just *imagined*. Perhaps the most wonderful description of Juliet, as she should be acted, occurs in Gabriele d'Annunzio's "Il Fuoco". In the book an Italian actress tells her friend how she played the part when she was a girl of fourteen in an open-air theatre near Verona. Could a girl of fourteen play such a part? Yes, if she were not youthful, only young with the youth of the poet, tragically old as some youth is.

Now I understand Juliet better. Now I know how she should be played. But time is inexorable. At sixty, know what one may, one cannot play Juliet.

I know that Henry Irving's production of "Romeo and Juliet" has been attributed to my ambition. What nonsense! Henry Irving now had in view the production of all Shakespeare's actable plays, and naturally "Romeo and Juliet" would come as early as possible in the programme.

The music was composed by Sir Julius Benedict, and was exactly right. There was no *leit-motiv*, no attempt to reflect the passionate emotion of the drama, but a great deal of Southern joy, of flutes and wood and wind. At a rehearsal which had lasted far into the night I asked Sir Julius, who was very old, if he wasn't sleepy.

"Sleepy! Good heavens, no! I never sleep more than two hours. It's the end of my life, and I don't want to waste it in sleep!"

There is generally some "old 'un" in a company now who complains of insufficient rehearsal, and says, perhaps, "Think of Irving's rehearsals! They were the real thing". While we were rehearsing "Romeo and Juliet" I remember that Mrs. Stirling, a charming and ripe old actress whom Henry had engaged to play the Nurse, was always groaning out that she had not rehearsed enough.

"Oh, these modern ways!" she used to say. "We never have any rehearsals at all. How am I going to play the Nurse?"

She played it splendidly—indeed, she as the Nurse and old Tom Mead as the Apothecary—the two "old 'uns" romped away with chief honours, had the play all to nothing.

I had one battle with Mrs. Stirling over "tradition". It was in the scene beginning—

> The clock struck twelve when I did send the nurse,
> And yet she is not here. . . .

Tradition said that Juliet must go on coquetting and clicking over the Nurse to get the news of Romeo out of her. Tradition said that Juliet must give imitations of the Nurse on the line "Where's your mother?" in order to get that cheap reward, "a safe laugh". I felt that it was wrong. I felt that Juliet was angry with the Nurse. Each time she delayed in answering I lost my temper, with genuine passion. At "Where's your mother?" I spoke with indignation, tears and rage. We were a long time coaxing Mrs. Stirling to let the scene be played on these lines, but this was how it *was* played eventually.

She was the only Nurse that I have ever seen who did not play the part like a female pantaloon. She did not assume any great decrepitude. In the "Cords" scene, where the Nurse tells Juliet of the death of Paris, she did not play for comedy at all, but was very emotional. Her parrot scream when she found me dead was horribly real and effective.

Years before I had seen Mrs. Stirling act at the Adelphi with Benjamin Webster, and had cried out: "*That's* my idea of an actress!" In those days she was playing Olivia (in a version of the "Vicar of Wakefield" by Tom Taylor), Peg Woffington, and other parts of the kind. She swept on to the stage and in that magical way, never, never to be learned, *filled* it. She had such breadth of style, such a lovely voice, such a beautiful expressive eye! When she played the Nurse at the Lyceum her voice had become a little jangled and harsh, but her eye was still bright and her art had not abated—not one little bit! Nor had her charm. Her smile was the most fascinating, irresistible thing imaginable.

The production was received with abuse by the critics. It was one of our failures, yet it ran a hundred and fifty nights!

Henry Irving's Romeo had more bricks thrown at it even than my Juliet! I remember that not long after we opened, a well-known politician who had enough wit and knowledge of the theatre to have taken a more original view, came up to me and said:

"I say, E. T., why is Irving playing Romeo?"

I looked at him distraught. "You should ask me why I am playing Juliet! Why are we any of us doing what we have to do?"

"Oh, *you're* all right. But Irving!"

"I don't agree with you," I said. I was growing a little angry by this time. "Besides, who would you have play Romeo?"

"Well, it's so obvious. You've got Terriss in the cast."

"*Terriss!*"

"Yes. I don't doubt Irving's intellectuality, you know. As Romeo he reminds me of a pig who has been taught to play the fiddle. He does it cleverly, but he would be better employed in squealing. He cannot shine in the part like the fiddler. Terriss in this case is the fiddler."

I was furious. "I am sorry you don't realise," I said, "that the worst thing Henry Irving could do would be better than the best of any one else."

When dear Terriss did play Romeo at the Lyceum two or three years later to the Juliet of Mary Anderson, he attacked the part with a good deal of fire. He was young, truly, and stamped his foot a great deal, was vehement and passionate. But it was so obvious that there was no intelligence behind his reading. He did not know what the part was about, and all the finer shades of meaning in it he missed. Yet the majority, with my political friend, would always prefer a Terriss as Romeo to a Henry Irving.

I am not going to say that Henry's Romeo was good. What I do say is that some bits of it were as good as anything he ever did. In the big emotional scene (in the Friar's cell), he came to grief precisely as he had done in Othello. He screamed, grew slower and slower, and looked older and older. When I begin to think it over I see that he often failed in such scenes through his very genius for impersonation. An actor of commoner mould takes such scenes rhetorically—recites them, and gets through them with some success. But the actor who impersonates, feels, and lives such anguish or passion or tempestuous grief, does for the moment in imagination nearly die. Imagination impeded Henry Irving in what are known as "strong" scenes.

He was a perfect Hamlet, a perfect Richard III, a perfect Shylock, except in the scene with Tubal, where I think his voice failed him. He was an imperfect Romeo; yet, as I have said, he did things in the part which were equal to the best of his perfect Hamlet.

His whole attitude before he met Juliet was beautiful. He came on from the very back of the stage and walked over a little bridge with a book in his hand, sighing and dying for Rosaline. In Iago he had been Italian. Then it was the Italy of Venice. As Romeo it was the Italy of Tuscany. His clothes were as Florentine as his bearing. He ignored the silly tradition that Romeo must wear a feather in his cap. In the course of his study of the part he had found that the youthful fops and gallants of the period put in their hats anything that they had been given—some souvenir "dallying with the innocence of love". And he wore in his hat a sprig of crimson oleander.

It is not unusual, I think, to make much of the Rosaline episode. Henry Irving chose with great care a tall dark girl to represent Rosaline at the ball. Can I ever forget his face when suddenly in pursuit of *her* he saw *me*. . . . Once more I reflect that a *face* is the chiefest equipment of the actor.

I know they said he looked too old—was too old for Romeo. In some scenes he looked aged as only a very young man can look. He was not boyish; but ought Romeo to be boyish?

I am not supporting the idea of an elderly Romeo. When it came to the scenes where Romeo "poses" and is poetical but insincere, Henry *did* seem elderly. He couldn't catch the youthful pose of melancholy with its extravagant expression. It was in the repressed scenes, where the melancholy was sincere, the feeling deeper, and the expression slighter, that he was at his best.

"He may be good, but he isn't Romeo," is a favourite type of criticism. But I have seen Duse and Bernhardt in "La Dame aux Camélias", and cannot say which is Marguerite Gauthier. Each has her own view of the character, and each *is* it *according to her imagination.*

According to his imagination, Henry Irving was Romeo.

Again in this play he used his favourite "fate" tree. It gloomed over the street along which Romeo went to the ball. It was in the scene with the Apothecary. Henry thought that it symbolised the destiny hanging over the lovers.

It is usual for Romeo to go in to the dead body of Juliet lying in Capulet's monument through a gate on the *level*, as if the Capulets were buried but a few feet from the road. At rehearsals Henry Irving kept on saying: "I must go *down* to the vault." After a great deal of consideration he had an inspiration. He had the exterior of the vault in one scene, the entrance to it down a flight of steps. Then the scene changed to the interior of the vault, and the steps now led from a height above the stage. At the close of the scene, when the Friar and the crowd came rushing down into the tomb, these steps were thronged with people, each one holding a torch, and the effect was magnificent.

At the opening of the Apothecary Scene, when Balthazar comes to tell Romeo of Juliet's supposed death, Henry was marvellous. His face grew whiter and whiter.

> Then she is well and nothing can be ill;
> Her body sleeps in Capulet's monument.

It was during the silence after those two lines that Henry Irving as Romeo had one of those sublime moments which an actor only achieves once or twice in his life. The only thing that I ever saw to compare with it was Duse's moment when she took Kellner's card in "Magda". There was absolutely no movement, but her face grew white, and the audience knew what was going on in her soul, as she read the name of the man who years before had seduced and deserted her.

As Juliet I did not *look* right. My little daughter Edy, a born archaeologist, said: "Mother, you oughtn't to have a fringe." Yet, strangely enough, Henry himself liked me as Juliet. After the first night, or was it the dress rehearsal—I am not quite clear which—he wrote to me that "beautiful as Portia was, Juliet leaves her far, far behind. Never anybody acted more exquisitely the part of the performance which I saw from the front. 'Hie to high fortune,' and 'Where spirits resort' were simply incomparable. . . . Your mother looked very radiant last night. I told her how proud she should be, and she was. . . . The play will be, I believe, a mighty 'go', for the beauty of it is bewildering. I am sure of this, for it dumbfounded them all last night. Now you—we—must make our task a delightful one by doing everything possible to make our acting easy and comfortable. We are in for a long run."

To this letter he added a very human postscript: "I have determined not to see a paper for a week—I know they'll cut me up, and I don't like it!"

Yes, he *was* cut up, and he didn't like it, but a few people knew. One of them was Mr. Frankfort Moore, the novelist, who wrote to me of this "revealing Romeo, full of originality and power".

"Are you affected by adverse criticism?" I was asked once. I answered then and I answer now, that legitimate adverse criticism has always been of use to me if only because it "gave me to think" furiously. Seldom does the outsider, however talented, as a writer and observer, recognise the actor's art, and often we are told that we are acting best when we are showing the works most plainly, and denied any special virtue when we are concealing our method. Professional criticism is most helpful, chiefly because it induces one to criticise oneself. "Did I give that impression to any one? Then there must have been something wrong somewhere." The "something" is often a perfectly different blemish from that to which the critic drew attention.

Unprofessional criticism is often more helpful still, but alas! one's friends are to one's faults more than a little blind, and to one's virtues very kind! It is through letters from people quite unknown to me that I have sometimes learned valuable lessons. During the run of "Romeo and Juliet" some one wrote and told me that if the dialogue at the ball could be taken in a lighter and *quicker* way, it would better express the manner of a girl of Juliet's age. The same unknown critic pointed out that I was too slow and studied in the Balcony Scene. She—I think it was a woman—was perfectly right.

On the hundredth night, although no one liked my Juliet very much, I received many flowers, little tokens, and poems. To one bouquet was pinned a note which ran:

To Juliet,
 As a mark of respect and Esteem
  From the Gasmen of the Lyceum Theatre.

That alone would have made my recollections of "Romeo and Juliet" pleasant. But there was more. At the supper on the stage after the hundredth performance, Sarah Bernhardt was present. She said nice things to me, and I was enraptured that my "vraies larmes" should have pleased and astonished her! I noticed that she hardly ever moved, yet all the time she gave the impression of swift, butterfly movement. While talking to Henry she took some red stuff out of her bag and rubbed it on her lips! This frank "making up" in public was a far more astonishing thing in the 'eighties than it would be now. But I liked Miss Sarah for it, as I liked her for everything.

How wonderful she looked in those days! She was as transparent as an azalea, only more so; like a cloud, only not so thick. Smoke from a burning paper describes her more nearly! She was hollow-eyed, thin, almost consumptive-looking. Her body was not the prison of her soul, but its shadow.

On the stage she has always seemed to me more a symbol, an ideal, an epitome than a *woman*. It is this quality which makes her so easy in such lofty parts as Phèdre. She is always a miracle. Let her play "L' Aiglon", and while matter-of-fact members of the audience are wondering if she looks *really* like the unfortunate King of Rome, and deciding against her and in favour of Maude Adams who did look the boy to perfection, more imaginative watchers see in Sarah's performance a truth far bigger than a mere physical resemblance. Rostand says in the foreword to his play, that in it he does not espouse this cause or that, but only tells the story of "one poor little boy". In another of his plays, "Cyrano de Bergerac", there is one poor little tune played on a pipe of which the hero says:

Écoutez, Gascons, c'est toute la Gascogne.

Though I am not French, and know next to nothing of the language, I thought when I saw Sarah's "L'Aiglon", that of that one poor little boy too might be said:

Écoutez, Français, c'est toute la France!

It is this extraordinary decorative and symbolic quality of Sarah's which makes her transcend all personal and individual feeling on the stage. No one plays a love scene better, but it is a *picture* of love that she gives, a strange orchidaceous picture rather than a suggestion of the ordinary human passion as felt by ordinary human people. She is exotic—well, what else should she be? One does not, at any rate one should not, quarrel with an exquisite tropical flower and call it unnatural because it is not a buttercup or a cowslip.

I have spoken of the face as the chief equipment of the actor. Sarah Bernhardt contradicts this at once. Her face does little for her. Her walk is not much. Nothing about her is more remarkable than the way she gets about the stage without one ever seeing her move. By what magic does she triumph without two of the richest possessions that an actress can have? Eleonora Duse has them. Her walk is the walk of the peasant, fine and free. She has the superb carriage of the head which goes with that fearless movement from the hips—and her face! There is nothing like it, nothing! But it is as the real woman, a particular woman, that Duse triumphs most. Her Cleopatra was insignificant compared with Sarah's— she is not so pictorial.

How futile it is to make comparisons! Better far to thank heaven for both these women.

Saturday, June 11, 1892—"To see 'Miss Sarah' as 'Cléopâtre' (Sardou superb!). She was inspired! The essence of Shakespeare's 'Cleopatra'. I went round and implored her to do Juliet. She said she was too old. She can *never* be old. 'Age cannot wither her.'

June 18—"Again to see Sarah—this time 'La Dame aux Camélias'. Fine, marvellous. Her writing the letter, and the last act the best.

July 11—"*Telegraph* says 'Frou-frou' was 'never at any time a character in which she (Sarah) excelled'. Dear me! When I saw it I thought it wonderful. It made me ashamed of ever having played it."

Sarah Bernhardt has shown herself the equal of any man as a manager. Her productions are always beautiful; she chooses her company with discretion, and sees to every detail of the stage-management. In this respect she differs from all other foreign artists that I have seen. I have always regretted that Duse should play as a rule with such a mediocre company and should be apparently so indifferent to her surroundings. In "Adrienne Lecouvreur" it struck me that the careless stage-management utterly ruined the play, and I could not bear to see Duse as Adrienne beautifully dressed while the Princess and the other Court ladies wore cheap red velveteen and white satin and brought the pictorial level of the performance down to that of a "fit-up" or booth.

Who could mention "Miss Sarah" (my own particular name for her) as being present at a supper-party without saying something about her by the way! Still, I have been a long time by the way. Now for Romeo and Juliet!

At that 100th-night celebration I saw Mrs. Langtry in evening dress for the first time, and for the first time realised how beautiful she was. Her neck and shoulders kept me so busy looking that I could neither talk nor listen.

"Miss Sarah" and I have always been able to understand one another, although I hardly know a word of French and her English is scanty. She too, liked my Juliet—she and Henry Irving! Well, that was charming, although I could not like it myself, except for my "Cords" scene, of which I shall always be proud.

My dresser, Sarah Holland, came to me, I think, during "Romeo and Juliet". I never had any other dresser at the Lyceum except Sally's sister Lizzie, who dressed me during the first few years. Sally stuck to me loyally until the Lyceum days ended. Then she perceived "a divided duty". On one side was "the Guv'nor" with "the Guv'nor's" valet Walter, to whom she was devoted; on the other was a precarious in and out job with me, for after the Lyceum I never knew what I was going to do next. She chose to go with Henry, and it was she and Walter who dressed him for the last time when he lay dead in the hotel bedroom at Bradford.

Sally Holland's two little daughters "walked on" in "Romeo and Juliet". Henry always took an interest in the children in the theatre, and was very kind to them. One night as we came down the stairs from our dressing-rooms to go home—the theatre was quiet and deserted—we found a small child sitting forlornly and patiently on the lowest step.

"Well, my dear, what are you doing here?" said Henry.

"Waiting for mother, sir."

"Are you acting in the theatre?"

"Yes, sir."

"And what part do you take?"

"Please, sir, first I'm a water-carrier, then I'm a little page, and then I'm a virgin."

Henry and I sat down on the stairs and laughed until we cried! Little Flo Holland was one of the troop of "virgins" who came to wake Juliet on her bridal morn. As time went on she was promoted to more important parts, but she never made us laugh so much again.

Her mother was a "character", a dear character. She had an extra-ordinarily open mind, and was ready to grasp each new play as it came along as a separate and entirely different field of operations! She was also extremely methodical, and only got flurried once in a blue moon. When we went to America and made the acquaintance of that dreadful thing a "one-night stand", she was as precise and particular about having everything nice and in order for me as if we were going to stay in the town a month. Down went my neat square of white drugget; all the lights in my dressing-room were arranged as I wished. Everything was unpacked and ironed. One day when I came into some American theatre to dress I found Sally nearly in tears.

"What's the matter with you, Sally?" I asked.

"I 'aven't 'ad a morsel to heat all day, dear, and I can't 'eat my iron."

"Eat your iron, Sally! What *do* you mean?"

"'Ow am I to iron all this, dear?" wailed Sally, picking up my Nance Oldfield apron and a few other trifles. "It won't get 'ot."

Until then I really thought that Sally was being sardonic about an iron as a substitute for victuals!

When she first began to dress me, I was very thin, so thin that it was really a grief to me. Sally would comfort me in my thin days by the terse compliment:

"Beautiful and fat tonight, dear."

As the years went on and I grew fat, she made a change in the compliment:

"Beautiful and thin tonight, dear."

Mr. Fernandez played Friar Laurence in "Romeo and Juliet". He was a very nervous actor, and it used to paralyse him with fright when I knelt down in the friar's cell with my back to the audience and put safety pins in the drapery I wore over my head to keep it in position while I said the lines,

> Are you at leisure, holy father, now
> Or shall I come to you at evening mass?

Not long after the production of "Romeo and Juliet" I saw the performance of a Greek play—the "Electra", I think—by some Oxford students. A young woman veiled in black with bowed head was brought in on a chariot. Suddenly she lifted her head and looked round, revealing a face of such pure classic beauty and a glance of such pathos that I called out:

"What a supremely beautiful girl!"

Then I remembered that there were no women in the cast! The face belonged to a young Oxford man, Frank Benson.

We engaged him to play Paris in "Romeo and Juliet", when George Alexander, the original Paris, left the Lyceum for a time. Already Benson gave promise of turning out quite a different person from the others. He had not nearly so much of the actor's instinct as Terriss, but one felt that he had far more earnestness. He was easily distinguished as a man with a purpose, one of those workers who "scorn delights and live laborious days". Those laborious days led him at last to the control of two or three companies, all travelling through Great Britain playing a Shakespearean répertoire. A wonderful organiser, a good actor (oddly enough, the more difficult the part the better he is—I like his *Lear*), and a man who has always been associated with high endeavour, Frank Benson's name is honoured all over England. He was only at the Lyceum for this one production, but he always regarded Henry Irving as the source of the good work that he did afterwards.

"Thank you very much," he wrote to me after his first night as Paris, "for writing me a word of encouragement. . . . I was very much ashamed and disgusted with myself all Sunday for my poverty-stricken and thin performance. . . . I think I was a little better last night. Indeed I was much touched at the kindness and sympathy of all the company and their efforts to make the awkward new boy feel at home . . . . I feel doubly grateful to you and Mr. Irving for the light you shed from the lamp of art on life now that I begin to understand the labour and weariness the process of trimming the Lamp entails."

X

LYCEUM PRODUCTIONS (*continued*)

"MUCH ADO ABOUT NOTHING" TO "FAUST"

OUR success with "The Belle's Stratagem" had pointed to comedy, to Beatrice and Benedick in particular, because in Mrs. Cowley's old comedy we had had some scenes of the same type. I have already told of my first appearance as Beatrice at Leeds, and said that I never played the part so well again; but the Lyceum production was a great success, and Beatrice a great personal success for me. It is only in high comedy that people seem to know what I am driving at!

The stage-management of the play was very good; the scenery nothing out of the ordinary except for the Church Scene. There was no question that it *was* a church, hardly a question that old Mead was a Friar. Henry had the art of making ceremonies seem very real.

This was the first time that we engaged a singer from outside. Mr. Jack Robertson came into the cast to sing "Sigh no more, ladies", and made an enormous success.

Johnston Forbes-Robertson made his first appearance at the Lyceum as Claudio. I had not acted with him since "The Wandering Heir", and his improvement as an actor in the ten years that had gone by since then was marvellous. I had once said to him that he had far better stick to his painting and become an artist instead of an actor. His Claudio made me "take it back". It was beautiful. I have seen many young actors play the part since then, but not one of them made it anywhere near as convincing. Forbes-Robertson put a touch of Leontes into it, a part which some years later he was to play magnificently, and through the subtle indication of consuming and insanely suspicious jealousy made Claudio's offensive conduct explicable at least. On the occasion of the performance at Drury Lane which the theatrical profession organised in 1906 in honour of my Stage Jubilee, one of the items in the programme was a scene from "Much Ado About Nothing". I then played Beatrice for the last time and Forbes-Robertson played his old part of Claudio.

During the run Henry commissioned him to paint a picture of the Church Scene, which was hung in the Beefsteak Room. The engravings printed from it were at one time very popular. When Johnston was asked why he had chosen that particular moment in the Church Scene, he answered modestly that it was the only moment when he could put himself as Claudio at the "side"! Some of the other portraits in the picture are Henry Irving, Terriss, who played Don Pedro; Jessie Millward as Hero, Mr. Glenny as Don John, Miss Amy Coleridge, Miss

Harwood, Mr. Mead, and his daughter "Charley" Mead, a pretty little thing who was one of the pages.

The Lyceum company was not a permanent one. People used to come, learn something, go away, and come back at a larger salary! Miss Emery left for a time, and then returned to play Hero and other parts. I liked her Hero better than Miss Millward's. Miss Millward had a sure touch; strength, vitality, interest; but somehow she was commonplace in the part.

Henry used to spend hours and hours teaching people. I used to think impatiently: "Acting can't be taught." Gradually I learned to modify this conviction and to recognise that there are two classes of actors:

1. Those who can only do what they are taught.

2. Those who cannot be taught, but can be helped by suggestion to work out things for themselves.

Henry said to me once: "What makes a popular actor? Physique! What makes a great actor? Imagination and sensibility." I tried to believe it. Then I thought to myself: "Henry himself is not quite what is understood by 'an actor of physique', and certainly he is popular. And that he is a great actor I know. He certainly has both imagination and 'sense and sensibility'." After the lapse of years I begin to wonder if Henry was ever really *popular*. It was natural to most people to dislike his acting—they found it queer, as some find the painting of Whistler—but he forced them, almost against their will and nature, out of dislike into admiration. They had to come up to him, for never would he go down to them. This is not popularity.

Brain allied with the instinct of the actor tells, but stupidity allied with the instinct of the actor tells more than brain alone. I have sometimes seen a clever man who was not a born actor play a small part with his brains, and have felt that the cleverness was telling more with the actors on the stage than with the audience.

Terriss, like Mrs. Pritchard, if we are to believe what Dr. Johnson said of her, often did not know what on earth he was talking about! One morning we went over and over one scene in "Much Ado"—at least a dozen times I should think—and each time when Terriss came to the speech beginning:

What needs the bridge much broader than the flood.

he managed to give a different emphasis. First it would be:

"What! *Needs* the bridge much broader than the flood!" Then:

"What needs the bridge *much* broader than the flood." After he had been floundering about for some time, Henry said:

"Terriss, what's the meaning of that?"

"Oh, get along, Guv'nor, *you* know!"

Henry laughed. He never could be angry with Terriss, not even when he came to rehearsal full of absurd excuses. One day, however, he was so late that it was past a joke, and Henry spoke to him sharply.

"I think you'll be sorry you've spoken to me like this, Guv'nor," said Terriss, casting down his eyes.

"Now no hanky-panky tricks, Terriss."

"Tricks, Guv'nor! I think you'll regret having said that when you hear that my poor mother passed away early this morning."

And Terriss wept.

Henry promptly gave him the day off. A few weeks later, when Terriss and I were looking through the curtain at the audience just before the play began, he said to me gaily:

"See that dear old woman sitting in the fourth row of stalls—that's my dear old mother."

The wretch had quite forgotten that he had killed her!

He was the only person who ever ventured to "cheek" Henry, yet he never gave offence, not even when he wrote a letter of this kind:

MY DEAR GUV., I hope you are enjoying yourself, and in the best of health. I very much want to play "Othello" with you next year (don't laugh). Shall I study it up, and will you do it with me on tour if possible? Say *yes*, and lighten the drooping heart of yours sincerely,

WILL TERRISS.

I have never seen any one at all like Terriss, and my father said the same. The only actor of my father's day, he used to tell me, who had a touch of the same insouciance and lawlessness was Leigh Murray, a famous *jeune premier*.

One night he came into the theatre soaked from head to foot.

"Is it raining, Terriss?" said some one who noticed that he was wet.

"Looks like it, doesn't it?" said Terriss carelessly.

Later it came out that he had jumped off a penny steam-boat into the Thames and saved a little girl's life. It was pretty brave, I think.

Mr. Pinero, who was no longer a member of the Lyceum company when "Much Ado" was produced, wrote to Henry after the first night that it was "as perfect a representation of a Shakespearean play as I conceive to be possible". "I think," he added, "that the work at your theatre does so much to create new playgoers—which is what we want, far more I fancy than we want new theatres and perhaps new plays."

A playgoer whose knowledge of the English stage extended over a period of fifty-five years, wrote another nice letter about "Much Ado" which was passed on to me because it had some ridiculously nice things about me in it.

145

SAVILE CLUB.
January 13, 1883.
MY DEAR HENRY, I were an imbecile ingrate if I did not hasten to give you my warmest thanks for the splendid entertainment of last night. Such a performance is not a grand entertainment merely, or a glorious pastime, although it was all that. It was, too, an artistic display of the highest character, elevating in the vast audience their art instinct—as well as purifying any developed art in the possession of individuals.

I saw the Kean revivals of 1855–57, and I suppose "The Winter's Tale" was the best of the lot. But it did not approach last night. . . .

I was impressed more strongly than ever with the fact that the plays of Shakespeare were meant to be *acted*. The man who thinks that he can know Shakespeare by reading him is a shallow ass. The best critic and scholar would have been carried out of himself last night into the poet's heart, his mind-spirit . . . The Terry was glorious. . . . The scenes in which she appeared—and she was in eight out of the sixteen—reminded me of nothing but the blessed sun that not only beautifies but creates. But she never acts so well as when I am there to see! That is a real lover's sentiment, and all lovers are vain men.

Terriss has "come on" wonderfully, and his Don Pedro is princely and manful.

I have thus set down, my dear Irving, one or two things merely to show that my gratitude to you is not that of a blind gratified idiot, but of one whose intimate personal knowledge of the English stage entitles him to say what he owes to you.

I am, affectionately yours,
A. J. DUFFIELD.

In 1891, when we revived "Much Ado", Henry's Benedick was far more brilliant than it was at first. In my diary, January 5, 1891, I wrote:

Revival of "Much Ado about Nothing". Went most brilliantly. Henry has vastly improved upon his *old* rendering of Benedick. Acts larger now—not so "finicking". His model (of manner) is the Duke of Sutherland. VERY good. I did some parts better, I think—made Beatrice a nobler woman. Yet I failed to please myself in the Cathedral Scene.

Two days later—Played the Church Scene all right at last. More of a *blaze*. The little scene in the garden, too, I did better (in the last act). Beatrice has *confessed* her love, and is now *softer*. Her voice should be beautiful now, breaking out into playful defiance now and again, as of old. The last scene, too, I made much more merry, happy, *soft*.

January 8—I must make Beatrice more *flashing* at first, and *softer* afterwards. This will be an improvement upon my old reading of the part. She must be always *merry* and by turns scornful, tormenting, vexed, self-communing, absent, melting, teasing, brilliant, indignant, *sad-merry*, thoughtful, withering, gentle, humorous, and gay, Gay, *Gay!* Protecting (to Hero), motherly, very intellectual—a gallant creature and complete in mind and feature.

After a run of two hundred and fifty nights, "Much Ado", although it was still drawing fine houses, was withdrawn as we were going to America in the autumn (of 1883) and Henry wanted to rehearse the plays that we were to do in the States by reviving them in London at the close of the summer season. It was during these revivals that I played Janette in "The Lyons Mail"—not a big part, and not well suited to me, but I played it well enough to support my theory that whatever I have *not* been, I *have* been a useful actress.

I always associate "The Lyons Mail" with old Mead, whose performance of the father, Jerome Lesurques, was one of the most impressive things that this fine actor ever did with us. (Before Henry was ever heard of, Mead had played Hamlet at Drury Lane!) Indeed when he "broke up", Henry put aside "The Lyons Mail" for many years because he dreaded playing Lesurques' scene with his father without Mead.

In the days just before the break-up, which came about because Mead was old, and—I hope there is no harm in saying of him what can be said of many men who have done finely in the world—too fond of "the wine when it is red", Henry used to suffer great anxiety in the scene, because he never knew what Mead was going to do or say next. When Jerome Lesurques is forced to suspect his son of crime, he has a line:

Am I mad, or dreaming? Would I were.

Mead one night gave a less poetic reading:

Am I mad or *drunk*? Would I were!

It will be remembered by those who saw the play that Lesurques, an innocent man, will not commit the Roman suicide of honour at his father's bidding, and refuses to take up his pistol from the table. "What! you refuse to die by your own hands, do you?" says the elder Lesurques. "Then die like a dog by mine!" (producing a pistol from his pocket).

One night, after delivering the line with his usual force and impressiveness, Mead, after prolonged fumbling in his coat-tail pockets, added another:

"D——, b——! God bless my soul! Where's the pistol? I haven't got the pistol!"

The last scene in the eventful history of "Meadisms" in "The Lyons Mail" was when Mead came on to the stage in his own top-hat, went over to the sofa, and lay down, apparently for a nap! Not a word could Henry get from him, and Henry had to play the scene by himself. He did it in this way:

"You say, father, that I," etc. "I answer you that it is false!"

Mead had a remarkable *foot*. Norman Forbes called it an *architectural* foot. Bunions and gout combined to give it a gargoyled effect! One night, I forget whether it was in this play or another, Henry, pawing the ground with his foot before an "exit"—one of the mannerisms which his imitators delighted to burlesque—came down on poor old Mead's foot, bunion, gargoyles and all! Hardly had Mead stopped cursing under his breath than on came Tyars, and brought down *his* weight heavily on the same foot. Directly Tyars came off the stage he looked for Mead in the wings and offered an apology.

"I beg your pardon—I'm really awfully sorry, Mead."

"Sorry! sorry!" the old man snorted. "It's a d——d conspiracy!"

It was the dignity and gravity of Mead which made everything he said so funny. I am afraid that those who never knew him will wonder where the joke comes in.

I forget what year he left us for good, but in a letter of Henry's dated September 1888, written during a provincial tour of "Faust", when I was ill and my sister Marion played Margaret instead of me, I find this allusion to him:

"Wenman does the Kitchen Witch now (I altered it this morning) and Mead the old one—the climber. Poor old chap, he'll not climb much longer!"

"Twelfth Night" was one of the least successful of Henry's Shake-spearean productions. Terriss looked all wrong as Orsino; many other people were miscast. Henry said to me a few years later when he thought of doing "The Tempest", "I can't do it without three great comedians. I ought never to have attempted 'Twelfth Night' without them".

I don't think that I played Viola nearly as well as my sister Kate. Her "I am the man" was very delicate and charming. I overdid that. My daughter says: "Well, you were far better than any Viola that I have seen since, but you were too simple to make a great hit in it. I think that if you had played Rosalind the public would have thought you too simple in that. Somehow people expect these parts to be acted in a 'principal boy' fashion, with sparkle and animation."

We had the curious experience of being "booed" on the first night. It was not a comedy audience, and I think the rollickings of Toby Belch and his fellows were thought "low". Then people were put out by Henry's attempt to reserve the pit. He thought that the public wanted it. When he found that it was against their wishes he immediately gave in. His pride was the service of the public.

His speech after the hostile reception of "Twelfth Night" was the only mistake that I ever knew him make. He was furious, and showed it. Instead of accepting the verdict, he trounced the first-night audience for giving it. He simply could not understand it!

My old friend Rose Leclercq, who was in Charles Kean's company at the Princess's when I made my first appearance upon the stage, joined the Lyceum company to play Olivia. Strangely enough she had lost the touch for the kind of part. She, who had made one of her early successes as the spirit of Astarte in "Manfred", was known to a later generation of playgoers as the aristocratic dowager of stately presence and incisive repartee. Her son, Fuller Mellish, was also in the cast as Curio, and when we played "Twelfth Night" in America was promoted to the part of Sebastian, my double. In London my brother Fred played it. Directly he walked on to the stage, looking as like me as possible, yet a *man* all over, he was a success. I don't think that I have ever seen anything so unmistakable and instantaneous.

In America "Twelfth Night" was liked far better than in London, but I never liked it. I thought our production dull, lumpy and heavy. Henry's Malvolio was fine and dignified, but not good for the play, and I never could help associating my Viola with physical pain. On the first night I had a bad thumb—I thought it was a whitlow—and had to carry my arm in a sling. It grew worse every night, and I felt so sick and faint from pain that I played most of my scenes sitting in a chair. One night Dr. Stoker, Bram Stoker's brother, came round between the scenes, and, after looking at my thumb, said:

"Oh, that'll be all right. I'll cut it for you."

He lanced it then and there, and I went on with my part for *that* night. George Stoker, who was just going off to Ireland, could not see the job through, but the next day I was in for the worst illness I ever had in my life. It was blood-poisoning, and the doctors were in doubt for a little as to whether they would not have to amputate my arm. They said that if George Stoker had not lanced the thumb that minute, I *should* have lost my arm.

A disagreeable incident in connection with my illness was that a member of my profession made it the occasion of an unkind allusion (in a speech at the Social Science Congress) to "actresses who feign illness and have straw laid down before their houses, while behind the drawn blinds they are having riotous supper-parties, dancing the can-can and drinking champagne". Upon being asked for "name", the speaker would neither assert nor deny that it was Ellen Terry (whose poor arm at the time was as big as her waist, and *that* has never been very small!) that she meant.

I think we first heard of the affair on our second voyage to America, during which I was still so ill that they thought I might never see Quebec, and Henry wrote a letter to the press—a "scorcher". He showed it to me on the boat. When I had read it, I tore it up and threw the bits into the sea.

"It hasn't injured me in any way," I said. "Any answer would be undignified."

Henry did what I wished in the matter, but, unlike me, whose heart I am afraid is of wax—no impression lasts long—he never forgot it, and never forgave. If the speech-maker chanced to come into a room where he was—he walked out. He showed the same spirit in the last days of his life, long after our partnership had come to an end. A literary club, not a hundred yards from Hyde Park Corner, "blackballed" me (although I was qualified for election under the rules) for reasons with which I was never favoured. The committee, a few months later, wished Henry Irving to be the guest of honour at one of the club dinners. The honour was declined.

The first night of "Olivia" at the Lyceum was about the only *comfortable* first night that I have ever had! I was familiar with the part, and two of the cast, Terriss and Norman Forbes, were the same as at the Court, which made me feel all the more at home. Henry left a great deal of the stage-management to us, for he knew that he could not improve on Mr. Hare's production. Only he insisted on altering the last act, and made a bad matter worse. The division into two scenes wasted time, and nothing was gained by it. *Never* obstinate, Henry saw his mistake and restored the original end after a time. It was weak and unsatisfactory but not pretentious and bad like the last act he presented at the first performance.

We took the play too slowly at the Lyceum. That was often a fault there. Because Henry was slow, the others took their time from him, and the result was bad.

The lovely scene of the vicarage parlour, in which we used a harpsichord and were accused of pedantry for our pains, did not look so well at the Lyceum as at the Court. The stage was too big for it.

The critics said that I played Olivia better at the Lyceum, but I did not feel this myself.

At first Henry did not rehearse the Vicar at all well. One day when he was stamping his foot very much, as if he were Mathias in "The Bells", my little Edy, who was a terrible child *and* a wonderful critic, said:

"Don't go on like that, Henry. Why don't you talk as you do to me and Teddy? At home you *are* the Vicar."

The child's frankness did not offend Henry, because it was illuminating. A blind man had changed his Shylock; a little child changed his Vicar. When the first night came he gave a simple, lovable performance. Many people now understood and liked him as they had never done before. One of the things I most admired in it was his sense of the period.

In this, as in other plays, he used to make his entrance in the *skin* of the part. No need for him to rattle a ladder at the side to get up excitement and illusion as Macready is said to have done. He walked on, and was the simple-minded old clergyman, just as he had walked on a prince in "Hamlet", a king in "Charles I", and a saint in "Becket".

A very handsome woman, descended from Mrs. Siddons and looking exactly like her, played the gipsy in "Olivia". The likeness was of no use, because the possessor of it had no talent. What a pity!

"Olivia" has always been a family play. Edy and Ted walked on the stage for the first time in the Court "Olivia". In later years Ted played Moses and Edy made her first appearance in a speaking part as Polly Flamborough, and has since played both Sophia and the Gipsy. My brother Charlie's little girl Beatrice made her first appearance as Bill, my sister Floss played Olivia on a provincial tour, and my sister Marion played it at the Lyceum when I was ill.

I saw Floss play it, and took from her a lovely and sincere bit of "business". In the third act, where the Vicar has found his erring daughter and has come to take her away from the inn, I had always hesitated at my entrance as if I were not quite sure what reception my father would give me after what had happened. Floss in the same situation came running in and went straight to her father, quite sure of his love if not of his forgiveness.

I did *not* take some business which Marion did on Terriss's suggestion. Where Thornhill tells Olivia that she is not his wife, I used to thrust him away with both hands as I said—"Devil!"

"It's very good, Nell, very fine," said Terriss to me, "but believe me, you miss a great effect there. You play it grandly, of course, but at that moment you miss it. As you say 'Devil!' you ought to strike me full in the face."

"Oh, don't be silly, Terriss," I said, "she's not a pugilist."

Of course I saw, apart from what was dramatically fit, what would happen.

However Marion, very young, very earnest, very dutiful, anxious to please Terriss, listened eagerly to the suggestion during an understudy rehearsal.

"No one could play this part better than your sister Nell," said Terriss to the attentive Marion, "but as I always tell her, she does miss one great effect. When Olivia says 'Devil!' she ought to hit me bang in the face."

"Thank you for telling me," said Marion gratefully.

"It will be much more effective," said Terriss.

It *was*. When the night came for Marion to play the part, she struck out, and Terriss had to play the rest of the scene with a handkerchief held to his bleeding nose!

151

I think it was as Olivia that Eleonora Duse first saw me act. She had thought of playing the part herself some time, but she said: "*Never now!*" No letter about my acting ever gave me the same pleasure as this from her:

MADAME,   Avec Olivia vous m'avez donné bonheur et peine. *Bonheur* par votre art que est noble et sincère . . . *peine* car je sens la tristesse au coeur quand je vois une belle et généreuse nature de femme, donner son âme à l'art—comme vous le faites—quand c'est la vie même, *votre* coeur même qui parle tendrement, douleureusement, noblement *sous* votre jeu. Je ne puis me débarrasser d'une certaine tristesse quand je vois des artistes si nobles et hauts tels que vous et Irving. . . . Si vous êtes si forts de soumettre (avec un travail continu) la vie à l'art, il faut donc vous admirer comme des forces de la nature même qui auraient pourtant le droit de vivre pour elles-mêmes et non pour la foule. Je n'ose pas vous déranger, Madame, et d'ailleurs j'ai tant à faire aussi qu'il m'est impossible de vous dire de vive voix tout le grand plaisir que vous m'avez donné, mais puisque j'ai senti votre coeur, veuillez, chère Madame, croire au mien qui ne demande pas mieux dans cet instant que de vous admirer et de vous le dire tant bien que mal d'une manière quelconque. Bien à vous.

E. DUSE.

When I wrote to Madame Duse the other day to ask her permission to publish this much-prized letter, she answered:

BUENOS AYRES,
Septembre 11, 1907.
CHÈRE ELLEN TERRY,   Au milieu du travail en Amérique, je reçois votre lettre envoyée à Florence.

Vous me demandez de publier mon ancienne lettre amicale. Oui, chère Ellen Terry; ce que j'ai donné vous appartient; ce que j'ai dit, je le peux encore, et je vous aime et admire comme toujours. . . .

J'espère que vous accepterez cette ancienne lettre que j'ai rendue plus claire et un peu mieux écrite. Vous en serez contente avec moi car, ainsi faisant, j'ai eu le moyen de vous dire que je vous aime et de vous le dire deux fois.

A vous de coeur,
E. DUSE.

Dear, noble Eleonora Duse, great woman, great artist—I can never appreciate you in words, but I store the delight that you have given me by your work, and the personal kindness that you have shown me, in the treasure-house of my heart!

When I celebrated my stage jubilee you travelled all the way from

Italy to support me on the stage at Drury Lane. When you stood near me, looking so beautiful with wings in your hair, the wings of glory they seemed to me, I could not thank you, but we kissed each other and you understood!

"Clap-trap" was the verdict passed by many on the Lyceum "Faust", yet Margaret was the part I liked better than any other—outside Shakespeare. I played it beautifully sometimes. The language was often very commonplace—not nearly as poetic or dramatic as that of "Charles I"—but the character was all right—simple, touching, sublime.

The Garden Scene I know was unsatisfactory. It was a bad, weak love-scene, but George Alexander as Faust played it admirably. Indeed he always acted like an angel with me; he was so malleable, ready to do anything. He was launched into the part at very short notice, after H. B. Conway's failure on the first night. Poor Conway! It was Coghlan as Shylock all over again.

Henry called a rehearsal the next day—on Sunday, I think. The company stood about in groups on the stage while Henry walked up and down, speechless, but humming a tune occasionally, always a portentous sign with him. The scene set was the Brocken Scene, and Conway stood at the top of the slope as far away from Henry as he could get! He looked abject. His handsome face was very red, his eyes full of tears. He was terrified at the thought of what was going to happen. The actor was summoned to the office, and presently Loveday came out and said that Mr. George Alexander would play Faust the following night. Alec had been wonderful as Valentine the night before, and as Faust he more than justified Henry's belief in him. After that he never looked back. He had come to the Lyceum for the first time in 1882, an unknown quantity from a stock company in Glasgow, to play Caleb Decie in "The Two Roses". He then left us for a time, returned for "Faust", and remained in the Lyceum company for some years playing all Terriss's parts.

Alexander had the romantic quality which was lacking in Terriss, but there was a kind of shy modesty about him which handicapped him when he played Squire Thornhill in "Olivia". "Be more dashing, Alec!" I used to say to him. "Well, I do my best," he said. "At the hotels I chuck all the barmaids under the chin, and pretend I'm a dog of a fellow for the sake of this part!" Conscientious, dear, delightful Alec! No one ever deserved success more than he did and used it better when it came, as the history of the St. James's Theatre under his management proves. He had the good luck to marry a wife who was clever as well as charming, and could help him.

The original cast of "Faust" was never improved upon. What Martha was ever so good as Mrs. Stirling? The dear old lady's sight had failed since "Romeo and Juliet", but she was very clever at concealing it.

153

When she let Mephistopheles in at the door, she used to drop her work on the floor so that she could find her way back to her chair. I never knew why she dropped it—she used to do it so naturally with a start when Mephistopheles knocked at the door—until one night when it was in my way and I picked it up, to the confusion of poor Mrs. Stirling, who nearly walked into the orchestra.

"Faust" was abused a good deal as a pantomime, a distorted caricature of Goethe, and a thoroughly inartistic production. But it proved the greatest of all Henry's financial successes. The Germans who came to see it, oddly enough, did not scorn it nearly as much as the English who were sensitive on behalf of the Germans, and the Goethe Society wrote a tribute to Henry Irving after his death, acknowledging his services to Goethe!

It is a curious paradox in the theatre that the play for which every one has a good word is often the play which no one is going to see, while the play which is apparently disliked and run down is crowded every night.

Our preparations for the production of "Faust" included a delightful "grand tour" of Germany. Henry, with his accustomed royal way of doing things, took a party which included my daughter Edy, Mr. and Mrs. Comyns Carr, and Mr. Hawes Craven, who was to paint the scenery. We bought nearly all the properties used in "Faust" in Nuremberg, and many other things which we did not use, that took Henry's fancy. One beautifully carved escutcheon, the finest armorial device I ever saw, he bought at this time and presented it in after years to the famous American connoisseur, Mrs. Jack Gardiner. It hangs now in one of the rooms of her palace at Boston.

It was when we were going in the train along one of the most beautiful stretches of the Rhine that Sally Holland, who accompanied us as my maid, said:—

"Uncommon pretty scenery, dear, I must say!"

When we laughed uncontrollably, she added:

"Well, dear, *I* think so!"

During the run of "Faust" Henry visited Oxford and gave his address on "Four Actors" (Burbage, Betterton, Garrick, Kean). He met there one of the many people who had recently been attacking him on the ground of too long runs and too much spectacle. He wrote me an amusing account of the duel between them:

> I had supper last night at New College after the affair. A—— was there, and I had it out with him—to the delight of all.
>
> *"Too much decoration,"* etc., etc.
>
> I asked him what there was in "Faust" in the matter of appointments, etc., that he would like left out?
>
> Answer: Nothing.

"Too long runs."

"You, sir, are a poet," I said. "Perhaps it may be my privilege some day to produce a play of yours. Would you like it to have a long run or a short one?" (Roars of laughter.)

Answer: "Well—er—well, of course, Mr. Irving, you—well—well, a short run, of course, for *art*, but——"

"Now, sir, you're on oath," said I. 'Suppose that the fees were rolling in £10 and more a night—would you rather the play were a failure or a success?"

"Well, well, as *you* put it—I must say—er—I would rather my play had a *long* run!"

A—— floored!

He has all his life been writing articles running down good work and crying up the impossible, and I was glad to show him up a bit!

The Vice-Chancellor made a most lovely speech after the address—an eloquent and splendid tribute to the stage.

Bourchier presented the address of the "Undergrads". I never saw a young man in a greater funk—because, I suppose, he had imitated me so often!

From the address:

"We have watched with keen and enthusiastic interest the fine intellectual quality of all these representations from Hamlet to Mephistopheles with which you have enriched the contemporary stage. To your influence we owe deeper knowledge and more reverent study of the master mind of Shake-speare."

All very nice indeed!

I never cared much for Henry's Mephistopheles—a two-pence coloured part, any way. Of course he had his moments—he had them in every part—but they were few. One of them was in the Prologue, when he wrote in the student's book, "Ye shall be as gods knowing good and evil". He never looked at the book, and the nature of the *spirit* appeared suddenly in a most uncanny fashion. Another was in the Spinning-wheel Scene when Faust defies Mephistopheles, and he silences him with, "*I am a spirit*". Henry looked to grow a gigantic height—to hover over the ground instead of walking on it. It was terrifying.

I made valiant efforts to learn to spin before I played Margaret. My instructor was Mr. Albert Fleming, who, at the suggestion of Ruskin, had recently revived hand-spinning and hand-weaving in the North of England. I had always hated that obviously "property" spinning-wheel in the opera, and Margaret's unmarketable thread. My thread always broke, and at last I had to "fake" my spinning to a certain extent; but at least I worked my wheel right, and gave an impression that I could spin my pound of thread a day with the best.

Two operatic stars did me the honour to copy my Margaret dress—

155

Madame Albani and Madame Melba. It was rather odd, by the way, that many mothers who took their daughters to see the opera of "Faust" would not bring them to see the Lyceum play. One of these mothers was Princess Mary of Teck, a constant patron of most of our plays.

Other people "missed the music". The popularity of an opera will often kill a play, although the play may have existed before the music was ever thought of. The Lyceum "Faust" held its own against Gounod. I liked our incidental music to the action much better. It was taken from many different sources and welded into an effective and beautiful whole by our clever musical director, Mr. Meredith Ball.

In many ways "Faust" was our heaviest production. About four hundred ropes were used, each rope with a name. The list of properties and instructions to the carpenters became a joke among the theatre staff. When Henry first took "Faust" into the provinces, the head carpenter at Liverpool, Myers by name, being something of a humorist, copied out the list on a long thin sheet of paper, which rolled up like a royal proclamation. Instead of "God save the Queen!" he wrote at the foot, with many flourishes: "God help Bill Myers!"

The crowded houses at "Faust" were largely composed of "repeaters", as Americans call those charming playgoers who come to see a play again and again. We found favour with the artists and musicians too, even in Faust! Here is a nice letter I got during the run (it *was* a long one) from that gifted singer and good woman, Madame Antoinette Sterling:—

> MY DEAR MISS TERRY, I was quite as disappointed as yourself that you were not at St. James's Hall last Monday for my concert. . . . Jean Ingelow said she enjoyed the afternoon very much. . . .
>
> I wonder if you would like to come to luncheon some day and have a little chat with her? But perhaps you already know her. I love her dearly. She has one fault—she never goes to the theatre. Oh my! What she misses, poor thing, poor thing! We have already seen "Faust" twice, and are going again soon, and shall take the George Macdonalds this time. The Holman Hunts were delighted. He is one of the most interesting and clever men I have ever met, and she is very charming and clever too. How beautifully plain you write! Give me the recipe.
>
> With many kind greetings, Believe me sincerely yours,
> ANTOINETTE STERLING MACKINLAY.

My girl Edy was one of the angels in the vision in the last act of "Faust", an event which Henry commemorated in a little rhyme that he sent me on Valentine's Day with some beautiful flowers:

White and red roses,
Sweet and fresh posies,
One bunch for Edy, *Angel* of mine—
One bunch for Nell, my dear Valentine.

Mr. Toole ran a burlesque on the Lyceum "Faust", called "Faust-and-Loose". Henry did not care for burlesques as a rule. He thought Fred Leslie's exact imitation of him, face, spectacles, voice—everything was like Henry except the ballet-skirt—in the worst taste. But everything that Toole did was to him adorable. Marie Linden gave a really clever imitation of me as Marguerite. She and her sister Laura both had the trick of taking me off. I recognised the truth of Laura's caricature in the burlesque of "The Vicar of Wakefield" when as Olivia she made her entrance, leaping impulsively over a stile!

There was a chorus of girl "mashers" in "Faust-and-Loose", dressed in tight black satin coats, who besides dancing and singing had lines in unison, such as "No, no!" "We will!" As one of these girls Violet Vanbrugh made her first appearance on the stage. In her case "we will!" proved prophetic. It was her plucky "I will get on" which finally landed her in her present successful position.

Violet Barnes was the daughter of Prebendary Barnes of Exeter, who, when he found his daughter stage-struck, behaved far more wisely than most parents. He gave her £100 and sent her to London with her old nurse to look after her, saying that if she really "meant business" she would find an engagement before the £100 was gone. Violet had inherited some talent from her mother, who was a very clever amateur actress, and the whole family were fond of getting up entertainments. But Violet didn't know quite how far £100 would go, or wouldn't go. I happened to call on her at her lodgings near Baker Street one afternoon, and found her having her head washed, and crying bitterly all the time! She had come to the end of the £100, she had not got an engagement, and thought she would have to go home defeated. There was something funny in the tragic situation. Vi was sitting on the floor, drying her hair, crying, and drinking port wine to cure a cold in her head!

I told her not to be a goose, but to cheer up and come and stay with me until something turned up. We packed the old nurse back to Devonshire. Violet came and stayed with me, and in due course something did turn up. Mr. Toole came to dinner, and Violet, acting on my instructions to ask every one she saw for an engagement, asked Mr. Toole! He said, "That's all right, my dear. Of course. Come down and see me tomorrow." Dear old Toole! The kindliest of men! Violet was with him for some time, and played at his theatre in Mr. Barrie's first piece "Walker, London". Her sister Irene, Seymour Hicks, and Mary Ansell (now Mrs. Barrie) were all in the cast.

This was all I did to "help" Violet Vanbrugh, now Mrs. Arthur Bourchier and one of our best actresses, in her stage career. She helped herself, as most people do who get on. I am afraid that I have discouraged more stage aspirants than I have encouraged. Perhaps I have snubbed really talented people, so great is my horror of girls taking to the stage as a profession when they don't realise what they are about. I once told an elderly aspirant that it was quite useless for any one to go on the stage who had not either great beauty or great talent. She wrote saying that my letter had been a great relief to her, as now she was not discouraged. "I have *both*."

There is one actress on the English stage whom I did definitely encourage, of whose talent I was *certain*.

When my daughter was a student at the Royal Academy of Music, Dr. (now Sir Alexander) Mackenzie asked me to distribute the medals to the Elocution Class at the end of the term. I was quite "new to the job", and didn't understand the procedure. No girl, I have learned since, can be given the gold medal until she has won both the bronze and the silver medals—that is, until she has been at the Academy three years. I was for giving the gold medallists, who only wanted certificates, *bronze* medals; and of one young girl who was in her first year and only entitled to a bronze medal, I said: "Oh, she must have the gold medal, of course!"

She was a queer-looking child, handsome, with a face suggesting all manner of possibilities. When she stood up to read the speech from "Richard II" she was nervous, but courageously stood her ground. She began slowly, and with a most "fetching" voice, to *think* out the words. You saw her think them, heard her speak them. It was so different from the intelligent elocution, the good recitation, but bad impersonation of the others! "A pathetic face, a passionate voice, a *brain*," I thought to myself. It must have been at this point that the girl flung away the book and began to act, in an undisciplined way, of course, but with such true emotion, such intensity, that the tears came to my eyes. The tears came to her eyes too. We both wept, and then we embraced, and then we wept again. It was an easy victory for her. She was incomparably better than any one. "She has to work," I wrote in my diary that day. "Her life must be given to it, and then she will—well, she will achieve just as high as she works." Lena Pocock was the girl's name, but she changed it to Lena Ashwell when she went on the stage.

In the days of the elocution class there was still some idea of her becoming a singer, but I strongly advised the stage, and wrote to my friend J. Comyns Carr, who was managing the Comedy Theatre, that I knew a girl with "supreme talent" whom he ought to engage. Lena was engaged. After that she had her fight for success, but she went steadily forward.

Henry Irving has often been attacked for not preferring Robert Louis Stevenson's "Macaire" to the version which he actually produced in 1883. It would have been hardly more unreasonable to complain of his producing "Hamlet" in preference to Mr. Gilbert's "Rosencrantz and Guildenstern". Stevenson's "Macaire" may have all the literary quality that is claimed for it, although I personally think Stevenson was only making a delightful idiot of himself in it. Anyhow, it is frankly a burlesque, a skit, a *satire* on the real Macaire. The Lyceum was *not* a burlesque house! Why should Henry have done it?

It was funny to see Toole and Henry rehearsing together for "Macaire". Henry was always *plotting* to be funny. When Toole as Jacques Strop hid the dinner in his pocket, Henry, after much labour, thought of his hiding the plate inside his waistcoat. There was much laughter later on when Macaire, playfully tapping Strop with his stick, cracked the plate, and the pieces fell out! Toole hadn't to bother about such subtleties, and Henry's deep-laid plans for getting a laugh must have seemed funny to dear Toole, who had only to come on and say "Whoop!" and the audience roared!

Henry's death as Macaire was one of a long list of splendid deaths. Macaire knows the game is up, and makes a rush for the French windows at the back of the stage. The soldiers on the stage shoot him before he gets away. Henry did not drop, but turned round, swaggered impudently down to the table, leaned on it, then suddenly rolled over, dead.

Henry's production of "Werner" for one matinée was to do some one a good turn, and when Henry did a "good turn", he did it magnificently.[1] We rehearsed the play as carefully as if we were in for a long run. Beautiful dresses were made for me by my friend Alice Carr. But when we had given that one matinée, they were put away for ever. The play may be described as gloom, gloom, gloom. It was worse than "The Iron Chest".

While Henry was occupying himself with "Werner", I was pleasing myself with "The Amber Heart", a play by Alfred Calmour, a young man who was at this time Wills's secretary. I wanted to do it, not only to help Calmour, but because I believed in the play and liked the part of Ellaline. I had thought of giving a matinée of it at some other theatre, but Henry, who at first didn't like my doing it at all, said: "You must do it at the Lyceum. I can't let you, or it, go out of the theatre."

So we had the matinée at the Lyceum. Mr. Willard and Mr. Beerbohm Tree were in the cast, and it was a great success. For the first time Henry saw me act—a whole part and from the "front" at least, for he had seen

[1] *From my Diary, June* 1, 1887—"Westland-Marston Benefit at the Lyceum. A triumphant success entirely due to the genius and admirable industry and devotion of H. I., for it is just the dullest play to read as ever was! He made it *intensely* interesting."

and liked scraps of my Juliet from the "side". Although he had known me such a long time, my Ellaline seemed to come quite as a surprise. "I wish I could tell you of the dream of beauty that you realised," he wrote after the performance. He bought the play for me, and I continued to do it "on and off" here and in America until 1902.

Many people said that I was good but the play was bad. This was hard on Alfred Calmour. He had created the opportunity for me, and few plays with the beauty of "The Amber Heart" have come my way since. "He thinks it's all his doing!" said Henry. "If he only knew!" "Well, that's the way of authors," I answered. "They imagine so much more about their work than we put into it, that although we may seem to the outsider to be creating, to the author we are, at our best, only doing our duty by him."

Our next production was "Macbeth". Meanwhile we had visited America three times. It is now my intention to give some account of my tours in America, of my friends there, and of some of the impressions that the vast, wonderful country made on me.

XI

AMERICA

THE FIRST OF EIGHT TOURS

THE first time that there was any talk of my going to America was, I think, in 1874, when I was playing in "The Wandering Heir". Dion Boucicault wanted me to go, and dazzled me with figures, but I expect the cautious Charles Reade influenced me against accepting the engagement.

When I did go in 1883, I was thirty-five and had an assured position in my profession. It was the first of eight tours, seven of which I went with Henry Irving. The last was in 1907 after his death. I also went to America one summer on a pleasure trip. The tours lasted three months at least, seven months at most. After a rough calculation, I find that I have spent not quite five years of my life in America. Five out of sixty is not a large proportion, yet I often feel that I am half American. This says a good deal for the hospitality of a people who can make a stranger feel so completely at home in their midst. Perhaps it also says something for my adaptableness!

"When we do not speak of things with a partiality full of love, what we say is not worth being repeated." That was the answer of a courteous Frenchman who was asked for his impressions of a country. In any case it is imprudent to give one's impressions of America. The country is so vast and complex that even those who have amassed mountains of impressions soon find that there still are mountains more! I have lived in New York, Boston and Chicago for a month at a time, and have felt that to know any of these great cities even superficially would take a year. I have become acquainted with this and that class of American, but I realise that there are thousands of other classes that remain unknown to me.

I set out in 1883 from Liverpool on board the *Britannic* with the fixed conviction that I should never, never return. For six weeks before we started, the word America had only to be breathed to me, and I burst into floods of tears! I was leaving my children, my bullfinch, my parrot, my "aunt" Boo, whom I never expected to see alive again, just because she said I never would; and I was going to face the unknown dangers of the Atlantic and of a strange, barbarous land. Our farewell performances in London had cheered me up a little—though I wept copiously at every one—by showing us that we should be missed. Henry Irving's position seemed to be confirmed and ratified by all that took place before his departure. The dinners he had to eat, the speeches that he had to make and to listen to, were really terrific!

One speech at the Rabelais Club had, it was said, the longest peroration on record. It was this kind of thing: Where is our friend Irving going? He is not going like Nares to face the perils of the far North. He is not going like A—— to face something else. He is not going to China, etc.,—and so on. After about the hundredth "he is not going", Lord Houghton, who was one of the guests, grew very impatient and interrupted the orator with: "Of course he isn't ! He's going to New York by the Cunard Line. It'll take him about a week!"

Many people came to see us off at Liverpool, but I only remember seeing Mrs. Langtry and Oscar Wilde. It was at this time that Oscar Wilde had begun to curl his hair in the manner of the Prince Regent. "Curly hair to match the curly teeth," said some one. Oscar Wilde *had* ugly teeth, and he was not proud of his mouth. He used to put his hand to his mouth when he talked so that it should not be noticed. His brow and eyes were very beautiful.

Well, I was not "disappointed in the Atlantic," as Oscar Wilde was the first to say, though many people have said it since without acknowledging its source.

My first voyage was a voyage of enchantment to me. The ship was laden with pig-iron, and she rolled and rolled and rolled. She could never roll too much for me! I have always been a splendid sailor, and I feel jolly at sea. The sudden leap from home into the wilderness of waves does not give me any sensation of melancholy.

What I thought I was going to see when I arrived in America I hardly remember. I had a vague idea that all American women wore red flannel shirts and carried bowie knives and that I might be sandbagged in the street! From somewhere or other I had derived an impression that New York was an ugly, noisy place.

Ugly! When I first saw that marvellous harbour I nearly cried—it was so beautiful. Whenever I come now to the unequalled approach to New York I wonder what Americans must think of the approach from the sea to London! How different are the mean, flat, marshy banks of the Thames and the wooden toy lighthouse at Dungeness to the vast, spreading Hudson with its busy multitude of steamboats, and ferryboats, its wharf upon wharf, and its tall statue of Liberty dominating all the racket and bustle of the sea traffic of the world!

That was one of the few times in America when I did not miss the poetry of the past. The poetry of the present, gigantic, colossal and enormous, made me forget it. The "sky-scrapers"—what a brutal name it is when one comes to think of it!—so splendid in the landscape now, did not exist in 1883, but I find it difficult to divide my early impressions from my later ones. There was Brooklyn Bridge though, hung up high in the air like a vast spider's web.

Between 1883 and 1893 I noticed a great change in New York and other cities. In ten years they seemed to have grown with the energy of tropical plants. But between 1893 and 1907 I saw no evidence of such feverish increase. It is possible that the Americans are arriving at a stage when they can no longer beat the records! There is a vast difference between one of the old New York brownstone houses and one of the fourteen-storied buildings near the river, but between this and the Times Square Building or the still more amazing Flat Iron Building, which is said to oscillate at the top—it is so far from the ground—there is very little difference. I hear that they are now beginning to build downwards into the earth, but this will not change the appearance of New York for a long time.

I had not to endure the wooden shed in which most people landing in America have to struggle with the Custom-house officials—a struggle as brutal as a "round in the ring", as Paul Bourget describes it. We were taken off the *Britannic* in a tug, and Mr. Abbey, Laurence Barrett, and many other friends met us—including the much-dreaded reporters.

They were not a bit dreadful, but very quick to see what kind of a man Henry was. In a minute he was on the best of terms with them. He had on what I used to call his best "Jingle" manner—a manner full of refinement, bonhomie, elegance and geniality.

"Have a cigar—have a cigar." That was the first remark of Henry's, which put every one at ease. He also wanted to be at ease and have a good smoke. It was just the right merry greeting to the press representatives of a nation whose sense of humour is far more to be relied on than its sense of reverence.

"Now come on, all of you!" he said to the interviewers. He talked to them all in a mass and showed no favouritism. It says much for his tact and diplomacy that he did not "put his foot in it". The Americans are suspicious of servile adulation from a stranger, yet are very sensitive to criticism.

"These gentlemen want to have a few words with you," said Henry to me when the reporters had done with him. Then with a mischievous expression he whispered: "Say something pleasant! Merry and bright!"

Merry and bright! I felt it! The sense of being a stranger entering a strange land, the rushing sense of loneliness and foreignness was overpowering my imagination. I blew my nose hard and tried to keep back my tears, but the first reporter said: "Can I send any message to your friends in England?"

I answered: "Tell them I never loved 'em so much as now," and burst into tears! No wonder that he wrote in his paper that I was "a woman of extreme nervous sensibility". Another of them said that "my figure was spare almost to attenuation". America soon remedied that. I began to put on flesh before I had been in the country a week, and it

163

was during my fifth American tour that I became really fat for the first time in my life.

When we landed I drove to the Hotel Dam, Henry to the Brevoort House. There was no Diana on the top of the Madison Square Building then. The building did not exist, to cheer the heart of a new arrival as the first evidence of *beauty* in the city. There were horse trams instead of cable cars, but a quarter of a century has not altered the peculiarly dilapidated carriages in which one drives from the dock, the muddy side-walks, and the cavernous holes in the cobble-paved streets. Had the elevated railway, the first sign of *power* that one notices after leaving the boat, begun to thunder through the streets? I cannot remember New York without it.

I missed then, as I miss now, the numberless *hansoms* of London plying in the streets for hire. People in New York get about in the cars, unless they have their own carriages. The hired carriage has no reason for existing, and when it does, it celebrates its unique position by charging two dollars (8s.) for a journey which in London would not cost fifty cents (2s.)!

I cried for two hours at the Hotel Dam! Then my companion, Miss Harries, came bustling in with: "Never mind! here's a piano!" and sat down and played "Annie Laurie" very badly until I screamed with laughter. Before the evening came my room was like a bower of roses, and my dear friends in America have been throwing bouquets at me in the same lavish way ever since. I had quite cheered up when Henry came to take me to see some minstrels who were performing at the Star Theatre, the very theatre where in a few days we were to open. I didn't understand many of the jokes which the American comedians made that night, but I liked their dry, cool way of making them. They did not "hand a lemon" of "skiddoo" in those days; American slang changes as quickly as thieves' slang, and only "Gee!" and "Gee-whiz!" seem to be permanent.

There were very few theatres in New York when we first went there. All that part of the city which is now "up town" did not exist, and what was then "up" is now more than "down" town. The American stage has changed almost as much. In those days their most distinguished actors were playing Shakespeare or old comedy, and their new plays were chiefly "imported" goods. Even then there was a liking for local plays which showed the peculiarities of the different States, but they were more violent and crude than now. The original American genius and the true dramatic pleasure of the people is, I believe, in such plays, where very complete observation of certain phases of American life and very real pictures of manners are combined with comedy almost child-like in its naïveté. The sovereignty of the young girl which is such a marked feature in social life is reflected in American plays.

This is by the way.

What I want to make clear is that in 1883 there was no living American drama as there is now, that such productions of romantic plays and Shakespeare as Henry Irving brought over from England were unknown, and that the extraordinary success of our first tours would be impossible now. We were the first and we were pioneers, and we were *new*. To be new is everything in America.

Such palaces as the Hudson Theatre, New York, were not dreamed of when we were at the Star, which was, however, quite equal to any theatre in London in front of the footlights. The stage itself, the lighting appliances, and the dressing-rooms were inferior.

Henry made his first appearance in America in "The Bells". He was not at his best on the first night, but he could be pretty good even when he was not at his best. I watched him from a box. Nervousness made the company very slow. The audience was a splendid one—discriminating and appreciative. We felt that the Americans *wanted* to like us. We felt in a few days so extraordinarily at home. The first sensation of entering a foreign city was quickly wiped out.

The difference in atmosphere disappears directly one understands it. I kept coming across duplicates of "my friends in England". "How this girl reminds me of Alice." "How like that one is to Gill!" We had transported the Lyceum three thousand miles—that was all.

On the second night in New York it was my turn. "Command yourself—this is the time to show you can act!" I said to myself as I went on to the stage of the Star Theatre, dressed as Henrietta Maria. But I could not command myself. I played badly and cried too much in the last act. But the people liked me, and they liked the play, perhaps because it was historical; and of history the Americans are passionately fond. The audience took many points which had been ignored in London. I had always thought Henry as Charles I most moving when he made that involuntary effort to kneel to his subject, Moray, but the Lyceum audiences never seemed to notice it. In New York the audience burst out into the most sympathetic spontaneous applause that I have ever heard in a theatre.

I know that there are some advanced stage reformers who prefer to think applause "vulgar" and would suppress it in the theatre if they could. If they ever succeed they will suppress a great deal of good acting. It is said that the American actor, Edwin Forrest, once walked down to the footlights and said to the audience very gravely and sincerely: "If you don't applaud, I can't act," and I do sympathise with him. Applause is an instinctive, unconscious act expressing the sympathy between actors and audience. Just as our art demands more instinct than intellect in its exercise, so we demand of those who watch us an appreciation of the simple unconscious kind which finds an outlet in clapping rather than the cold, intellectual approval which would self-consciously think applause derogatory. I have yet to meet the actor who was *sincere* in saying that he disliked applause.

My impression of the way the American women dressed in 1883 was not favourable. Some of them wore Indian shawls and diamond earrings. They dressed too grandly in the street and too dowdily in the theatre. All this has changed. The stores in New York are now the most beautiful in the world, and the women are dressed to perfection. They are as clever at the *demi-toilette* as the Parisian, and the extreme neatness and smartness of their walking-gowns are very refreshing after the floppy, blowsy, trailing dresses, accompanied by the inevitable feather boa of which English girls, who used to be so tidy and "tailor-made", now seem so fond. The universal white "waist" is very pretty and trim on the American girl. It is one of the distinguishing marks of a land of the free, a land where "class" hardly exists. The girl in the store wears the white waist; so does the rich girl on Fifth Avenue. It costs anything from seventy-five cents to fifty dollars!

London when I come back from America always seems at first like an ill-lighted village, strangely tame, peaceful and backward. Above all, I miss the sunlight of America, and the clear blue skies of an evening.

"Are you glad to get back?" said an English friend.

"Very."

"It's a land of vulgarity, isn't it?"

"Oh yes, if you mean by that a wonderful land—a land of sunshine and light, of happiness, of faith in the future!" I answered. I saw no misery or poverty there. Every one looked happy. What hurts me on coming back to England is the *hopeless* look on so many faces; the dejection and apathy of the people standing about in the streets. Of course there is poverty in New York, but not among the Americans. The Italians, the Russians, the Poles—all the host of immigrants washed in daily on the bosom of the Hudson—these are poor, but you don't see them unless you go Bowery-ways, and even then you can't help feeling that in their sufferings there is always hope. The barrow man of today is the millionaire of tomorrow! Vulgarity? I saw little of it. I thought that the people who had amassed large fortunes used their wealth beautifully.

When a man is rich enough to build himself a big new house, he remembers some old house which he once admired, and he has it imitated with all the technical skill and care that can be had in America. This accounts for the odd jumble of styles in Fifth Avenue, along the lakeside in Chicago, in the new avenues in St. Louis and elsewhere. One millionaire's house is modelled on a French château, another on an old Colonial house in Virginia, another on a monastery in Mexico, another is like an Italian palazzo. And their imitations are never weak or pretentious. The architects in America seem to me to be far more able than ours, or else they have a freer hand and more money. It is sad to remember that Mr. Stanford White was one of the best of these splendid architects.

It was Stanford White with Saint-Gaudens—that great sculptor, whose work dignifies nearly all the great cities in America—who had most to do with the Exhibition buildings of the World's Fair in Chicago in 1893. It was odd to see that fair dream city rising out of the lake, so far more beautiful in its fleeting beauty than the Chicago of the stock-yards and the Pit which had provided the money for its beauty. The millionaires did not interfere with the artists at all. They gave their thousands—and stood aside. The result was one of the loveliest things conceivable. Saint-Gaudens and the rest did their work as well as though the buildings were to endure for centuries instead of being burned in a year to save the trouble of pulling down! The World's Fair always recalled to me the story of Michael Angelo, who carved a figure in snow which, says the chronicler who saw it, "was superb".

Saint-Gaudens gave me a cast of his medallion of Bastien-Lepage, and wrote to a friend of mine that "Bastien had '*le coeur au métier*'. So had Miss Terry, and I will place that saying in the frame that is to replace the present unsatisfactory one." He was very fastidious about this frame, and took such a lot of trouble to get it right. It must have been very irritating to Saint-Gaudens when he fell a victim to that extraordinary official Puritanism which sometimes excercises a petty censorship over works of art in America. The medal that he made for the World's Fair was rejected at Washington because it had on it a beautiful little nude figure of a boy holding an olive branch, emblematical of young America. I think a commonplace wreath and some lettering were substituted.

Saint-Gaudens did the fine bas-relief of Robert Louis Stevenson which was chosen for the monument in St. Giles's Cathedral, Edinburgh. He gave my daughter a medallion cast from this, because he knew that she was a great lover of Stevenson. The bas-relief was dedicated to his friend Joe Evans. I knew Saint-Gaudens first through Joe Evans, an artist who, while he lived, was to me and to my daughter the dearest of all in America. His character was so fine and noble—his nature so perfect. Many were the birthday cards he did for me, original in design, beautiful in execution. Whatever he did he put the best of himself into it. I wrote to my daughter soon after his death:—

> I heard on Saturday that our dear Joe Evans is dangerously ill. Yesterday came the worst news. Joe was not happy, but he was just heroic, and this world wasn't half good enough for him. I keep on getting letters about him. He seems to have been so glad to die. It was like a child's funeral, I am told,

and all his American friends seem to have been there—Saint-Gaudens, Taber, etc. A poem about the dear fellow by Mr. Gilder has one very good line in which he says the grave "might snatch a brightness from his presence there". I thought that was very happy, the love of light and gladness being the most remarkable thing about him, the dear sad Joe.

Robert Taber, dear, and rather sad too, was a great friend of Joe's. They both came to me first in the shape of a little book in which was inscribed, "Never anything can be amiss when simpleness and duty tender it". "Upon this hint I spake," the book began. It was all the work of a few boys and girls who from the gallery of the Star Theatre, New York, had watched Irving's productions and learned to love him and me. Joe Evans had done a lovely picture by way of a frontispiece of a group of eager heads hanging over the gallery's edge, his own and Taber's among them. Eventually Taber came to England and acted with Henry Irving in "Peter the Great" and other plays.

Like his friend Joe, he too was heroic. His health was bad and his life none too happy—but he struggled on. His career was cut short by consumption, and he died in the Adirondacks in 1904.

I cannot speak of all my friends in America, or anywhere, for the matter of that, *individually*. My personal friends are so many, and they are *all* wonderfully staunch to me! I have "tried" them so, and they have never given me up as a bad job.

My first friends of all in America were Mr. Bayard, afterwards the American Ambassador in London, and his sister, Mrs. Benoni Lockwood, her husband and their children. Now after all these years they are still my friends, and I can hope for none better to the end.

William Winter, poet, critic and exquisite man, was one of the first to write of Henry with whole-hearted appreciation. But all the criticism in America, favourable and unfavourable, surprised us by the scholarly knowledge it displayed. In Chicago the notices were worthy of the *Temps* or the *Journal des Débats*. There was no attempt to force the personality of the writer into the foreground nor to write a style that should attract attention to the critic and leave the thing criticised to take care of itself. William Winter, and, of late years, Allan Dale, have had their personalities associated with their criticisms, but they are exceptions. Curiously enough the art of acting appears to bore most dramatic critics, the very people who might be expected to be interested in it. The American critics, however, at the time of our early visits, were keenly interested, and showed it by their observation of many points which our English critics had passed over. For instance, writing of "Much Ado about Nothing", one of the Americans said of Henry in the Church Scene that "something of him as a subtle interpreter of doubtful situations was exquisitely shown in the early part of this fine scene by his suspicion of Don John—felt by him alone, and expressed only by a quick covert look, but a look so full of intelligence as to proclaim him a sharer in the secret with his audience."

"Wherein does the superiority lie?" wrote another critic in comparing our productions with those which had been seen in America up to 1884. "Not in the amount of money expended, but in the amount of brains;—in the artistic intelligence and careful and earnest pains with which every detail is studied and worked out. Nor is there any reason why Mr. Irving or any other foreigner should have a monopoly of either intelligence or pains. They are common property, and one man's money can buy them as well as another's. The defect in the American manager's policy heretofore has been that he has squandered his money upon high salaries for a few of his actors and costly, because unintelligent, expenditure for mere dazzle and show."

William Winter soon became a great personal friend of ours, and visited us in England. He was one of the few *sad* people I met in America. He could have sat upon the ground and told "sad stories of the deaths of kings" with the best. He was very familiar with the poetry of the *immediate* past—Cowper, Coleridge, Gray, Wordsworth, Shelley, Keats, and the rest. He *liked* us, so everything we did was right to him. He could not help being guided entirely by his feelings. If he disliked a thing, he had no use for it. Some men can say, "I hate this play, but of its kind it is admirable". Willie Winter could never take that unemotional point of view. In England he loved going to see graveyards, and knew where every poet was buried.

His children came to stay with me in London. When we were all coming home from the theatre one night after "Faust" (the year must have been 1886) I said to little Willie:

"Well, what do you think of the play?"

"Oh my!" said he, "it takes the cake."

"Takes the *cake!*" said his little sister scornfully, "it takes the ice-cream!"

"Won't you give me a kiss?" said Henry to the same young miss one night. "No, I *won't*, with all that blue stuff on your face." (He was made up for Mephistopheles.) Then, after a pause, "But why—why don't you *take* it!" She was only five years old at the time!

I love the American papers, especially the Sunday ones, although they do weigh nearly half a ton! As for the interviewers, I never cease to marvel at their cleverness. I tell them nothing, and the next day I read their "story" and find that I have said the most brilliant things! The following delightful "skit" on one of these interviews suggested itself to my clever friend Miss Aimée Lowther:—

169

WHAT CONSTITUTES CHARM.

An Illustrated Interview with Miss Ellen Terry.

"Yes, I know that I am very charming," said Miss Ellen Terry, "a perfectly delightful creature, a Queen of Hearts, a regular witch!" she added thoughtfully, at the same time projecting a pip of the orange she was chewing, with inimitable grace and accurate aim into

THE REPORTER'S EYE.

"You know, at all events, that you have charm?" I said.

"What do you think, you idiot! I exercise absolute power over my audiences—I cast over them an irresistible spell—I do with them what I will. . . . I am omnipotent, enthralling—and no wonder!"

I looked at her across the table, wondering at so much simple modesty.

"But feeling your power, you must often be tempted to experiment with it," I ventured.

"Yes, now and then I am," replied Miss Terry. "Once, I remember, when I was to appear as Ophelia, on making my entrance and seeing the audience waiting breathlessly—as they always do—for what I was going to do next, I said to myself, 'You silly fools, you shall have a treat tonight—I will give you something you will appreciate more than Shakespeare!' Hastily slipping on a

FALSE NOSE

which I always carry in my pocket, I struck an attitude, and then turned

A SOMERSAULT.

"Ah! the applause, the delirious, intoxicating applause! That night I felt my power, that night I knew that I had wished I could have held them indefinitely! But I am only one of several gifted beings on the stage who are blessed with this mysterious quality. Dan Leno, Herbert Campbell, and Little Tich all have it. Dan Leno, in particular, rivets the attention of his audience by his entrancing by-play, even when he doesn't speak. And yet it is

NOT HIS BEAUTY

precisely that does it."

At that moment Miss Terry's little grandchild, who was playing about the room,

BEGAN TO HOWL

most dismally.

"Here is a little maid who was a charmer from her cradle," said the delightful actress, picking up the child and

PLAYFULLY TOSSING

it out of the third-floor window. Seeing me look relieved, though somewhat surprised, she said merrily: "I have plenty more of them at home, and they are

ALL CHARMING,

every one of them! If you want to be charming you must be natural—I always am. Even in my cradle I was

QUITE NATURAL.

And now, please go. Your conversation bores me inexpressibly, and your countenance, which is at once vacuous and singularly plain, disagrees with me thoroughly. Go! or I shall

BE SICK!"

So saying the great actress gave me a

VIGOROUS KICK

which landed me outside her room, considerably shaken, and entirely under the spell of her matchless charm.

For "quite a while" during the first tour I stayed in Washington with my friend Miss Olive Seward, and all the servants of that delightful household were coloured. This was my first introduction to the negroes, whose presence more than anything else in the country, makes America seem foreign to European eyes. They are more sharply divided into high and low types than white people, and are not in the least alike in their types. It is safe to call any coloured man "George". They all love it, perhaps because of George Washington, and most of them are really named George. I never met such perfect service as they can give. *Some* of them are delightful. The beautiful, full voice of the "darkey" is so attractive, so soothing, and they are so deft and gentle. Some of the women are beautiful, and all the young appeared to me to be well-formed. As for the babies! I washed two or three little piccaninnies when I was in the South, and the way they rolled their gorgeous eyes at me was "too cute", which means in British-English "fascinating".

At the Washington house, the servants danced a cake-walk for me—the coloured cook, a magnificent type, who "took the cake", saying, "that was because I chose a good handsome boy to dance with, Missie".

They sang too. Their voices were beautiful—with such illimitable power, yet as sweet as treacle.

The little page-boy had a pet of a woolly head. Henry once gave him a tip—"fee", as they call it in America—and said: "There, that's for a new wig when this one is worn out," gently pulling the astrakhan-like hair. The tip would have bought him many wigs, I think!

"Why, Uncle Tom, how your face shines tonight!" said my hostess to one of the very old servants.

"Yes, Missie, glycerine and rose-water, Missie!"

He had taken some from her dressing-table to shine up his face in honour of me! A shiny complexion is considered to be a great beauty among the negroes! The dear old man! He was very bent and very old; and looked like one of the logs that he used to bring in for the fire—a log from some hoary, lichened tree whose life was long since past. He would produce pins from his head when you wanted one; he had them stuck in his pad of white woolly hair: "Always handy then, Missie," he would say.

"Ask them to sing 'Sweet Violets', Uncle Tom."

He was acting as a sort of master of the ceremonies at the entertainment the servants were giving me.

"Don't think they know dat, Miss Olly."

"Why, I heard them singing it the other night!" And she hummed the tune.

"Oh, dat was 'Sweet Vio-*letts*,' Miss Olly!"

Washington was the first city I had seen in America where the people did not hurry, and where the social life did not seem entirely the work of women. The men asserted themselves here as something more than machines in the background untiringly turning out the dollars, while their wives and daughters give luncheons and teas at which only women are present.

Beautifully as the women dress, they talk very little about clothes. I was much struck by their culture—by the evidences that they had read far more and developed a more fastidious taste than most young English-women. Yet it is all mixed up with extraordinary naïveté. The vivacity, the appearance, at least, of *reality*, the animation, the energy of American women delighted me. They are very sympathetic, too, in spite of a certain callousness which comes of regarding everything in life, even love, as "lots of fun". I did not think that they, or the men either, had much natural sense of beauty. They admire beauty in a curious way through their intellect. Nearly every American girl has a cast of the winged Victory of the Louvre in her room. She makes it a point of her *education* to admire it.

There! I am beginning to generalise—the very thing I was resolute to avoid. How silly to generalise about a country which embraces such extremes of climate as the sharp winters of Boston and New York and the warm winds of Florida which blow through palms and orange groves!

XII

SOME LIKES AND DISLIKES

IT is only human to make comparisons between American and English institutions, although they are likely to turn out as odious as the proverb says! The first institution in America that distressed me was the steam heat. It is far more manageable now than it was both in hotels and theatres, because there are more individual heaters. But how I suffered from it at first I cannot describe! I used to feel dreadfully ill, and when we could not turn the heat off at the theatre, the play always went badly. My voice was affected too. At Toledo once, it nearly went altogether. Then the next night, after a good fight for it, we got the theatre cool, and the difference that it made to the play was extraordinary. I was in my best form, feeling well and jolly!

No wonder the Americans drink ice-water and wear very thin clothes indoors. Their rooms are hotter than ours ever are, even in the height of the summer—when we have a summer! But no wonder, either, that Americans in England shiver at our cold, draughty rooms. They are brought up in hot-houses.

If I did not like steam heat, I loved the ice which is such a feature at American meals. Everything is served on ice, and the ice-water, however pernicious the Europeans may consider it as a drink, looks charming and cool in the hot rooms.

I liked the travelling; but then we travelled in a very princely fashion. The Lyceum company and baggage occupied eight cars, and Henry's private parlour car was lovely. The only thing that we found was better understood in England, so far as railway travelling is concerned, was *privacy*. You may have a *private* car in America, but all the conductors on the train, and there is one to each car, can walk through it. So can any official, baggage man or newsboy who has the mind!

The "parlour car" in America is more luxurious than our first class, but you travel in it (if you have no "private" car) with thirty other people.

"What do you want to be private for?" asked an American, and you don't know how to answer, for you find that with them that privacy means concealment. For this reason, I believe, they don't have hedges or walls round their estates and gardens. "Why should we? We have nothing to hide!"

In the cars, as in the rooms at one's hotel, the "cuspidor" is always with you as a thing of beauty! When I first went to America the "Ladies' Entrance" to the hotel was really necessary, because the ordinary entrance was impassable! Since then very severe laws against spitting in public places have been passed, and there is a *great* improvement. But the habit, I suppose due to the dryness of the climate, or to the very strong cigars smoked, or to chronic catarrh, or to a feeling of independence— "This is a free country and I can spit if I choose!"—remains sufficiently disgusting to a stranger visiting the country.

The American voice is the one thing in the country that I find unbearable; yet the truly terrible variety only exists in one State, and is not widely distributed. I suppose it is its very assertiveness that makes one forget the very sweet voices that also exist in America. The Southern voice is very low in tone and soothing, like the "darkey" voice. It is as different from Yankee as the Yorkshire burr is from the Cockney accent.

This question of accent is a very funny one. I had not been in America long when a friend said to me:

"We like your voice. You have so little English accent!"

This struck me as rather cool. Surely English should be spoken with an *English* accent, not with a French, German, or double-dutch one! Then I found that what they meant by an English accent was an English affectation of speech—a drawl with a tendency to "aw" and "ah" everything. They thought that every one in England who did not miss out aspirates where they should be, and put them in where they should not be, talked of "the rivah", "ma brothar", and so on. Their conclusion was, after all, quite as well founded as ours about *their* accent. The American intonation, with its freedom from violent emphasis, is, I think, rather pretty when the quality of the voice is sweet.

Of course the Americans would have their jokes about Henry's method of speech. Ristori followed us once in New York, and a newspaper man said he was not sure whether she or Mr. Irving was the more difficult for an American to understand.

"He pronounces the English tongue as it is pronounced by no other man, woman, or child," wrote the critic, and proceeded to give a phonetically spelled version of Irving's delivery of Shylock's speech of Antonio.

> Wa thane, eet no eperes
> Ah! um! yo ned m'elp
> Ough! ough! Gaw too thane! Ha! um!
> Yo com'n say
> Ah! Shilok, um! ouch! we wode hev moanies!

I wonder if the clever American reporter stopped to think how *his* delivery of the same speech would look in print! As for the ejaculations, the interjections and grunts with which Henry interlarded the text, they often helped to reveal the meaning of Shakespeare to his audience—a meaning which many a perfect elocutionist has left perfectly obscure. The use of "m'" or "me" for "my" has often been hurled in my face as a reproach, but I never contracted "my" without good reason. I had a line in Olivia which I began by delivering as—

My sorrows and my shame are my own.

Then I saw that the "mys" sounded ridiculous, and abbreviated the two first ones into "me's".

There were of course people ready to say that the Americans did not like Henry Irving as an actor, and that they only accepted him as a manager—that he triumphed in New York as he had done in London, through his lavish spectacular effects. This is all moonshine. Henry made his first appearance in "The Bells", his second in "Charles I", his third in "Louis XI". By that time he had conquered, and without the aid of anything at all notable in the mounting of the plays. It was not until we did "The Merchant of Venice" that he gave the Americans anything of a "production".

My first appearance in America in Shakespeare was as Portia, and I could not help feeling pleased by my success. A few weeks later I played Ophelia at Philadelphia. It is in Shakespeare that I have been best liked in America, and I consider that Beatrice was the part about which they were most enthusiastic.

During our first tour we visited in succession New York, Philadelphia, Boston, Baltimore, Brooklyn, Chicago, Cincinnati, St. Louis, Detroit, and Toronto. To most of these places we paid return visits.

"To what do you attribute your success, Mr. Irving?"

"To my acting," was the simple reply.

We never had poor houses except in Baltimore and St. Louis. Our journey to Baltimore was made in a blizzard. They were clearing the snow before us all the way from New Jersey, and we took forty-two hours to reach Baltimore! The bells of trains before us and behind us sounded very alarming. We opened in Baltimore on Christmas Day. The audience was wretchedly small, but the poor things who were there had left their warm firesides to drive or tramp through the slush of melting snow, and each one who managed to reach the theatre was worth a hundred on an ordinary night.

At the hotel I put up holly and mistletoe, and produced from my trunks a real Christmas pudding that my mother had made. We had it for supper, and it was very good.

It never does to repeat an experiment. Next year at Pittsburg my little son Teddy brought me out another pudding from England. For once we were in an uncomfortable hotel, and the Christmas dinner was deplorable. It began with *burned hare soup*.

"It seems to me," said Henry, "that we aren't going to get anything to eat, but we'll make up for it by drinking!"

He had brought his own wine out with him from England, and the company took him at his word and *did* make up for it!

"Never mind!" I said, as the soup was followed by worse and worse. "There's my pudding!"

It came on blazing, and looked superb. Henry tasted a mouthful.

"Very odd," he said, "but I think this is a camphor pudding."

He said it so politely, as if he might easily be mistaken!

My maid in England had packed the pudding with my furs! It simply reeked of camphor.

So we had to dine on Henry's wine and L. F. Austin's wit. This dear, brilliant man, now dead, acted for many years as Henry's secretary, and one of his gifts was the happy knack of hitting off people's peculiarities in rhyme. This dreadful Christmas dinner at Pittsburg was enlivened by a collection of such rhymes, which Mr. Austin called a "Lyceum Christmas Play".

Every one roared with laughter until it came to the verse of which he was the victim, when suddenly he found the fun rather laboured!

The first verse was spoken by Loveday, who announces that the "Governor" has a new play which is *"Wonderful!"* a great word of Loveday's.

George Alexander replies:

> But I say, Loveday, have I got a part in it,
> That I can wear a cloak in and look smart in it?
> Not that I care a fig for gaudy show, dear boy—
> But juveniles must *look* well, don't you know, dear boy.
> And shall I lordly hall and tuns of claret own?
> And may I murmur love in dulcet baritone?
> Tell me at least, this simple fact of it—
> Can I beat Terriss hollow in one act of it?[1]

Norman Forbes:

> Pooh for Wenman's bass![2] Why should he make a boast of it?
> If he has a voice, I have got the ghost of it!
> When I pitch it low, you may say how weak it is,
> When I pitch it high, heavens! what a squeak it is!
> But I never mind; for what does it signify?
> See my graceful hands, they're the things that dignify;
> All the rest is froth, and egotism's dizziness—

---

[1] Alexander had just succeeded Terriss as our leading young man.
[2] Wenman had a rolling bass voice of which he was very proud. He was a valuable actor, yet somehow never interesting. Young Norman Forbes-Robertson played Sir Andrew Aguecheek with us on our second American tour.

Have I not played with Phelps?
  (To Wenman)
I'll teach you all the business!

T. Mead:
(Of whom much has already been written in these pages)

What's this about a voice? Surely you forget it, or
Wilfully conceal that *I* have no competitor!
I do not know the play, or even what the title is,
But safe to make success a charnel-house recital is!
So please to bear in mind, if I am not to fail in it,
That Hamlet's father's ghost must rob the Lyons Mail in it!
No! that's not correct! But you may spare your charity—
A good sepulchral groan's the thing for popularity!

H. Howe:
(The "agricultural" actor, as Henry called him.)

Boys, take my advice, the stage is not the question,
But whether at three score you'll all have my digestion.
Why yearn for plays, to pose as Brutuses or Catos in,
When you may get a garden to grow the best potatoes in?
You see that at my age by Nature's shocks unharmed I am!
Tho' if I sneeze but thrice, good heavens, how alarmed I am!
But act your parts like men, and tho' you all great sinners are,
You're sure to act like men wherever Irving's dinners are!

J. H. Allen (our prompter):

Whatever be the play, *I* must have a hand in it,
For won't I teach the supers how to stalk and stand in it?
Tho' that blessed Shakespeare never gives a ray to them,
I explain the text, and then it's clear as day to them![1]

———————

[1] Once when Allen was rehearsing the supers in the Church Scene in "Much Ado about Nothing", we overheard him show the sense in Shakespeare like this:
"This 'Ero let me tell you is a perfect lady, a nice, innercent young thing, and when the feller she's engaged to calls 'er an 'approved wanton', you naturally claps yer 'ands to yer swords. A wanton is a kind of—well, you know she ain't what she ought to be!"
Allen would then proceed to read the part of Claudio:
". . . not to knit my soul to an approved wanton."
Seven or eight times the supers clapped their " 'ands to their swords" without giving Allen satisfaction.
"No, no, no, that's not a bit like it, not a bit! If any of your sisters was 'ere and you 'eard me call 'er a ——, would yer stand gapin' at me as if this was a bloomin' tea party!"

Plain as A B C is a plot historical,
When *I* overhaul allusions allegorical!
Shakespeare's not so bad; he'd have more pounds and pence in him,
If actors stood aside, and let me show the sense in him!

Louis Austin's little "Lyceum Play" was presented to me with a silver water-jug, a souvenir from the company, and ended up with the following pretty lines spoken by Katie Brown, a clever little girl who played all the small pages' parts at this time:

> Although I'm but a little page,
>   Who waits for Portia's kind behest,
> Mine is the part upon this stage
>   To tell the plot you have not guessed.
>
> Dear lady, oft in Belmont's hall,
>   Whose mistress is so sweet and fair,
> Your humble slaves would gladly fall
>   Upon their knees, and praise you there.
>
> To offer you this little gift,
>   Dear Portia, now we crave your leave,
> And let it have the grace to lift
>   Our hearts to yours this Christmas eve.
>
> And so we pray that you may live
>   Thro' many, many, happy years,
> And feel what you so often give—
>   The joy that is akin to tears!

How nice of Louis Austin! It quite made up for my mortification over the camphor pudding!

Pittsburg has been called "hell with the lid off", and other insulting names. I have always thought it beautiful, especially at night when its furnaces make it look like a city of flame. The lovely park that the city has made on the heights that surround it is a lesson to Birmingham, Sheffield, and our other black towns. George Alexander said that Pittsburg reminded him of his native town of Sheffield. "Had he said Birmingham, now, instead of Sheffield," wrote a Pittsburg newspaper man, "he would have touched our tender spot exactly. As it is, we can be as cheerful as the Chicago man was who boasted that his sweetheart 'came pretty near calling him "honey",' when in fact she had called him 'Old Beeswax'!"

When I played Ophelia for the first time in Chicago, I played the part better than I had ever played it before, and I don't believe I ever played it so well again. *Why*, it is almost impossible to say. I had heard a good deal of the crime of Chicago, that the people were a rough, murderous, sand-bagging crew. I ran on to the stage in the mad scene, and never have I felt such sympathy! This frail wraith, this poor demented thing, could hold them in the hollow of her hand . . . It was splendid! "How long can I hold them?" I thought. "For ever!" Then I laughed. That was the best Ophelia laugh of my life—my life that is such a perfect kaleidoscope with the people and the places turning round and round.

At the risk of being accused of indiscriminate flattery I must say that I liked *all* the American cities. Every one of them has a joke at the expense of the others. They talk in New York of a man who lost both his sons—"One died and the other went to live in Philadelphia." Pittsburg is the subject of endless criticism, and Chicago is "the limit". To me, indeed, it seemed "the limit"—of the industry, energy, and enterprise of man. In 1812 this vast city was only a frontier post—Fort Dearborn. In 1871 the town that first rose on these great plains was burned to the ground. The growth of the present Chicago began when I was a grown woman. I have celebrated my jubilee. Chicago will not do that for another fifteen years!

I never visited the stock-yards. Somehow I had no curiosity to see a live pig turned in fifteen minutes into ham, sausages, hair-oil, and the binding for a Bible! I had some dread of being made sad by the spectacle of so much slaughter— of hating the Chicago of the "abattoir" as much as I had loved the Chicago of the Lake with the white buildings of the World's Fair shining on it, the Chicago built on piles in splendid isolation in the middle of the prairie, the Chicago of Marshall Field's beautiful palace of a store, the Chicago of my dear friends, the Chicago of my son's first appearance on the stage! Was it not a Chicago man who wrote of my boy, tending the roses in the stage garden in "Eugene Aram", that he was "a most beautiful lad"!

His eyes are full of sparkle, his smile is a ripple over his face, and his laugh is as cheery and natural as a bird's song. . . . This Joey is Miss Ellen Terry's son, and the apple of her eye. On this Wednesday night, January 14, 1885, he spoke his first lines upon the stage. His mother has high hopes of this child's dramatic future. He has the instinct and the soul of art in him. Already the theatre is his home. His postures and his playfulness with the gardener, his natural and graceful movements, had been the subject of much drilling, of study and practice. He acquitted himself beautifully and received the wise congratulations of his mother, of Mr. Irving, and of the company.

That is the nicest newspaper notice I have ever read!

At Chicago I made my first speech. The Haverley Theatre, at which we first appeared in 1884, was altered and rechristened the "Columbia" in 1885. I was called upon for a speech after the special performance in honour of the occasion, consisting of scenes from "Charles I", "Louis XI", "The Merchant of Venice", and "The Bells", had come to an end. I think it must be the shortest speech on record:

> Ladies and Gentlemen, I have been asked to christen your beautiful theatre. "Hail Columbia!"

When we acted in Brooklyn we used to stay in New York and drive over that wonderful bridge every night. There were no trolley cars on it then. I shall never forget how it looked in winter, with the snow and ice on it—a gigantic trellis of dazzling white, as incredible as a dream. The old stone bridges were works of *art*. This bridge, woven of iron and steel for a length of over 500 yards, and hung high in the air over the water so that great ships can pass beneath it, is the work of *science*. It looks as if it had been built by some power, not by men at all.

It was during our week at Brooklyn in 1885 that Henry was ill, too ill to act for four nights. Alexander played Benedick, and got through it wonderfully well. Then old Mr. Mead did (*did* is the word) Shylock. There was no intention behind his words or what he did.

I had such a funny batch of letters on my birthday that year. "Dear, sweet Miss Terry, etc., etc. Will you give me a piano?"!! etc., etc. Another: "Dear Ellen. Come to Jesus. Mary." Another, a lovely letter of thanks from a poor woman in the most ghastly distress, and lastly an offer of a *two years'* engagement in America. There was a simple coming in for one woman acting at Brooklyn on her birthday!

Brooklyn is as sure a laugh in New York as the mother-in-law in a London music hall. "All cities begin by being lonesome," a comedian explained, "and Brooklyn has never gotten over it."

My only complaint against Brooklyn was that they would not take Fussie in at the hotel there. Fussie, during these early American tours, was still *my* dog. Later on he became Henry's. He had his affections alienated by a course of chops, tomatoes, strawberries, "ladies' fingers" soaked in a champagne, and a beautiful fur rug of his own presented by the Baroness Burdett-Coutts!

How did I come by Fussie? I went to Newmarket with Rosa Corder, whom Whistler painted. She was one of those plain-beautiful women who are so far more attractive than some of the pretty ones. She had wonderful hair—like a fair, pale veil, a white, waxen face, and a very good figure; and she wore very odd clothes. She had a studio in Southampton Row, and another at Newmarket where she went to paint horses. I went to Cambridge once and drove back with her across the heath to her studio.

"How wonderfully different are the expressions on terriers' faces," I said to her, looking at a painting of hers of a fox-terrier pup. "That's the only sort of dog I should like to have."

"That one belonged to Fred Archer," Rosa Corder said. "I daresay he could get you one like it."

We went to find Archer. Curiously enough I had known the famous jockey at Harpenden when he was a little boy, and I believe used to come round with vegetables.

"I'll send you a dog, Miss Terry, that won't be any trouble. He's got a very good head, a first-rate tail, stuck in splendidly, but his legs are too long. He'd follow you to America."

Prophetic words! On one of our departures for America, Fussie was left behind by mistake at Southampton. He could not get across the Atlantic, but he did the next best thing. He found his way back from there to his own theatre in the Strand, London!

Fred Archer sent him originally to the stage-door at the Lyceum. The man who brought him out from there to my house in Earl's Court said:

"I'm afraid he gives tongue, Miss. He don't like music, anyway. There was a band at the bottom of your road, and he started hollering."

We were at luncheon when Fussie made his début into the family circle, and I very quickly saw his *stomach* was his fault. He had a great dislike to "Charles I"; we could never make out why. Perhaps it was because Henry wore armour in one act—and Fussie may have barked his shins against it. Perhaps it was the firing off of the guns; but more probably it was because the play once got him into trouble. As a rule Fussie had the most wonderful sense of the stage, and at rehearsal would skirt the edge of it, but never cross it. But at Brooklyn one night when we were playing "Charles I"—the last act, and that most pathetic part of it where Charles is taking a last farewell of his wife and children—Fussie, perhaps excited by his run over the bridge from New York, suddenly bounded on to the stage! The good children who were playing Princess Mary and Prince Henry didn't even smile; the audience remained solemn, but Henry and I nearly went into hysterics. Fussie knew directly that he had done wrong. He lay down on his stomach, then rolled over on his back, whimpering an apology—while carpenters kept on whistling and calling to him from the wings. The children took him up to the window at the back of the scene, and he stayed there cowering between them until the end of the play.

America seems to have been always fatal to Fussie. Another time when Henry and I were playing in some charity performance in which John Drew and Maude Adams were also acting, he disgraced himself again. Henry having "done his bit" and put on hat and coat to leave the theatre, Fussie thought the end of the performance must have come; the stage had no further sanctity for him, and he ran across it to the stage door barking! John Drew and Maude Adams were playing "A Pair of Lunatics". Maude Adams, sitting looking into the fire, did not see Fussie, but was amazed to hear John Drew departing madly from the text:

> Is this a dog I see before me,
> His tail towards my hand?
> Come, let me clutch thee.

She began to think that he had really gone mad!

When Fussie first came, Charlie was still alive, and I have often gone into Henry's dressing-room and seen the two dogs curled up in both the available chairs, Henry *standing* while he made up, rather than disturb them!

When Charlie died, Fussie had Henry's idolatry all to himself. I have caught them often sitting quietly opposite each other at Grafton Street, just adoring each other! Occasionally Fussie would thump his tail on the ground to express his pleasure.

Wherever we went in America the hotel people wanted to get rid of the dog. In the paper they had it that Miss Terrry asserted that Fussie was a little terrier, while the hotel people regarded him as a pointer, and funny caricatures were drawn of a very big me with a very tiny dog, and a very tiny me with a dog the size of an elephant! Henry often walked straight out of an hotel where an objection was made to Fussie. If he wanted to stay, he had recourse to strategy. At Detroit the manager of the hotel said that dogs were against the rules. Being very tired Henry let Fussie go to the stables for the night, and sent Walter to look after him. The next morning he sent for the manager.

"Yours is a very old-fashioned hotel, isn't it?"

"Yes, sir, very old and ancient."

"Got a good chef? I didn't think much of the supper last night; but still—the beds are comfortable enough—I am afraid you don't like animals?"

"Yes, sir, in their proper place."

"It's a pity," said Henry meditatively, "because you happen to be overrun by rats!"

"Sir, you must have made a mistake. Such a thing couldn't——"

"Well, I couldn't pass another night here without my dog," Henry interrupted. "But there are, I suppose, other hotels?"

"If it will be any comfort to you to have your dog with you, sir, do by all means, but I assure you that he'll catch no rat here."

"I'll be on the safe side," said Henry calmly.

And so it was settled. That very night Fussie supped off, not rats, but terrapin and other delicacies in Henry's private sitting-room.

It was the 1888 tour, the great blizzard year, that Fussie was left behind by mistake at Southampton. He jumped out at the station just before Southampton, where they stop to collect tickets. After this long separation, Henry naturally thought that the dog would go nearly mad with joy when he saw him again. He described to me the meeting in a letter.

My dear Fussie gave me a terrible shock on Sunday night. When we got in, J——, Hatton, and I dined at the Café Royal. I told Walter to bring Fussie there. He did, and Fussie burst into the room while the waiter was cutting some mutton, when, what d'ye think—one bound at me—another instantaneous bound at the mutton, and from the mutton nothing would get him until he'd got his plateful.

Oh, what a surprise it was indeed! He never now will leave my side, my legs, or my presence, but I cannot but think, alas, of that seductive piece of mutton!

Poor Fussie! He met his death through the same weakness. It was at Manchester, I think. A carpenter had thrown down his coat with a ham sandwich in the pocket, over an open trap on the stage. Fussie, nosing and nudging after the sandwich, fell through and was killed instantly. When they brought up the dog after the performance, every man took his hat off . . . Henry was not told until the end of the play.

He took it so very quietly that I was frightened, and said to his son Laurence who was on that tour:

"Do let's go to his hotel and see how he is."

We drove there and found him sitting eating his supper with the poor dead Fussie, who would never eat supper any more, curled up in his rug on the sofa. Henry was talking to the dog exactly as if it were alive. The next day he took Fussie back in the train with him to London, covered with a coat. He is buried in the dogs' cemetery, Hyde Park.

His death made an enormous difference to Henry. Fussie was his constant companion. When he died, Henry was really alone. He never spoke of what he felt about it, but it was easy to know.

We used to get hints how to get this and that from watching Fussie! His look, his way of walking! He *sang*, whispered eloquently and low— then barked suddenly and whispered again! Such a lesson in the law of contrasts!

The first time that Henry went to the Lyceum after Fussie's death, every one was anxious and distressed, knowing how he would miss the dog in his dressing-room. Then an odd thing happened. The wardrobe cat, who had never been near the room in Fussie's lifetime, came down and sat on Fussie's cushion! No one knew how the "Governor" would take it. But when Walter was sent out to buy some meat for it, we saw that Henry was not going to resent it! From that night onwards the cat always sat night after night in the same place, and Henry liked its companionship. In 1902, when he left the theatre for good, he wrote to me:

The place is now given up to the rats—all light cut off, and only Barry[1] and a foreman left. Everything of mine I've moved away, including the Cat!

I have never been to America yet without going to Niagara. The first time I saw the great falls I thought it all more wonderful than beautiful. I got away by myself from my party, and looked and looked at it, and I listened—and at last it became dreadful and I was *frightened* at it. I wouldn't go alone again, for I felt queer and wanted to follow the great flow of it. But at twelve o'clock with the "sun upon the topmost height of the day's journey", most of Nature's sights appear to me to be at their plainest. In the evening, when the shadows grow long and all hard lines are blurred, how soft, how different, everything is! It was noontide, that garish cruel time of day, when I first came in sight of the falls. I'm glad I went again in other lights—but one should live by the side of all this greatness to learn to love it. Only once did I catch Niagara in *beauty*, with pits of colour in its waters, no one colour definite—all was wonderment, allurement, fascination. The *last* time I was there it was wonderful, but not beautiful any more. The merely stupendous, the merely marvellous, have always repelled me. I cannot *realise*, and become terribly weak and doddering. No terrific scene gives me pleasure. The great canyons give me unrest, just as the long low lines of my Sussex marshland near Winchelsea give me rest.

At Niagara William Terriss slipped and nearly lost his life. At night when he appeared as Bassanio, he shrugged his shoulders, lowered his eyelids, and said to me—

"Nearly gone, dear,"—he would call everybody "dear"—"But Bill's luck! Tempus fugit!"

What tempus had to do with it, I don't quite know!

When we were first in Canada I tobogganed at Rosedale. I should say it was like flying! The start! Amazing! "Farewell to this world," I thought, as I felt my breath go. Then I shut my mouth, opened my eyes, and found myself at the bottom of the hill in a jiffy—"over hill, over dale, through bush, through briar!" I rolled right out of the toboggan when we stopped. A very nice Canadian man was my escort, and he helped me up the hill afterwards. I didn't like *that* part of the affair quite so much!

Henry Irving would not come, much to my disappointment. He said that quick motion through the air always gave him the ear-ache. He had to give up swimming (his old Cornish Aunt Penberthy told me he delighted in swimming as a boy) just because it gave him most violent pains in the ear.

Philadelphia, as I first knew it, was the most old-world place I saw in America, except perhaps Salem. Its red-brick side-walks, the trees in the

[1] The stage-door keeper.

184

streets, the low houses with their white marble cuffs and collars, the pretty design of the place, all give it a character of its own. The people, too, have a character of their own. They dress, or at least *did* dress, very quietly. This was the only sign of their Quaker origin, except a very fastidious taste—in plays as in other things.

Mrs. Gillespie, the great-grandchild of Benjamin Franklin, was one of my earliest Philadelphia friends—a splendid type of the independent woman, a bit of a martinet, but immensely full of kindness and humour. She had a word to say in all Philadelphian matters. It would be difficult to imagine a greater contrast to Mrs. Gillespie of Philadelphia than Mrs. Fields of Boston, that other great American lady whom to know is a liberal education.

Mrs. Fields reminded me of Lady Tennyson, Mrs. Tom Taylor, and Miss Hogarth (Dickens's sister-in-law) all rolled into one. Her house is full of relics of the past. There is a portrait of Dickens as a young man with long hair. He had a feminine face in those days, for all its strength. Hard by is a sketch of Keats by Severn, with a lock of the poet's hair. Opposite is a head of Thackeray, with a note in his hand-writing fastened below. "Goodbye, Mrs. Fields; goodbye, my dear Fields; goodbye to all. I go home."

Thackeray left Boston abruptly because a sudden desire to see his children had assailed him at Christmas time!

As you sit in Mrs. Fields' spacious room overlooking the Bay, you realise suddenly that before you ever came into it, Dickens and Thackeray were both here, that this beautiful old lady who so kindly smiles on you has smiled on them and on many other great men of letters long since dead. It is here that they seem most alive. This is the house where the culture of Boston seems no fad to make a joke about, but a rare and delicate reality.

This—and Fen Court, the home of that wonderful woman Mrs. Jack Gardiner, who represents the present worship of beauty in Boston as Mrs. Fields represents its former worship of literary men. Fen Court is a house of enchantment, a palace, and Mrs. Gardiner is like a great princess in it. She had "great possessions" indeed, but her best, to my mind, is her most beautiful voice, even though I remember her garden by moonlight with the fountain playing, her books and her pictures, the Sargent portrait of herself presiding over one of the most splendid of those splendid rooms, where everything great in old art and new art is represented. What a portrait it is! Some one once said of Sargent that "behind the individual he finds the real, and behind the real, a whole social order".

He has painted "Mrs. Jack" in a tight-fitting black dress with no ornament but her world-famed pearl necklace round her waist, and on her shoes rubies like drops of blood. The daring, intellectual face seems to say: "I have possessed everything that is worth possession, through the energy and effort and labour of the country in which I was born."

Mrs. Gardiner represents all the *poetry* of the millionaire.

Mrs. Gardiner's house filled me with admiration, but if I want rest and peace I just think of the houses of Mrs. James Fields and Oliver Wendell Holmes. He was another personage in Boston life when I first went there. Oh, the visits I inflicted on him—yet he always seemed pleased to see me, the cheery, kind man. It was generally winter when I called on him. At once it was "four feet upon a fender!" Four feet upon a fender was his idea of happiness, he told me, during one of these lengthy visits of mine to his house in Beacon Street.

He came to see us in "Much Ado about Nothing" and, next day sent me some little volumes of his work with a lovely inscription on the front page. I miss him very much when I go to Boston now.

In New York, how much I miss Mrs. Beecher I could never say. The Beechers were the most wonderful pair. What an actor he would have made! He read scenes from Shakespeare to Henry and me at luncheon one day. He sat next to his wife, and they held hands nearly all the while; I thought of that time when the great preacher was tried, and all through the trial his wife showed the world her faith in his innocence by sitting by his side and holding his hand.

He was indeed a great preacher. I have a little faded card in my possession now: "Mrs. Henry W. Beecher." "Will ushers of Plymouth Church please seat the bearer in the Pastor's pew." And in the Pastor's pew I sat, listening to that magnificent bass-viol voice with its persuasive low accent, its torrential scorn! After the sermon I went to the Beecher's home. Mr. Beecher sat with a saucer of uncut gems by him on the table. He ran his hand through them from time to time, held them up to the light, admiring them and speaking of their beauty and colour as eloquently as an hour before he had spoken of sin and death and redemption.

He asked me to choose a stone, and I selected an aquamarine, and he had it splendidly mounted for me in Venetian style to wear in "The Merchant of Venice". Once when he was ill, he told me, his wife had some few score of his jewels set up in lead—a kind of small stained-glass window—and hung up opposite his bed. "It did me more good than the doctor's visits," he laughed out!

Mrs. Beecher was very remarkable. She had a way of lowering her head and looking at you with a strange intentness—gravely—kindly and quietly. At her husband she looked a world of love, of faith, of undying devotion. She was fond of me, although I was told she disliked women generally and had been brought up to think all actresses children of Satan. Obedience to the iron rules which had always surrounded her had endowed her with extraordinary self-control. She would not allow herself ever to feel heat or cold, and could stand any pain or discomfort without a word of complaint.

She told me once that when she and her sister were children, a friend had given them some lovely bright blue silk, and as the material was so fine they thought they would have it made up a little more smartly than was usual in their sombre religious home. In spite of their father's hatred of gaudy clothes, they ventured on a little "V" at the neck, hardly showing more than the throat; but still, in a household where blue silk itself was a crime, it was a bold venture. They put on the dresses for the first time for five o'clock dinner, stole downstairs with trepidation, rather late, and took their seats as usual one each side of their father. He was eating soup and never looked up. The little sisters were relieved. He was not going to say anything.

No, he was not going to say anything, but suddenly he took a ladleful of the hot soup and dashed it over the neck of one sister; another ladleful followed quickly on the neck of the other.

"Oh, father, you've burned my neck!"

"Oh, father, you've spoiled my dress!"

"Oh, father, why did you do that?"

"I thought you might be cold," said the severe father significantly—malevolently.

That a woman who had been brought up like this should form a friendship with me naturally caused a good deal of talk. But what did she care! She remained my true friend until her death, and wrote to me constantly when I was in England—such loving, wise letters, full of charity and simple faith. In 1889, after her husband's death, I wrote to her and sent my picture, and she replied:

MY DARLING NELLIE, You cannot know how it soothes my extreme heart-loneliness to receive a token of remembrance, and word of cheer from those I have faithfully loved, and who knew and reverenced my husband. . . . Ellen Terry is very sweet as Ellaline, but dearer far as my dear Nellie.

The Daly players were a revelation to me of the pitch of excellence which American acting had reached. My first night at Daly's was a night of enchantment. I wrote to Mr. Daly and said: "You've got a girl in your company who is the most lovely, humorous darling I have ever seen on the stage." It was Ada Rehan! Now of course I didn't "discover" her or any rubbish of that kind; the audience were already mad about her, but I did know her for what she was, even in that brilliant "all-star" company and before she had played in the classics and won enduring fame. The audacious, superb, quaint, Irish creature! Never have I seen such splendid high comedy! Then the charm of her voice—a little like Ethel Barrymore's when Miss Ethel is speaking very nicely—her smiles and dimples, and provocative, inviting *coquetterie*! Her Rosalind, her Country Wife, her Helena, her performance in "The Railroad of Love"! And above all, her Katherine in "The Taming of the Shrew"! I can only exclaim, not explain! Directly she came on I knew how she was going to do the part. She had such shy, demure fun. She understood, like all great comedians, that you must not pretend to be serious so sincerely that no one in the audience sees through it!

As a woman off the stage Ada Rehan was even more wonderful than as a shrew on. She had a touch of dignity, of nobility, of beauty, rather like Eleonora Duse's. The mouth and the formation of the eye were lovely. Her guiltlessness of make-up off the stage was so attractive! She used to come in to a supper with a lovely shining face which scorned a powder puff. The only thing one missed was the red hair which seemed such a part of her on the stage.

Here is a dear letter from the dear, written in 1890:

> MY DEAR MISS TERRY, Of course the first thing I was to do when I reached Paris was to write and thank you for your lovely red feathers. One week is gone. Today it rains and I am compelled to stay at home, and at last I write. I thought you had forgotten me and my feathers long ago. So imagine my delight when they came at the very end. I liked it so. It seemed as if I lived all the time in your mind: and they came as a goodbye.
>
> I saw but little of you, but in that little I found no change. That was gratifying to me, for I am over-sensitive, and would never trouble you if you had forgotten me. How I shall prize those feathers—Henry Irving's, presented by Ellen Terry to me for my Rosalind Cap. I shall wear them once and then put them by as treasures. Thank you so much for the pretty words you wrote me about "As You Like It". I was hardly fit on that matinée. The great excitement I went through during the London season almost killed me. I am going to try and rest, but I fear my nerves and heart won't let me.
>
> You must try and read between the lines all I feel. I am sure you can if any one ever did, but I cannot put into words my admiration for you—and that comes from deep down in my heart. Goodbye, with all good wishes for your health and success.
>
> I remain, yours most affectionately,
> ADA REHAN.

I wish I could just once have played with Ada Rehan. When Mr. Tree could not persuade Mrs. Kendal to come and play in "The Merry Wives of Windsor" a second time, I hoped that Ada Rehan would come and rollick with me as Mrs. Ford—but it was not to be.

Mr. Daly himself interested me greatly. He was an excellent manager, a man in a million. But he had no artistic sense. The productions of

Shakespeare at Daly's were really bad from the pictorial point of view. But what pace and "ensemble" he got from his company!

May Irwin was the low comedian who played the servants' parts in Daly's comedies from the German. I might describe her, except that she was far more genial, as a kind of female Rutland Barrington. On and off the stage her geniality distinguished her like a halo. It is a rare quality on the stage, yet without it the comedian has up-hill work. I should say that May Irwin and J. B. Buckstone (the English actor and manager of the Haymarket Theatre during the 'sixties) had it equally. Generous May Irwin! Lucky those who have her warm friendship and jolly, kind companionship!

John Drew, the famous son of a famous mother, was another Daly player whom I loved. With what loyalty he supported Ada Rehan! He never played for his own hand but for the good of the piece. His mother Mrs. John Drew, had the same quiet methods as Mrs. Alfred Wigan. Everything that she did told. I saw Mrs. Drew play Mrs. Malaprop, and it was a lesson to people who overact. Her daughter, Georgie Drew, Ethel Barrymore's mother, was also a charming actress. Maurice Barrymore was a brilliantly clever actor. Little Ethel, as I still call her, though she is a big "star", is carrying on the family traditions. She ought to play Lady Teazle. She may take it from me that she would make a success in it.

Modjeska, who, though she is a Polish actress, lives in America and is associated with the American stage, made a great impression on me. She was exquisite in many parts, but in none finer than in "Adrienne Lecouvreur". Her last act electrified me. I have never seen it better acted, although I have seen all the great ones do it since. Her Marie Stuart, too, was a beautiful and distinguished performance. Her Juliet had lovely moments, but I did not so much care for that, and her broken English interfered with the verse of Shakespeare. Some years ago I met Modjeska and she greeted me so warmly and sweetly, although she was very ill.

During my more recent tours in America Maude Adams is the actress of whom I have seen most, and "to see her is to love her!" In "The Little Minister" and in "Quality Street" I think she is at her best, but above all parts she herself is most adorable. She is just worshipped in America, and has an extraordinary effect—an *educational* effect upon all American girlhood.

I never saw Mary Anderson act. That seems a strange admission, but during her wonderful reign at the Lyceum Theatre, which she rented from Henry Irving, I was in America, and another time when I might have seen her act I was very ill and ordered abroad. I have, however, had the great pleasure of meeting her, and she has done me many little kindnesses. Hearing her praises sung on all sides, and her beauties spoken of everywhere, I was particularly struck by her modest evasion of publicity *off* the stage. I personally only knew her as a most beautiful woman—as kind as beautiful—constantly working for her religion—*always* kind, a good daughter, a good wife, a good woman.

She cheered me before I first sailed for America by saying that her people would like me.

"Since seeing you in Portia and Letitia," she wrote, "I am convinced you will take America by storm." Certainly *she* took *England* by storm! But she abandoned her triumphs almost as soon as they were gained. They never made her happy, she once told me, and I could understand her better than most since I had had success too, and knew that it did not mean happiness. I have a letter from her, written from St. Raphael soon after her marriage. It is nice to think that she is just as happy now as she was then—that she made no mistake when she left the stage, where she had such a brief and brilliant career.

GRAND HÔTEL DE VALESCURE,
ST. RAPHAEL, FRANCE.

DEAR MISS TERRY, I am saying all kinds of fine things about your beautiful work in my book—which will appear shortly; but I cannot remember the name of the small part you made so attractive in the "Lyons Mail". It was the first one I had seen you in, and I wish to write my delightful impressions of it.

Will you be so very kind as to tell me the name of your character and the two Mr. Irving acted so wonderfully in that play?

There is a brilliant blue sea before my windows, with purple mountains as a background and silver-topped olives and rich green pines in the middle distance. I wish you could drop down upon us in this golden land for a few days' holiday from your weary work.

I would like to tell you what a big darling my husband is, and how perfectly happy he makes my life—but there's no use trying.

The last time we met I promised you a photo—here it is! One of my latest! And won't you send me one of yours in private dress? DO!

Forgive me for troubling you, and believe me your admirer.

MARY ANDERSON DE NAVARRO.

Henry and I were so fortunate as to gain the friendship and approval of Dr. Horace Howard Furness, perhaps the finest Shakespearean scholar in America, and editor of the "Variorum Shakespeare", which Henry considered the best of all editions—"the one which counts". It was in Boston, I think, that I disgraced myself at one of Dr. Furness's lectures. He was discussing "As You Like It" and Rosalind, and proving with much elaboration that English in Shakespeare's time was pronounced like a broad country dialect, and that Rosalind spoke

Warwickshire! A little girl who was sitting in the row in front of me had lent me her copy of the play a moment before, and now, absorbed in Dr. Furness's argument, I forgot the book wasn't mine and began scrawling controversial notes in it with my very thick and blotty fountain pen.

"Give me back my book! Give me my book!" screamed the little girl. "How dare you write in my book!" She began to cry with rage.

Her mother tried to hush her up: "Don't, darling. Be quiet! It's Miss Ellen Terry."

"I don't care! She's spoilt my nice book!"

I am glad to say that when the little girl understood, she forgave me; and the spoilt book is treasured very much by a tall Boston young lady of eighteen who has replaced the child of seven years ago! Still, it was dreadful of me, and I did feel ashamed at the time.

I saw "As You Like It" acted in New York once with every part (except the man who let down the curtain) played by a woman, and it was extraordinarily well done. The most remarkable bit of acting was by Janauschek, who played Jacques. I have never heard the speech beginning "All the world's a stage" delivered more finely, not even by Phelps, who was fine in the part.

Mary Shaw's Rosalind was good, and the Silvius (who played it, now?) was charming.

Unfortunately that one man, poor creature (no wonder he was nervous!), spoiled the end of the play by failing to ring down the curtain, at which the laughter was immoderate! Janauschek used to do a little sketch from the German called "Come Here!" which I afterwards did in England.

In November 1901 I wrote in my diary: "*Philadelphia.*—Supper at Henry's. Jefferson there, sweeter and more interesting than ever—and younger."

Dear Joe Jefferson—actor, painter, courteous gentleman, *profound* student of Shakespeare! When the Bacon-Shakespeare controversy was raging in America (it really *did* rage there!) Jefferson wrote the most delicious doggerel about it. He ridiculed, and his ridicule killed the Bacon enthusiasts all the more dead because it was barbed with erudition.

He said that when I first came into the box to see him as "Rip" he thought I did not like him, because I fidgeted and rustled and moved my place, as is my wicked way. "But I'll get her, and I'll hold her," he said to himself. I was held indeed—enthralled.

In manner Jefferson was a little like Norman Forbes-Robertson. Perhaps that was why the two took such a fancy to each other. When Norman was walking with Jefferson one day, some one who met them said:

"Your son?"

"No," said Jefferson, "but I wish he were! The young man has such good manners!"

Our first American tours were in 1883 and 1884; the third in 1887–88, the year of the great blizzard. Henry fetched us at half-past ten in the morning! His hotel was near the theatre where we were to play at night. He said the weather was stormy, and we had better make for his hotel while there was time! The German actor Ludwig Barnay was to open in New York that night, but the blizzard affected his nerves to such an extent that he did not appear at all, and returned to Germany directly the weather improved!

Most of the theatres closed for three days, but we remained open, although there was a famine in the town and the streets were impassable. The cold was intense. Henry sent Walter out to buy some violets for Barnay, and when he brought them in to the dressing room—he had only carried them a few yards—they were frozen so hard that they could have been chipped with a hammer!

We rang up on "Faust" three-quarters of an hour late! This was not bad considering all things. Although the house was sold out, there was hardly any audience, and only a harp and two violins in the orchestra. Discipline was so strong in the Lyceum company that every member of it reached the theatre by eight o'clock, although some of them had had to walk from Brooklyn Bridge.

The Mayor of New York and his daughter managed to reach their box somehow. Then we thought it was time to begin. Some members of Daly's company, including John Drew, came in, and a few friends. It was the oddest, scantiest audience! But the enthusiasm was terrific!

Five years went by before we visited America again. Five years in a country of rapid changes is a long time, long enough for friends to forget! But they didn't forget. This time we made new friends, too, in the Far West. We went to San Francisco, among other places. We attended part of a performance at the Chinese theatre. Oh, those rows of impenetrable faces gazing at the stage with their long, shining, inexpressive eyes! What a look of the everlasting the Chinese have! "We have been before you—we shall be after you," they seem to say.

Just as we were getting interested in the play, the interpreter rose and hurried us out. Something that was not for the ears of women was being said, but we did not know it!

The chief incident of the fifth American tour was our production at Chicago of Laurence Irving's one-act play "Godefroi and Yolande". I regard that little play as an inspiration. By instinct the young author did everything right. The Chicago folk, in spite of the unpleasant theme of the play, recognised the genius of it, and received it splendidly.

In 1901 I was ill, and hated the parts I was playing in America. The Lyceum was not what it had been. Everything was changed.

In 1907—only the other day—I toured in America for the first time on my own account—playing modern plays for the first time. I made new friends and found my old ones still faithful.

But this tour was chiefly momentous to me because at Pittsburg I was married for the third time, and married to an American. My marriage was my own affair, but very few people seemed to think so, and I was overwhelmed with "inquiries", kind and otherwise. Kindness and loyalty won the day. "If any one deserves to be happy, you do," many a friend wrote. Well, I am happy, and while I am happy, I cannot feel old.

XIII

THE MACBETH PERIOD

PERHAPS Henry Irving and I might have gone on with Shakespeare to the end of the chapter if he had not been in such a hurry to produce "Macbeth".

We ought to have done "As You Like It" in 1888, or "The Tempest". Henry thought of both these plays. He was much attracted by the part of Caliban in "The Tempest", but, he said, "the young lovers are everything, and where are we going to find them?" He would have played Touchstone in "As You Like It", not Jacques, because Touchstone is in the vital part of the play.

He might have delayed both "Macbeth" and "Henry VIII". He ought to have added to his list of Shakespearean productions "Julius Caesar", "King John", "As You Like It", "Antony and Cleopatra"', "Richard II", and "Timon of Athens". There were reasons "against", of course. In "Julius Caesar" he wanted to play Brutus. "That's the part for the actor," he said, "because it needs acting. But the actor-manager's part is Antony—Antony scores all along the line. Now when the actor and actor-manager fight in a play, and when there is no part for you in it, I think it's wiser to leave it alone."

Every one knows when the luck first began to turn against Henry Irving. It was in 1896 when he revived "Richard III". On the first night he went home, slipped on the stairs in Grafton Street, broke a bone in his knee, aggravated the hurt by walking on it, and had to close the theatre. It was that year, too, that his general health began to fail. For the ten years preceding his death he carried on an indomitable struggle against ill-health. Lungs and heart alike were weak. Only the spirit in that frail body remained as strong as ever. Nothing could bend it, much less break it.

But I have not come to that sad time yet.

"We all know when we do our best," said Henry once. "We are the only people who know." Yet he thought he did better in "Macbeth" than in "Hamlet"!

Was he right after all?

His *view* of "Macbeth", though attacked and derided and put to shame in many quarters, is as clear to me as the sunlight itself. To me it seems as stupid to quarrel with the conception as to deny the nose on one's face. But the carrying out of the conception was unequal. Henry's imagination was sometimes his worst enemy.

When I think of his "Macbeth", I remember him most distinctly in the last act after the battle when he looked like a great famished wolf, weak

194

with the weakness of a giant exhausted, spent as one whose exertions have been ten times as great as those of commoner men of rougher fibre and coarser strength.

> Of all men else I have avoided thee.

Once more he suggested, as he only could suggest, the power of Fate. Destiny seemed to hang over him, and he knew that there was no hope, no mercy.

The rehearsals for "Macbeth" were very exhausting, but they were splendid to watch. In this play Henry brought his manipulation of crowds to perfection. My acting edition of the play is riddled with rough sketches by him of different groups. Artists to whom I have shown them have been astonished by the spirited impressionism of these sketches. For his "purpose" Henry seems to have been able to do anything, even to drawing, and composing music! Sir Arthur Sullivan's music at first did not quite please him. He walked up and down the stage humming, and showing the composer what he was going to do at certain situations. Sullivan, with wonderful quickness and open-mindedness, caught his meaning at once.

"Much better than mine, Irving—much better—I'll rough it out at once!"

When the orchestra played the new version, based on that humming of Henry's it was exactly what he wanted!

Knowing what a task I had before me, I began to get anxious and worried about "Lady Mac". Henry wrote me such a nice letter about this:

> Tonight, if possible, the last act. I want to get these great multitudinous scenes over and then we can attack *our* scenes. . . . Your sensitiveness is so acute that you must suffer sometimes. You are not like anybody else—you see things with such lightning quickness and unerring instinct that dull fools like myself grow irritable and impatient sometimes. I feel confused when I'm thinking of one thing, and disturbed by another. That's all. But I do feel very sorry afterwards when I don't seem to heed what I so much value. . . .
>
> I think things are going well, considering the time we've been at it, but I see so much that is wanting that it seems almost impossible to get through properly. "Tonight commence, Matthias. If you sleep, you are lost!"[1]

At this time we were able to be of the right use to each other. Henry could never have worked with a very strong woman. I might have deteriorated, in partnership with a weaker man whose ends were less fine, whose motives were less pure. I had the taste and artistic knowledge

[1] A quotation from "The Bells."

that his upbringing had not developed in him. For years he did things to please me. Later on I gave up asking him. In "King Lear" Mrs. Nettleship made him a most beautiful cloak, but he insisted on wearing a brilliant purple velvet cloak with spangles all over it which swamped his beautiful make-up and his beautiful acting. Poor Mrs. Nettleship was almost in tears.

"I'll never make you anything again—never!"

One of Mrs. "Nettle's" greatest triumphs was my Lady Macbeth dress, which she carried out from Mrs. Comyns Carr's design. I am glad to think it is immortalised in Sargent's picture. From the first I knew that picture was going to be splendid. In my diary for 1888 I was always writing about it:

> The picture of me is nearly finished, and I think it magnificent. The green and blue of the dress is splendid, and the expression as Lady Macbeth holds the crown over her head is quite wonderful.
>
> Henschel is sitting to Sargent. His concerts, I hear, can't be carried on another year for want of funds. What a shame!
>
> Mr. Sargent is painting a head of Henry—very good, but mean about the chin at present.
>
> Sargent's picture is talked of everywhere and quarrelled about as much as my way of playing the part.
>
> Sargent's "Lady Macbeth" in the New Gallery is a great success. The picture is the sensation of the year. Of course opinions differ about it, but there are dense crowds round it day after day. There is talk of putting it on exhibition by itself.

Since then it has gone over nearly the whole of Europe, and now is resting for life at the Tate Gallery. Sargent suggested by this picture all that I should have liked to be able to convey in my acting as Lady Macbeth.

My Diary—Everybody hates Sargent's head of Henry. Henry also. I like it, but not altogether. I think it perfectly wonderfully painted and like him, only not at his best by any means. There sat Henry and there by his side the picture, and I could scarce tell one from t'other. Henry looked white, with tired eyes, and holes in his cheeks and bored to death! And there was the picture with white face, tired eyes, holes in the cheeks and boredom in every line. Sargent tried to paint his smile and gave it up.

Sargent said to me, I remember, upon Henry Irving's first visit to the studio to see the Macbeth picture of me, "What a Saint!" This to my mind promised well—that Sargent should see *that* side of Henry so swiftly. So then I never left off asking Henry to sit to Sargent, who wanted to paint him too, and said to me continually, "What a head!"

From my Diary—Sargent's picture is almost finished, and it is really splendid. Burne-Jones yesterday suggested two or three alterations about the colour which Sargent immediately adopted, but Burne-Jones raves about the picture.

It ("Macbeth") is a most tremendous success, and the last three days' advance booking has been greater than ever was known, even at the Lyceum. Yes, it is a success, and I am a success, which amazes me, for never did I think I should be let down so easily. Some people hate me in it; some, Henry among them, think it my best part, and the critics differ, and discuss it hotly, which in itself is my best success of all! Those who don't like me in it are those who don't want, and don't like to read it fresh from Shakespeare, and who hold by the "fiend" reading of the character. . . . One of the best things ever written on the subject, I think, is the essay of J. Comyns Carr. That is as hotly discussed as the new "Lady Mac"—all the best people agreeing with it. Oh, dear! It is an exciting time!

From a letter I wrote to my daughter, who was in Germany at the time:

I wish you could see my dresses. They are superb, especially the first one: green beetles on it, and such a cloak! The photographs give no idea of it at all, for it is in colour that it is so splendid. The dark red hair is fine. The whole thing is Rossetti—rich stained-glass effects. I play some of it well, but, of course, I don't do what I want to do yet. Meanwhile I shall not budge an inch in the reading of it, for that I know is right. Oh, it's fun, but it's precious hard work, for I by no means make her a "gentle, lovable woman" as some of 'em say. That's all pickles. She was nothing of the sort, although she was *not* a fiend, and *did* love her husband. I have to what is vulgarly called "sweat at it", each night.

The few people who liked my Lady Macbeth, liked it very much. I hope I am not vain to quote this letter from Lady Pollock:

. . . Burne-Jones has been with me this afternoon: he was at "Macbeth" last night, and you filled his whole soul with your beauty and your poetry. . . . He says you were a great Scandinavian queen; that your presence, your voice, your movement made a marvellously poetic harmony; that your dress was grandly imagined and grandly worn—and that he cannot criticise—he can only remember.

But Burne-Jones by this time had become one of our most ardent admirers, and was prejudiced in my favour because my acting appealed to his *eye*. Still, the drama is for the eye as well as for the ear and the mind.

Very early I learned that one had best be ambitious merely to please oneself in one's work a little—quietly. I coupled with this the reflection that one "gets nothing for nothing, and damned little for sixpence!"

Here I was in the very noonday of life, fresh from Lady Macbeth and still young enough to play Rosalind, suddenly called upon to play a rather uninteresting mother in "The Dead Heart". However, my son Teddy made his first appearance in it, and had such a big success that I soon forgot that for me the play was rather "small beer".

It had been done before, of course, by Benjamin Webster and George Vining. Henry engaged Bancroft for the Abbé, a part of quite as much importance as his own. It was only a melodrama, but Henry could always invest a melodrama with life, beauty, interest, mystery, by his methods of production.

I'm full of French Revolution [he wrote to me when he was preparing the play for rehearsal], and could pass an examination. In our play, at the taking of the Bastille we must have a starving crowd—hungry, eager, cadaverous faces. If that can be well carried out, the effect will be very terrible, and the contrast to the other crowd (the red and fat crowd—the blood-gorged ones who look as if they'd been all drinking wine—*red* wine, as Dickens says) would be striking. . . . It's tiresome stuff to read, because it depends so much on situations. I have been touching the book up though, and improved it here and there, I think.

A letter this morning from the illustrious Blank offering me his prompt book to look at. . . . I think I shall borrow the treasure. Why not? Of course he will say that he has produced the play and all that sort of thing; but what does that matter, if one can only get one hint out of it?

The longer we live, the more we see that if we only do our own work thoroughly well, we can be independent of everything else or anything that may be said. . . .

I see in Landry a great deal of Manette—that same vacant gaze into years gone by when he crouched in his dungeon nursing his wrongs. . . .

I shall send you another book soon to put any of your alterations and additions in. I've added a lot of little things with a few lines for you—very good, I think, though I say it as shouldn't—I know you'll laugh! They are perhaps not startlingly original, but better than the original, anyhow! Here they are—last act!

"Ah, Robert, pity me. By the recollections of our youth, I implore you to save my boy!" (*Now* for 'em!)

"If my voice recalls a tone that ever fell sweetly upon your ear, have pity on me! If the past is not a blank, if you once loved, have pity on me!" (Bravo!)

Now I call that very good, and if the "If" and the "pitys" don't bring down the house, well it's a pity! I pity the pittites!

. . . I've just been copying out my part in an account book—a little more handy to put in one's pocket. It's really very short, but difficult to act, though, and so is yours. I like this "piling up" sort of acting, and I am sure you will, when you play the part. It's restful. "The Bells" is that sort of thing.

The crafty old Henry! All this was to put me in conceit with my part! Many people at this time put me in conceit with my son, including dear Burne-Jones with his splendid gift of impulsive enthusiasm.

> THE GRANGE,
> WEST KENSINGTON, W.
> *Sunday.*

MOST DEAR LADY, I thought all went wonderfully last night, and no sign could I see of hitch or difficulty; and as for your boy, he looked a lovely little gentleman—and in his cups was perfect, not overdoing by the least touch a part always perilously easy to overdo. I too had the impertinence to be a bit nervous for you about him, but not when he appeared—so altogether I was quite happy.

. . . Irving was very noble—I thought I had never seen his face so beatified before—no, that isn't the word, and to hunt for the right one would be so like judicious criticism that I won't. Exalted and splendid it was—and you were you—YOU—and so all was well. I rather wanted more shouting and distant roar in the Bastille Scene—since the walls fell, like Jericho, by noise. A good dreadful growl always going on would have helped, I thought—and that was the only point where I missed anything.

And I was very glad you got your boy back again and that Mr. Irving was ready to have his head cut off for you; so it had what I call a good ending, and I am in bright spirits today, and ever

> Your real friend,
> E. B-J.

I would come and growl gladly.

There were terrible strikes all over England when we were playing "The Dead Heart". I could not help sympathising with the strikers . . . yet reading all about the French Revolution as I did then, I can't understand how the French nation can be proud of it when one remembers how they butchered their own great men, the leaders of the movement—Camille Desmoulins, Danton, Robespierre and the others. My man is Camille Desmoulins. I just love him.

Plays adapted from novels are generally unsatisfactory. A whole story cannot be conveyed in three hours, and every reader of the story looks for something not in the play. Wills took from "The Vicar of Wake-field" an episode and did it right well, but there was no *episode* in "The Bride of Lammermoor" for Merivale to take. He tried to traverse the whole ground, and failed. But he gave me some lovely things to do in Lucy Ashton. I had to lose my poor wits, as in Ophelia, in the last act, and with hardly a word to say I was able to make an effect. The love scene at the well I did nicely too.

Seymour Lucas designed splendid dresses for this play. My "Ravens-wood" riding dress set a fashion in ladies' coats for quite a long time. Mine was copied by Mr. Lucas from a leather coat of Lord Mohun's. He is said to have had it on when he was killed. At any rate there was a large stab in the back of the coat, and a blood-stain.

This was my first speculation in play-buying! I saw it acted, and thought I could do something with it. Henry would not buy it, so I did! He let me do it first in front of a revival of "The Corsican Brothers" in 1891. It was a great success, although my son and I did not know a word on the first night and had our parts written out and pinned all over the furniture on the stage! Dear old Mr. Howe wrote to me that Teddy's performance was "more than creditable; it was exceedingly good and full of character, and with your own charming performance the piece was a great success." Since 1891 I must I played "Nance Oldfield" hundreds of times, but I never had an A xander Oldworthy so good as my own son, although such talented young actors as Martin Harvey, Laurence Irving and, more recently, Harcourt Williams have all played it with me.

Henry's pride as Cardinal Wolsey seemed to eat him. How wonderful he looked (though not fat and self-indulgent like the pictures of the real Wolsey) in his flame-coloured robes! He had the silk dyed specially by the dyers to the Cardinals' College in Rome. Seymour Lucas designed the clothes. It was a magnificent production, but not very interesting to me. I played Katherine much better ten years later at Stratford-on-Avon at the Shakespeare Memorial Festival. I was stronger then, and more reposeful. This letter from Burne-Jones about "Henry VIII" is a delightful tribute to Henry Irving's treatment of the play:

MY DEAR LADY, We went last night to the play (at my theatre) to see Henry VIII.—Margaret and Mackail and I. It was delicious to go out again and see mankind, after such evil days. How kind they were to me no words can say—I went in at a private door and then into a cosy box and back the same way, swiftly, and am marvellously the better for the adventure. No YOU, alas!

I have written to Mr. Irving just to thank him for his great kindness in making the path of pleasure so easy, for I go tremblingly at present. But I could not say to him what I thought of the Cardinal—a sort of shame keeps one from saying to an artist what one thinks of his work—but to you I can say how nobly he warmed up the story of the old religion to my exacting mind in that impersonation. I shall think always of dying monarchy in his Charles—and always of dying hierarchy in his Wolsey. How Protestant and dull all grew when that noble type had gone!

I can't go to church till red cardinals come back (and may they be of exactly that red) nor to Court till trumpets and banners come back— nor to evening parties till the dances are like that dance. What a lovely young Queen has been found. But there was no YOU. . . . Perhaps it was as well. I couldn't have you slighted even in a play, and put aside. When I go back to see you, as I soon will, it will be easier. Mr. Irving let me know you would not act, and proposed that I should go later on—wasn't that like him? So I sat with my children and was right happy; and, as usual, the streets looked dirty and all the people muddy and black as we came away. Please not to answer this stuff.

Ever yours affectionately,
E. B.-J.

—I wish that Cardinal could have been made Pope, and sat with his foot on the Earl of Surrey's neck. Also I wish to be a Cardinal; but then I sometimes want to be a pirate. We can't have all we want.

Your boy was very kind—I thought the race of young men who are polite and attentive to old fading ones had passed away with antique pageants—but it isn't so.

When the Duke and Duchess of Devonshire gave the famous fancy dress ball at Devonshire House, Henry attended it in the robes which had appealed so strongly to Burne-Jones's imaginative eye. I was told by one who was present at this ball that as the Cardinal swept up the staircase, his long train held magnificently over his arm, a sudden wave of reality seemed to sweep upstairs with him, and reduce to the pettiest make-believe all the aristocratic masquerade that surrounded him.

I renewed my acquaintance with "Henry VIII" in 1902, when I played Queen Katherine for Mr. Benson during the Shakespeare Memorial performances in April. I was pretty miserable at the time— the Lyceum reign was dying, and taking an unconscionably long time about it, which made the position all the more difficult. Henry Irving was reviving "Faust"—a wise step, as it had been his biggest "money-maker"—and it was impossible that I could play Margaret. There are some young parts that the actress can still play when she is no longer young: Beatrice, Portia, and many others come to mind. But I think that when the character is that of a young girl the betrayal of whose innocence is the main theme of the play, no amount of skill on the part of the actress can make up for the loss of youth.

Suggestions were thrown out to me (not by Henry Irving, but by others concerned) that although I was too old for Margaret, I might play *Martha!* Well! well! I didn't quite see *that*. So I redeemed a promise given in jest at the Lyceum to Frank Benson twenty years earlier, and went off to Stratford-upon-Avon to play in Henry VIII.

Mr. Benson was wonderful to work with. "I am proud to think," he wrote me just before our few rehearsals began, "that I have trained my folk (as I was taught by my elders and betters at the Lyceum) to be pretty quick at adapting themselves to anything that may be required of them, so that you need not be uneasy as to their not fitting in with your business."

"My folk," as Mr. Benson called them, were excellent, especially Surrey (Harcourt Williams), Norfolk (Matheson Lang), Caperius (Fitzgerald), and Griffith (Nicholson). "Harcourt Williams," I wrote in my diary on the day of the dress-rehearsal, "will be heard of very shortly. He played Edgar in 'Lear' much better than Terriss, although not so good an actor yet."

I played Katherine on Shakespeare's Birthday—such a lovely day, bright and sunny and warm. The performance went finely—and I made a little speech afterwards which was quite a success. I was presented publicly on the stage with the Certificate of Governorship of the Memorial Theatre.

During these pleasant days at Stratford, I went about in between the performances of "Henry VIII"—which was, I think, given three times a week for three weeks—seeing the lovely country and lovely friends who live there. A visit to Broadway and to beautiful Madame de Navarro (Mary Anderson) was particularly delightful. To see her looking so handsome, robust and fresh—so happy in her beautiful home, gave me the keenest pleasure. I also went to Stanways—the Elchos' home—a fascinating place. Lady Elcho showed me all over it, and she was not the least lovely thing in it.

In Stratford I was rebuked by the permanent inhabitants for being kind to a little boy in professionally ragged clothing who made me, as he has made hundreds of others, listen to a long, made-up history of Stratford-on-Avon, Shakespeare, the Merchant of Venice, Julius Caesar, and other things—the most hopeless mix! The inhabitants assured me that the boy was a little rascal, who begged and extorted money from visitors by worrying them with his recitation until they paid him to leave them alone.

Long before I knew that the child was such a reprobate I had given him a pass to the gallery and a Temple Shakespeare! I derived such pleasure from his version of the "Mercy" speech from "The Merchant of Venice" that I still think he was ill-paid!

The quality of mercy is not strange
It droppeth as *the* gentle rain from 'Eaven
Upon *the* place beneath; it is twicet bless.
It blesseth in that gives and in that takes
It is in the mightiest—in the mightiest
It becomes the throned monuk better than its crownd.
It's an appribute to God inself
It is in the thorny 'earts of kings
But not in the fit and dread of kings.

I asked the boy what he meant to be when he was a man. He
answered with decision: "A reciterer."

I also asked him what he liked best in the play ("Henry VIII").

"When the blind went up and down and you smiled," he replied—
surely a naïve compliment to my way of "taking a call"! Further
pressed, he volunteered: "When you lay on the bed and died to please
the angels."

XIV

LAST DAYS AT THE LYCEUM

I HAD exactly ten years more with Henry Irving after "Henry VIII". During that time we did "King Lear", "Becket", "King Arthur", "Cymbeline", "Madame Sans-Gêne", "Peter the Great" and "The Medicine Man". I feel too near to these productions to write about them. The first night of "Cymbeline" I felt almost dead. Nothing seemed right. "Everything is so slow, so slow," I wrote in my diary. "I don't feel a bit inspired, only dull and hide-bound." Yet Imogen was, I think, the *only* inspired performance of these later years. On the first night of "Sans-Gêne" I acted *courageously* and fairly well. Every one seemed to be delighted. The old Duke of Cambridge patted, or rather *thumped*, me on the shoulder and said kindly: "Ah, my dear, *you* can act!" Henry quite effaced me in his wonderful sketch of Napoleon. "It seems to me some nights," I wrote in my diary at the time, "as if I were watching Napoleon trying to imitate H. I., and I find myself immensely interested and amused in the watchings."

"The Medicine Man" was, in my opinion, our only *quite* unworthy production.

> *From my Diary*—Poor Taber has such an awful part in the play, and mine is even worse. It is short enough, yet I feel I can't cut too much of it. . . . The gem of the whole play is my hair! Not waved at all, and very filmy and pale. Henry, I admit, is splendid; but oh, it is all such rubbish! . . . If "Manfred" and a few such plays are to succeed this, I simply must do something else.

But I did not! I stayed on, as every one knows, when the Lyceum as a personal enterprise of Henry's was no more—when the farcical Lyceum Syndicate took over the theatre. I played a wretched part in "Robes-pierre", and refused £12,000 to go to America with Henry in "Dante".

In these days Henry was a changed man. He became more republican and less despotic as a producer. He left things to other people. As an actor he worked as faithfully as ever. Henley's stoical lines might have been written of him as he was in these last days:

> Out of the night that covers me,
> Black as the Pit from pole to pole,
> I thank whatever gods there be
> For my unconquerable soul.

In the fell clutch of circumstance
I have not winced nor cried aloud:
Beneath the bludgeonings of chance
My head is bloody but unbowed.

Henry Irving did not treat me badly. I hope I did not treat him badly.
He revived "Faust" and produced "Dante". I would have liked to stay
with him to the end of the chapter, but there was nothing for me to act
in either of these plays. But we never quarrelled. Our long partnership
dissolved naturally. It was all very sad, but it could not be helped.

It has always been a reproach against Henry Irving in some mouths
that he neglected the modern English playwright; and of course the
reproach included me to a certain extent. I was glad, then, to show that
I *could* act in the new plays when Mr. Barrie wrote "Alice-sit-by-the-
Fire" for me, and after some years' delay I was able to play in Mr.
Bernard Shaw's "Captain Brassbound's Conversion". Of course I could
not have played in "little" plays of this school at the Lyceum with
Henry Irving, even if I had wanted to! They are essentially plays for
small theatres.

In Mr. Shaw's "A Man of Destiny" there were two good parts, and
Henry, at my request, considered it, although it was always difficult to
fit a one-act play into the Lyceum bill. For reasons of his own Henry
never produced Mr. Shaw's play, and there was a good deal of fuss
made about it at the time (1897). But ten years ago Mr. Shaw was not so
well known as he is now, and the so-called "rejection" was probably of
use to him as an advertisement!

"A Man of Destiny" has been produced since, but without any great
success. I wonder if Henry and I could have done more with it?

At this time Mr. Shaw and I frequently corresponded. It began by
my writing to ask him, as musical critic of the *Saturday Review*, to tell
me frankly what he thought of the chances of a composer-singer friend
of mine. He answered "characteristically", and we developed a perfect
fury for writing to each other! Sometimes the letters were on business,
sometimes they were not, but always his were entertaining, and mine
were, I suppose, "good copy", as he drew the character of Lady Cecily
Waynflete in "Brassbound" entirely from my letters. He never met me
until after the play was written. In 1902 he sent me this ultimatum:

April 3, 1902.

Mr. Bernard Shaw's compliments to Miss Ellen Terry.

Mr. Bernard Shaw has been approached by Mrs. Langtry with a view to the
immediate and splendid production of "Captain Brassbound's Conversion."

Mr. Bernard Shaw, with the last flash of a trampled-out love, has
repulsed Mrs. Langtry with a petulance bordering on brutality.

Mr. Bernard Shaw has been actuated in this ungentlemanly and un-businesslike course by an angry desire to seize Miss Ellen Terry by the hair and make her play Lady Cicely.

Mr. Bernard Shaw would be glad to know whether Miss Ellen Terry wishes to play Martha at the Lyceum instead.

Mr. Bernard Shaw will go to the length of keeping a minor part open for Sir Henry Irving when "Faust" fails, if Miss Ellen Terry desires it.

Mr. Bernard Shaw lives in daily fear of Mrs. Langtry's recovering sufficiently from her natural resentment of his ill manners to reopen the subject.

Mr. Bernard Shaw begs Miss Ellen Terry to answer this letter.

Mr. Bernard Shaw is looking for a new cottage or house in the country, and wants advice on the subject.

Mr. Bernard Shaw craves for the sight of Miss Ellen Terry's once familiar handwriting.

The first time he came to my house I was not present, but a young American lady who had long adored him from the other side of the Atlantic took my place as hostess (I was at the theatre as usual); and I took great pains to have everything looking nice! I spent a long time putting out my best blue china, and ordered a splendid dinner, quite forgetting the honoured guest generally dined off a Plasmon biscuit and a bean!

Mr. Shaw read "Arms and the Man" to my young American friend (Miss Satty Fairchild) without even going into the dining-room where the blue china was spread out to delight his eye. My daughter Edy was present at the reading, and appeared so much absorbed in some embroidery, and paid the reader so few compliments about his play, that he expressed the opinion that she behaved as if she had been married to him for twenty years!

The first time I ever saw Mr. Shaw in the flesh—I hope he will pardon me such an anti-vegetarian expression—was when he took his call after the first production of "Captain Brassbound's Conversion" by the Stage Society. He was quite unlike what I had imagined from his letters.

When at last I was able to play in "Captain Brassbound's Conversion", I found Bernard Shaw wonderfully patient at rehearsal. I look upon him as a good, kind, gentle creature whose "brain-storms" are just due to the Irishman's love of a fight; they never spring from malice or anger. It doesn't answer to take Bernard Shaw seriously. He is not a man of convictions. That is one of the charms of his plays—to me at least. One never knows how the cat is really jumping. But it *jumps*. Bernard Shaw is alive, with nine lives, like that cat!

★   ★   ★

On Whit Monday, 1902, I received a telegram from Mr. Tree saying that he was coming down to Winchelsea to see me on "an important matter of business". I was at the time suffering from considerable depression about the future.

The Stratford-on-Avon visit had inspired me with the feeling that there was life in the old 'un yet, and had distracted my mind from the strangeness of no longer being at the Lyceum permanently with Henry Irving. But there seemed to be nothing ahead, except two matinées a week with him at the Lyceum, to be followed by a provincial tour in which I was only to play twice a week, as Henry's chief attraction was to be "Faust". This sort of "dowager" engagement did not tempt me. Besides, I hated the idea of drawing a large salary and doing next to no work.

So when Mr. Tree proposed that I should play Mrs. Page (Mrs. Kendal being Mrs. Ford) in "The Merry Wives of Windsor" at His Majesty's, it was only natural that I should accept the offer joyfully. I telegraphed to Henry Irving, asking him if he had any objection to my playing at His Majesty's. He answered: "Quite willing if proposed arrangements about matinées are adhered to."

I have thought it worth while to give the facts about this engagement, because so many people seemed at the time, and afterwards, to think that I had treated Henry Irving badly by going to play in another theatre, and that theatre one where a certain rivalry with the Lyceum as regards Shakespearean productions had grown up. There was absolutely no foundation for the rumours that my "desertion" caused further estrangement between Henry Irving and me.

"Heaven give you many, many merry days and nights," he telegraphed to me on the first night; and after that first night (the jolliest that I ever saw), he wrote delighting in my success.

It *was* a success—there was no doubt about it! Some people accused the Merry Wives of rollicking and "mafficking" overmuch—but these were the people who forgot that we were acting in a farce, and that farce is farce, even when Shakespeare is the author.

All the summer I enjoyed myself thoroughly. It was all such *good fun*—Mrs. Kendal was so clever and delightful to play with, Mr. Tree so indefatigable in discovering new funny "business".

After the dress-rehearsal I wrote in my diary: "Edy has real genius for dresses for the stage." My dress for Mrs. Page was such a *real* thing—it helped me enormously—and I was never more grateful for my daughter's gift than when I played Mrs. Page.

It was an admirable all-round cast—almost a "star" cast: Oscar Asche as Ford, poor Henry Kemble (since dead) as Dr. Caius, Courtice Pounds as Sir Hugh Evans, and Mrs. Tree as sweet Anne Page all rowed in the boat with precisely the right swing. There were no "passengers" in the cast. The audience at first used to seem rather amazed! This thwacking rough-and-tumble, Rabelaisian horse-play—Shakespeare! Impossible! But as the evening went on we used to capture even the most civilised, and force them to return to a simple Elizabethan frame of mind.

In my later career I think I have had no success like this! Letters rained on me—yes, even love-letters, as if, to quote Mrs. Page, I were still in "the holiday-time of my beauty". As I would always rather make an audience laugh than see them weep, it may be guessed how much I enjoyed the hearty laughter at His Majesty's during the run of the madcap absurdity of "The Merry Wives of Windsor".

All the time I was at His Majesty's I continued to play in matinées of "Charles I" and "The Merchant of Venice" at the Lyceum with Henry Irving. We went on negotiating, too, about the possibility of my appearing in "Dante", which Sardou had written specially for Irving, and on which he was relying for his next tour in America.

On the 19th of July, 1902, I acted at the Lyceum for the very last time, although I did not know it then. These last Lyceum days were very sad. The reception given by Henry to the Indian Princes, who were in England for the Coronation, was the last flash of the splendid hospitality which had for so many years been one of the glories of the theatre.

During my provincial tour with Henry Irving in the autumn of this year I thought long and anxiously over the proposition that I should play in "Dante". I heard the play read, and saw no possible part for me in it. I refused a large sum of money to go to America with Henry Irving because I could not consent to play a part even worse than the one that I had played in "Robespierre". As things turned out, although "Dante" did fairly well at Drury Lane, the Americans would have none of it and Henry had to fall back upon his répertoire.

Having made the decision against "Dante", I began to wonder what I should do. My partnership with Henry Irving was definitely broken, most inevitably and naturally "dissolved". There were many roads open to me. I chose one which was, from a financial point of view, *madness*.

Instead of going to America, and earning £12,000, I decided to take a theatre with my son, and produce plays in conjunction with him.

I had several plays in view—an English translation of a French play about the patient Griselda, and a comedy by Miss Clo Graves among them. Finally, I settled upon Ibsen's "Vikings".

We read it aloud on Christmas Day, and it seemed *tremendous*. Not in my most wildly optimistic moments did I think Hiordis, the chief female character—a primitive, fighting, free, open-air person—suited to me, but I saw a way of playing her more *brilliantly* and less *weightily*

208

than the text suggested, and anyhow I was not thinking so much of the play for me as for my son. He had just produced Mr. Laurence Housman's Biblical play "Bethlehem" in the hall of the Imperial Institute, and every one had spoken highly of the beauty of his work. He had previously applied the same principles to the mounting of operas by Handel and Purcell.

It had been a great grief to me when I lost my son as an actor. I have never known any one with so much natural gift for the stage. Unconsciously he did everything right—I mean all the technical things over which some of us have to labour for years. The first part that he played at the Lyceum, Arthur St. Valery in "The Dead Heart," was good, and he went on steadily improving. The last part that he played at the Lyceum—Edward IV in "Richard III"—was, maternal prejudice quite apart, a most remarkable performance.

His record for 1891, when he was still a mere boy, was: Claudio (in "Much Ado about Nothing"), Mercutio, Modus, Charles Surface, Alexander Oldworthy, Moses (in "Olivia"), Lorenzo, Malcolm, Beauchamp, Meynard, and the Second Grave-Digger!

Later on he played Hamlet, Macbeth, and Romeo on a small provincial tour. His future as an actor seemed assured, but it wasn't! One day when he was with William Nicholson, the clever artist and one of the Beggarstaff Brothers of poster fame, he began chipping at a wood-block in imitation of Nicholson, and produced in a few hours and admirable wood-cut of Walt Whitman, then and always his particular hero. From that moment he had the "black and white" fever badly. Acting for a time seemed hardly to interest him at all. When his interest in the theatre revived, it was not as an actor but as a stage director that he wanted to work.

What more natural than that his mother should give him the chance of exploiting his ideas in London? Ideas he had in plenty—"unpractical" ideas people called them; but what else should *ideas* be?

At the Imperial Theatre, where I spent my financially unfortunate season in April 1903, I gave my son a free hand. I hope it will be remembered, when I am spoken of by the youngest critics after my death as a "Victorian" actress, lacking in enterprise, an actress belonging to the "old school", that I produced a spectacular play of Ibsen's in a manner which possibly anticipated the scenic ideas of the future by a century, of which at any rate the orthodox theatre managers of the present age would not have dreamed.

Naturally I am not inclined to criticise my son's methods. I think there is a great deal to be said for the views that he has expressed in his pamphlet on "The Art of the Theatre", and when I worked with him I found him far from unpractical. It was the modern theatre which was unpractical when he was in it! It was wrongly designed, wrongly built.

We had to disembowel the Imperial behind scenes before he could even start, and then the great height of the proscenium made his lighting lose all its value. He always considered the pictorial side of the scene before its dramatic significance, arguing that this significance lay in the picture and in movement—the drama having originated not with the poet but with the dancer.

When his idea of dramatic significance clashed with Ibsen's, strange things would happen.

Mr. Bernard Shaw, though impressed by my son's work and the beauty that he brought on to the stage of the Imperial, wrote to me that the symbolism of the first act according to Ibsen should be Dawn, youth rising with the morning sun, reconciliation, rich gifts, brightness, lightness, pleasant feelings, peace. On to this sunlit scene stalks Hiordis, a figure of gloom, revenge, of feud eternal, of relentless hatred and uncompromising unforgetfulness of wrong. At the Imperial, said Mr. Shaw, the curtain rose on profound gloom. When you *could* see anything you saw eld and severity—old men with white hair personating the gallant young sons of Ornulf—everywhere murky cliffs and shadowy spears, melancholy—darkness!

Into this symbolic night enter, in a blaze of limelight, a fair figure robed in complete fluffy white fur, a gay and bright Hiordis with a timid and hesitating utterance.

The last items in the topsy-turviness of my son's practical significance were entirely my fault! Mr. Shaw was again moved to compliments when I revived "Much Ado about Nothing" under my son's direction at the Imperial. "The dance was delightful, but I would suggest the substitution of trained dancers for untrained athletes," he wrote.

I singed my wings a good deal in the Imperial limelight, which, although our audience complained of the darkness on the stage, was the most serious drain on my purse. But a few provincial tours did something towards restoring some of the money that I had lost in management.

On one of these tours I produced "The Good Hope", a play by the Dutch dramatist, Heijermans, dealing with life in a fishing village. Done into simple and vigorous English by Christopher St. John, the play proved a great success in the provinces. This was almost as new a departure for me as my season at the Imperial. The play was essentially modern in construction and development—full of action, but the action of incident rather than the action of stage situation. It had no "star" parts, but every part was good, and the gloom of the story was made bearable by the beauty of the atmosphere—of the *sea*, which played a bigger part in it than any of the visible characters.

For the first time I played an old woman, a very homely old peasant woman too. It was not a big part, but it was interesting, and in the last act I had a little scene in which I was able to make the same kind of effect that I had made years before in the last act of "Ravenswood"—an effect of *quiet* and stillness.

I flattered myself that I was able to assume a certain roughness and solidity of the peasantry in "The Good Hope", but although I stumped about heavily in large sabots, I was told by the critics that I walked like a fairy and was far too graceful for a Dutch fisherwoman! It is a case of "Give a dog a bad name and hang him"—the bad name in my case being "a womanly woman"! What this means I scarcely apprehend, but I fancy it is intended to signify (in an actress) something sweet, pretty, soft, appealing, gentle and *underdone*. Is it possible that I convey that impression when I try to assume the character of a washerwoman or a fisherwoman? If so I am a very bad actress!

My last Shakespearean part was Hermione in "A Winter's Tale". By some strange coincidence it fell to me to play it exactly fifty years after I had played the little boy Mamilius in the same play. I sometimes think that Fate is the best of stage managers! Hermione is a gravely beautiful part—well-balanced, difficult to act, but certain in its appeal. If only it were possible to put on the play in a simple way and arrange the scenes to knit up the ravelled interest, I should hope to play Hermione again.

MY STAGE JUBILEE

When I had celebrated my stage jubilee in 1906, I suddenly began to feel exuberantly young again. It was very inappropriate, but I could not help it.

The recognition of my fifty years of stage life by the public and by my profession was quite unexpected. Henry Irving had said to me not long before his death in 1905 that he believed that they (the theatrical profession) "intended to celebrate our jubilee". (If he had lived he would have completed his fifty years on the stage in the autumn of 1906.) He said that there would be a monster performance at Drury Lane, and that already the profession were discussing what form it was to take.

After his death, I thought no more of the matter. Indeed I did not want to think about it, for any recognition of my jubilee which did not include his, seemed to me very unnecessary.

Of course I was pleased that others thought it necessary. I enjoyed all the celebrations. Even the speeches that I had to make did not spoil my enjoyment. But all the time I knew perfectly well that the great show of honour and "friending" was not for me alone. Never for one instant did I forget this, nor that the light of the great man by whose side I had worked for a quarter of a century was still shining on me from his grave.

The difficulty was to thank people as they deserved. Stammering speeches could not do it, but I hope that they all understood. "I were but little happy, if I could say how much."

Kindness on kindness's head accumulated! There was *The Tribune* testimonial. I can never forget that London's youngest newspaper first conceived the idea of celebrating my Stage Jubilee.[1]

The matinée given in my honour at Drury Lane by the theatrical profession was a wonderful sight. The two things about it which touched me most deeply were my reception by the crowd who were waiting to get into the gallery when I visited them at two in the morning, and the presence of Eleonora Duse, who came all the way from Florence just to honour me. She told me afterwards that she would have come from South Africa or from Heaven, had she been there! I appreciated very much too, the kindness of Signor Caruso in singing for me. I did not know him at all, and the gift of his service was essentially the impersonal desire of an artist to honour another artist.

I was often asked during these jubilee days, "how I felt about it all", and I never could answer sensibly. The strange thing is that I don't know even now what was in my heart. Perhaps it was one of my chief joys that I had not to say goodbye at any of the celebrations. I could still speak to my profession as a fellow-comrade on the active list, and to the public as one still in their service.

One of those little things almost too good to be true happened at the close of the Drury Lane matinée. A four-wheeler was hailed for me by the stage-door keeper, and my daughter and I drove off to Lady Bancroft's in Berkeley Square to leave some flowers. Outside the house, the cabman told my daughter that in old days he had often driven Charles Kean from the Princess's Theatre, and that sometimes the little Miss Terrys were put inside the cab too and given a lift! My daughter thought it such an extraordinary coincidence that the old man should have come to the stage-door of Drury Lane by a mere chance on my jubilee day that she took his address, and I was to send him a photograph and remuneration. But I promptly lost the address, and was never able to trace the old man.

APOLOGIA

I have now nearly finished the history of my fifty years upon the stage.

A good deal has been left out through want of skill in selection. Some things have been included which perhaps it would have been wiser to omit.

I have tried my best to tell "all things faithfully", and it is possible that I have given offence where offence was not dreamed of; that some people

[1] I am sorry to say that since I wrote this *The Tribune*, after a gallant fight for life, has gone to join the company of courageous enterprises which have failed.

will think that I should not have said this, while others, approving of "this", will be quite certain that I ought not to have said "that".

One said it thundered . . . another that an angel spake.

It's the point of view, for I have "set down naught in malice".

During my struggles with my refractory, fragmentary, and unsatisfactory memories, I have realised that life itself is a point of view: is, to put it more clearly, imagination.

So if any one said to me at this point in my story: "And is this, then, what you call your life?" I should not resent the question one little bit.

"We have heard," continues my imaginary and disappointed interlocutor, "a great deal about your life in the theatre. You have told us of plays and parts and rehearsals, of actors good and bad, of critics and of playwrights, of success and failure, but after all, your whole life has not been lived in the theatre. Have you nothing to tell us about your different homes, your family life, your social diversions, your friends and acquaintances? During your life there have been great changes in manners and customs; political parties have altered; a great Queen has died; your country has been engaged in two or three serious wars. Did all these things make no impression on you? Can you tell us nothing of your life in the world?"

And I have to answer that I have lived very little in the world. After all, the life of an actress belongs to the theatre, as the life of a soldier belongs to the army, the life of a politician to the State, and the life of a woman of fashion to society.

Certainly I have had many friends outside the theatre, but I have had very little time to see them.

I have had many homes, but I have had very little time to live in them!

When I am not acting, the best part of my time is taken up by the most humdrum occupations. Dealing with my correspondence, even with the help of a secretary, is no insignificant work. The letters, chiefly consisting of requests for my autograph, or appeals to my charity, have to be answered. I have often been advised to ignore them—surely a course that would be both bad policy and bad taste on the part of a servant of the public. It would be unkind, too, to those ignorant of my busy life and the calls upon my time.

Still, I sometimes wish that the cost of a postage stamp were a sovereign at least!

*　　*　　*

In 1887, the year of Queen Victoria's Jubilee, I find that I wrote in my diary:— "I am not yet forty, but am pretty well worn out."

It is twenty years since then, and I am still not worn out. Wonderful!

213

THE DEATH OF HENRY IRVING

It is commonly known, I think, that Henry Irving's health first began to fail in 1896.

He went home to Grafton Street after the first night of the revival of "Richard III" and slipped on the stairs, injuring his knee. With characteristic fortitude, he struggled to his feet unassisted and walked to his room. This made the consequences of the accident far more serious, and he was not able to act for weeks.

It was a bad year at the Lyceum.

In 1898 when we were on tour he caught a chill. Inflammation of the lungs, bronchitis, pneumonia followed. His heart was affected. He was never really well again.

When I think of his work during the next seven years, I could weep! Never was there a more admirable, extraordinary worker; never was any one more splendid-couraged and patient.

The seriousness of his illness in 1898 was never really known. He nearly died.

> I am still fearfully anxious about H. [I wrote to my daughter at the time]. It will be a long time at the best before he gains strength. . . . But now I do hope for the best. I'm fairly well so far. All he wants is for me to keep my health, not my *head*. He knows I'm doing that! Last night I did three acts of "Sans-Gêne" and "Nance Oldfield" thrown in! That is a bit too much—awful work—and I can't risk it again.
>
> A telegram just come: "Steadily improving . . ." You should have seen Norman[1] as Shylock! It was not a bare "get-through". It was—the first night—an admirable performance, as well as a plucky one. . . . H. is more seriously ill than any one dreams. . . . His look! Like the last act of Louis XI.

In 1902, on the last provincial tour that we ever went together, he was ill again, but he did not give in. One night when his cough was rending him, and he could hardly stand up from weakness, he acted so brilliantly and strongly that it was easy to believe in the triumph of mind over matter—in Christian science, in fact!

Strange to say, a newspaper man noticed the splendid power of his performance that night and wrote of it with uncommon discernment— a *provincial* critic, by the way.

In London at the time they were always urging Henry Irving to produce new plays by new playwrights. But in the face of the failure of most of the new work, and of his departing strength, and of the extraordinary support given him in the old plays (during this 1902 tour

[1] Mr. Norman Forbes Robertson.

we took £4,000 at Glasgow in one week!), Henry took the wiser course in doing nothing but the old plays to the end of the chapter.

I realised how near, not only the end of the chapter but the end of the book was, when he was taken ill at Wolverhampton in the spring of 1905.

We had not acted together for more than two years then, and times were changed indeed.

I went down to Wolverhampton when the news of his illness reached London. I arrived late and went to an hotel. It was not a good hotel, nor could I find a very good florist when I got up early the next day and went out with the intention of buying Henry some flowers. I wanted some bright-coloured ones for him—he had always liked bright flowers—and this florist dealt chiefly in white flowers—*funeral* flowers.

At last I found some daffodils—my favourite flower. I bought a bunch, and the kind florist, whose heart was in the right place if his flowers were not, found me a nice simple glass to put it in. I knew the sort of vase that I should find at Henry's hotel.

I remembered, on my way to the doctor's—for I had decided to see the doctor first—that in 1892 when my dear mother died, and I did not act for a few nights, when I came back I found my room at the Lyceum filled with daffodils. "To make it look like sunshine," Henry said.

The doctor talked to me quite frankly.

"His heart is dangerously weak," he said.

"Have you told him?" I asked.

"I had to, because the heart being in that condition he must be careful."

"Did he understand *really*?"

"Oh, yes. He said he quite understood."

Yet a few minutes later when I saw Henry, and begged him to remember what the doctor had said about his heart, he exclaimed: "Fiddle! It's not my heart at all! It's my *breath*!" (Oh the ignorance of great men about themselves!)

"I also told him," the Wolverhampton doctor went on, "that he must not work so hard in future."

I said: "He will, though,—and he's stronger than any one."

Then I went round to the hotel.

I found him sitting up in bed, drinking his coffee.

He looked like some beautiful grey tree that I have seen in Savannah. His old dressing-gown hung about his frail yet majestic figure like some mysterious grey drapery.

We were both very much moved, and said little.

"I'm glad you've come. Two Queens have been kind to me this morning. Queen Alexandra telegraphed to say how sorry she was I was ill, and now you——"

He showed me the Queen's gracious message.

I told him he looked thin and ill, but *rested*.

"Rested! I should think so. I have plenty of time to rest. They tell me I shall be here eight weeks. Of course I sha'n't, but still—— It was that rug in front of the door. I tripped over it. A commercial traveller picked me up—a kind fellow, but d——n him, he wouldn't leave me afterwards—wanted to talk to me all night."

I remembered his having said this, when I was told by his servant, Walter Collinson, that on the night of his death at Bradford, he stumbled over the rug when he walked into the hotel corridor.

We fell to talking about work. He said he hoped that I had a good manager . . . agreed very heartily with me about Frohman, saying he was always so fair—more than fair.

"What a wonderful life you've had, haven't you?" I exclaimed, thinking of it all in a flash.

"Oh, yes," he said quietly . . . "a wonderful life—of work."

"And there's nothing better, after all, is there?"

"Nothing."

"What have you got out of it all. . . . You and I are 'getting on', as they say. Do you ever think, as I do sometimes, what you have got out of life?"

"What have I got out of it?" said Henry, stroking his chin and smiling slightly. "Let me see. . . . Well, a good cigar, a good glass of wine—good friends." Here he kissed my hand with courtesy. Always he was so courteous; always his actions, like this little one of kissing my hand, were so beautifully timed. They came just before the spoken words, and gave them peculiar value.

"That's not a bad summing-up of it all," I said. "And the end. . . . How would you like that to come?"

"How would I like that to come?" He repeated my question lightly yet meditatively too. Then he was silent for some thirty seconds before he snapped his fingers—the action again before the words.

"Like that!"

I thought of the definition of inspiration—"A calculation rapidly made." Perhaps he had never thought of the manner of his death before. Now he had an inspiration as to how it would come.

We were silent a long time, I thinking how like some splendid Doge of Venice he looked, sitting up in bed, his beautiful mobile hand stroking his chin.

I agreed, when I could speak, that to be snuffed out like a candle would save a lot of trouble.

After Henry Irving's sudden death in October of the same year, some of his friends protested against the statement that it was the kind of death that he desired—that they knew, on the contrary, that he thought sudden death inexpressibly sad.

216

I can only say what he told me.

I stayed with him about three hours at Wolverhampton. Before I left I went back to see the doctor again—a very nice man by the way, and clever.

He told me that Henry ought never to play "The Bells" again, even if he acted again, which he said ought not to be.

It was clever of the doctor to see what a terrible emotional strain "The Bells" put upon Henry—how he never could play the part of Mathias with ease as he could Louis XI, for example.

Every time he heard the sound of the bells, the throbbing of his heart must have nearly killed him. He used always to turn quite white—there was no trick about it. It was imagination acting physically on the body.

His death as Mathias—the death of a strong, robust man—was different from all his other stage deaths. He did really almost die—he imagined death with such horrible intensity. His eyes would disappear upwards, his face grow grey, his limbs cold.

No wonder, then, that the first time that the Wolverhampton doctor's warning was disregarded, and Henry played "The Bells" at Bradford, his heart could not stand the strain. Within twenty-four hours of his last death as Mathias, he was dead.

What a heroic thing was that last performance of Becket which came between! I am told by those who were in the company at the time that he was obviously suffering and dazed, this last night of life. But he went through it all as usual. The courteous little speech to the audience, the signing of a worrying boy's drawing at the stage-door—all that he had done for years, he did faithfully for the last time.

Yes, I know it seems sad to the ordinary mind that he should have died in the entrance to an hotel in a country town with no friend, no relation near him. Only his faithful and devoted servant Walter Collinson (whom, as was not his usual custom, he had asked to drive back to the hotel with him that night) was there. Do I not feel the tragedy of the beautiful body, for so many years the house of a thousand souls, being laid out in death by hands faithful and devoted enough, but not the hands of his kindred either in blood or in sympathy!

I do feel it, yet I know it was more appropriate to such a man than the deathbed where friends and relations weep.

Henry Irving belonged to England, not to a family. England showed that she knew it when she buried him in Westminster Abbey.

Years before I had discussed, half in joke, the possibility of this honour. I remember his saying to me with great simplicity, when I asked him what he expected of the public after his death: "I should like them to do their duty by me. And they will—they will!"

There was not a touch of arrogance in this, just as I hope there was no touch of heartlessness in me because my chief thought during the

217

funeral in Westminster Abbey was: "How Henry would have liked it!" The right note was struck, as I think was not the case at Tennyson's funeral thirteen years earlier.

> Tennyson is buried today in Westminster Abbey [I wrote in my diary, October 12, 1892]. His majestic life and death spoke of him better than the service. . . . The music was poor and dull and weak, while he was *strong*. The triumphant should have been the sentiment expressed. . . . Faces one knew everywhere. Lord Salisbury looked fine. His massive head and sad eyes were remarkable. No face there, however, looked anything by the side of Henry's. . . . He looked very pale and slim and wonderful!

How terribly I missed that face at Henry's own funeral! I kept on expecting to see it, for indeed it seemed to me that he was directing the whole most moving and impressive ceremony. I could almost hear him saying, "Get on! get on!" in the parts of the service that dragged. When the sun—such a splendid, tawny sun—burst across the solemn misty grey of the Abbey, at the very moment when the coffin, under its superb pall of laurel leaves,[1] was carried up the choir, I felt that it was an effect which he would have loved.

I can understand any one who was present at Henry Irving's funeral thinking that this was his best memorial, and that any attempt to honour him afterwards would be superfluous and inadequate.

Yet when some further memorial was discussed, it was not always easy to sympathise with those who said: "We got him buried in Westminster Abbey. What more do you want?"

After all it was Henry Irving's commanding genius, and his devotion of it to high objects, his personal influence on the English people, which secured him burial among England's great dead. The petition for the burial presented to the Dean and Chapter, and signed, on the initiative of Henry Irving's leading fellow-actors, by representative personages of influence, succeeded only because of Henry's unique position.

"We worked very hard to get it done," I heard said—more than once. And I often longed to answer: "Yes, and all honour to your efforts, but you worked for it between Henry's death and his funeral. *He* worked for it all his life!"

I have always desired some other memorial to Henry Irving than his honoured grave, not so much for *his* sake as for the sake of those who loved him and would gladly welcome the opportunity of some great test of their devotion.

Henry Irving's profession decided last year, after much belated

[1] Every lover of beauty and every lover of Henry Irving must have breathed a silent thanksgiving that day to the friends who had that inspiration and made the pall with their own hands.

discussion, to put up a statue to him in the streets of London. I believe that it is to take the form of a portrait statue in academic robes. A statue can never at any time be a very happy memorial to an actor, who does not do his work in his own person, but through his imagination of many different persons. If statue it had to be, the work should have had a symbolic character. My dear friend Alfred Gilbert, one of the most gifted sculptors of this or any age, expressed a similar opinion to the committee of the memorial, and later on wrote to me as follows:

> I should never have attempted the representation of Irving as a mummer, nor literally as Irving disguised as this one or that one, but as *Irving*—the artistic exponent of other great artists' conceptions—*Irving*, the greatest illustrator of the greatest men's creations—he himself being a creator.
>
> I had no idea of making use of Irving's facial and physical peculiarities as a means to perpetuate his life's work. The spirit of this work was worship of an ideal, and it was no fault of his that his strong personality dominated the honest conviction of his critics. These judged Irving as the man masquerading, not as the Artist interpreting, for the simple reason that they were themselves overcome by the magic personality of a man above their comprehension.
>
> I am convinced that Irving, when playing the rôle of whatever character he undertook to represent, lived in that character, and not as the actor playing the part for the applause of those in front—Charles I was a masterpiece of conception as to the representation of a great gentleman. His Cardinal Wolsey was the most perfect presentation of greatness, of self-abnegation, and of power to suffer I can realize. . . . Jingle and Mathias were in Comedy and Tragedy combined, masterpieces of histrionic art. I could write volumes upon Irving as an actor, but to write of him as a *man*, and as a very great Artist, I should require more time than is still allotted to me of man's brief span of life and far, far more power than that which was given to those who wrote of him in a hurry during his lifetime. . . . Do you wonder, then, that I should rather elect to regard Irving in the abstract, when called upon to suggest a fitting monument, than to promise a faithful portrait? . . . Let us be grateful, however, that a great artist is to be commemorated at all, side by side with the effigies of great Butchers of mankind, and ephemeral statesmen, the instigators of useless bloodshed. . . .

ALFRED GILBERT AND OTHERS

Alfred Gilbert was one of Henry's sincere admirers in the old Lyceum days, and now if you want to hear any one talk of those days brilliantly, delightfully, and whimsically, if you want to live first nights and Beefsteak Room suppers over again—if you want to have Henry Irving at the Garrick

Club recreated before your eyes, it is only Alfred Gilbert who can do it for you!

He lives now in Bruges, that beautiful dead city of canals and Hans Memlings, and when I was there a few years ago I saw him. I shall never forget his welcome! I let him know of my arrival, and within a few hours he sent a carriage to my hotel to bring me to his house. The seats of the *fiacre* were hidden by flowers! He had not long been in his house, and there were packing-cases still lying about in the spacious, desolate rooms looking into an old walled garden. But on the wall of the room in which we dined was a sketch by Raffaele, and the dinner, chiefly cooked by Mr. Gilbert himself—the Savoy at its best!

Some people regret that he has "buried" himself in Bruges, and that England has practically lost her best sculptor. I think that he will do some of the finest work of his life there, and meanwhile England should be proud of Alfred Gilbert.

In a city which can boast of some of the ugliest and weakest statues in the world, he has, in the fountain erected to the memory of the good Lord Shaftesbury in Piccadilly Circus, created a thing of beauty which will be a joy to future generations of Londoners.

The other day Mr. Frampton, one of the leaders of the younger school of English sculptors, said of the Gilbert fountain that it could hold its own with the finest work of the same kind done by the masters of the past. "They tell me," he said, "that it is inappropriate to its surroundings. It is. That's the fault of the surroundings. In a more enlightened age than this, Piccadilly Circus will be destroyed and rebuilt merely as a setting for Gilbert's jewel."

"The name of Gilbert is honoured in this house," went on Mr. Frampton. We were at the time looking at Henry Irving's death-mask which Mr. Frampton had taken, and a replica of which he had just given me. I thought of Henry's living face, alive with raffish humour and mischief, presiding at a supper in the Beefsteak Room—and of Alfred Gilbert's Beethoven-like head with its splendid lion-like mane of tawny hair. Those days were dead indeed.

Now it seems to me that I did not appreciate them half enough—that I did not observe enough. Yet players should observe, if only for their work's sake. The trouble is that only certain types of men and women—the expressive types which are useful to us—appeal to our observation.

I remember one supper very well at which Bastien-Lepage was present, and "Miss Sarah" too. The artist was lost in admiration of Henry's face, and expressed a strong desire to paint him. The Bastien-Lepage portrait originated that evening, and is certainly a Beefsteak Room portrait, although Henry gave two sittings for it afterwards at Grafton Street. At the supper itself Bastien-Lepage drew on a half-sheet of paper for me two little sketches, one of Sarah Bernhardt and the other of Henry, which are among my most precious relics.

My portrait as Lady Macbeth by Sargent used to hang in the alcove in the Beefsteak Room when it was not away at some exhibition, and the artist and I have often supped under it—to me no infliction, for I have always loved the picture, and think it is far more like me than any other. Mr. Sargent first of all thought that he would paint me at the moment when Lady Macbeth comes out of the castle to welcome Duncan. He liked the swirl of the dress, and the torches and the women bowing down on either side. He used to make me walk up and down his studio until I nearly dropped in my heavy dress, saying suddenly as I got the swirl:— "That's it, that's it!" and rushing off to his canvas to throw on some paint in his wonderful inimitable fashion!

But he had to give up *that* idea of the Lady Macbeth picture all the same. I was the gainer, for he gave me the unfinished sketch, and it is certainly very beautiful.

By this sketch hangs a tale of Mr. Sargent's great-heartedness. When the details of my jubilee performance at Drury Lane were being arranged, the Committee decided to ask certain distinguished artists to contribute to the programme. They were all delightful about it, and such busy men as Sir Laurence Alma-Tadema, Mr. Abbey, Mr. Byam Shaw, Mr. Walter Crane, Mr. Bernard Partridge, Mr. James Pryde, Mr. Orpen, and Mr. William Nicholson all gave some of their work to me. Mr. Sargent was asked if he would allow the first Lady Macbeth study to be reproduced. He found that it would not reproduce well, so in the height of the season and of his work with fashionable sitters, he did an entirely new painting of the same subject, which *would* reproduce! This act of kind friendship I could never forget even if the picture were not in front of me at this minute to remind me of it. "You must think of me as one of the people bowing down to you in the picture," he wrote to me when he sent the new version for the programme. Nothing during my jubilee celebrations touched me more than this wonderful kindness of Mr. Sargent's.

Burne-Jones would have done something for my jubilee programme too, I think, had he lived. He was one of my kindest friends, and his letters—he was a heaven-born letter-writer—were like no one else's; full of charm and humour and feeling. Once when I was starting for a long tour in America he sent me a picture with this particularly charming letter:

THE GRANGE,
July 14, 1897.

MY DEAR MISS TERRY,   I never have the courage to throw you a huge bouquet as I should like to—so in default I send you a little sign of my homage and admiration. I made it purposely for you, which is its only excellence, and thought nothing but gold good enough to paint with for you—and now it's done, I am wofully disappointed. It looks such a poor little wretch of a thing, and there is no time to make another before you go, so look mercifully upon it—it did mean so well—as you would upon a foolish friend, not holding it up to the light, but putting it in a corner and never showing it.

As to what it is about, I think it's a little scene in Heaven (I am always pretending to know so much about that place!), a sort of patrol going to look to the battlements, some such thought as in Marlowe's lovely line: "Now walk the angels on the walls of Heaven." But I wanted it to be so different, and my old eyes cannot help me to finish it as I want—so forgive it and accept it with all its accompanying crowd of good wishes to you. They were always in my mind as I did it.

And come back soon from that America and stay here, and never go away again. Indeed I do wish you boundless happiness, and for our sake, such a length of life that you might shudder if I were to say how long.

Ever your poor artist,
E. B.-J.

If it is so faint that you can scarcely see it, let that stand for modest humility and shyness—as if I had only dared to whisper.

Another time, when I had sent him a trifle for some charity, he wrote:

DEAR LADY, This morning came the delightful crinkly paper that always means you! If anybody else ever used it, I think I should assault them! I certainly wouldn't read their letter or answer it.

And I know the cheque will be very useful. If I thought much about those wretched homes, or saw them often, I should do no more work, I know. There is but one thing to do—to help with a little money if you can manage it, and then try hard to forget. Yes, I am certain that I should never paint again if I saw much of those hopeless lives that have no remedy. I know of such a dear lad about my Phil's age who has felt this so sharply that he has given up his happy, lucky, petted life to give himself wholly to share their squalor and unlovely lives—doing all he can, of evenings when his work is over, to amuse such as have the heart to be amused, reading to them and telling them about histories and what not—anything he knows that can entertain them. And this he has daily done for above a year, and if he carries it on for his life time he shall have such a nimbus that he will look top-heavy with it.

No, you would always have been lovely and made some beauty about you if you had been born there—but I should have got drunk and beaten my family and been altogether horrible! When everything goes just as I like, and

222

painting prospers a bit, and the air is warm and friends well and everything perfectly comfortable, I can just manage to behave decently, and a spoilt fool I am—that's the truth. But wherever you were, some garden would grow.

Yes, I know Winchelsea and Rye and Lymm and Hythe—all bonny places, and Hythe has a church it may be proud of. Under the sea is another Winchelsea, a poor drowned city—about a mile out at sea, I think, always marked in old maps as "Winchelsea Dround". If ever the sea goes back on that changing coast there may be great fun when the spires and towers come up again. It's a pretty land to drive in.

I am growing downright stupid—I can't work at all, nor think of anything. Will my wits ever come back to me?

And when are you coming back—when will the Lyceum be in its rightful hands again? I refuse to go there till you come back. . . .

DEAR LADY, I have finished four pictures: come and tell me if they will do. I have worked so long at them that I know nothing about them, but I want you to see them—and like them if you can.

All Saturday and Sunday and Monday they are visible. Come any time you can that suits you best—only come.

I do hope you will like them. If you don't, you must really pretend to, else I shall be heartbroken. And if I knew what time you would come and which day, I would get Margaret here.

I have had them about four years—long before I knew you, and now they are done and I can hardly believe it. But tell me pretty, pacifying lies and say you like them, even if you find them rubbish.

Your devoted and affectionate,
E. B.-J.

I went the next day to see the pictures with Edy. It was the "Briar Rose" series. They were *beautiful*. The lovely Lady Granby (now Duchess of Rutland) was there—reminding me, as always, of the reflection of something in water on a misty day. When she was Miss Violet Lindsay she did a drawing of me as Portia in the doctor's robes, which is I think very like me, as well as having all the charming qualities of her well-known pencil portraits.

The artists all loved the Lyceum, not only the old school, but the young ones, who could have been excused for thinking that Henry Irving and I were a couple of old fogeys! William Nicholson and James Pryde, who began by working together as "The Beggarstaff Brothers", and in this period did a poster of Henry for "Don Quixote" and another for "Becket", were as enthusiastic about the Lyceum as Burne-Jones had been. Mr. Pryde has done an admirable portrait of me as Nance Oldfield, and his "Irving as Dubosc" shows the most extraordinary insight.

223

"I have really tried to draw his *personality*," he wrote to me thanking me for having said I liked the picture (it was done after Henry's death). . . . "Irving's eyes in Dubosc always made my hair stand on end, and I paid great attention to the fact that one couldn't exactly say whether they were *shut* or *open*. Very terrifying. . . ."

Mr. Rothenstein, to whom I once sat for a lithograph, was another of the young artists who came a good deal to the Lyceum. I am afraid that I must be a very difficult "subject", yet I sit easily enough, and don't mind being looked at—an objection which makes some sitters constrained and awkward before the painter. Poor Mr. Rothenstein was much worried over his lithograph, yet "it was all right on the night", as actors say.

DEAR MISS TERRY, My nights have been sleepless—my drawing sitting gibbering on my chest. I knew how fearfully I should stumble—that is why I wanted to do more drawings earlier. I have been working on the thing this morning, and I believe I improved it slightly. What I want now is a cloak— the simplest you have (perhaps the green one?), which I think would be better than the less simple and worrying lace fallalas in the drawing. I can put it on the lay figure and sketch it into the horror over the old lines. I think the darker stuff will make the face blonde—more delicate. Please understand how nervously excited I have been over the wretched drawing, how short it falls of any suggestion of that personality of which I cannot speak to you—which I should some day like to give a shadow of. . . .

You were altogether charming and delightful and sympathetic. Perhaps if you had looked like a bear and behaved like a harpy, who knows what I might not have done!

. . . . You shall have a sight of a proof at the end of the week, if you have any address out of town. Meanwhile I will do my best to improve the stone.

Always yours, dear Miss Terry,
WILL ROTHENSTEIN.

My dear friend Graham Robertson painted two portraits of me, and I was Mortimer Menpes' first subject in England.

Sir Laurence Alma-Tadema did the designs for the scenery and dresses in "Cymbeline", and incidentally designed for Imogen one of the loveliest dresses that I ever wore. It was made by Mrs. Nettleship. So were the dresses that Burne-Jones designed for me to wear in "King Arthur".

Many of my most effective dresses have been what I may call "freaks". The splendid dress that I wore in the Trial Scene in "Henry VIII" is one example of what I mean. Mr. Seymour Lucas designed it, and there was great difficulty in finding a material rich enough and sombre enough at the same time. No one was so clever on such quests as Mrs. Comyns Carr. She was never to be misled by the appearance of the stuff in the hand, nor impressed by its price by the yard, if she did not think it would look right on the stage. As Katherine she wanted me to wear steely silver and bronzy gold, but all the brocades had such insignificant designs. If they had a silver design on them it looked under the lights like a scratch in white cotton! At last Mrs. Carr found a black satin which on the right side was timorously and feebly patterned with a meandering rose and thistle. On the wrong side of it was a sheet of silver—just the *right* steely silver because it was the *wrong* side! Mrs. Carr then started on another quest for gold that should be as right as that silver. She found it at last in some gold-lace antimacassars at Whiteley's! From these base materials she and Mrs. Nettleship constructed a magnificent queenly dress. Its only fault was that it was *heavy*.

But the weight that I can carry on the stage has often amazed me. I remember that for "King Arthur" Mrs. Nettleship made me a splendid cloak embroidered all over with a pattern in jewels. At the dress-rehearsal when I made my entrance the cloak swept magnificently and I daresay looked fine, but I knew at once that I should never be able to act in it. I called out to Mrs. Nettleship and Alice Carr, who were in the stalls, and implored them to lighten it of some of the jewels.

"Oh, do keep it as it is," they answered, "it looks splendid."

"I can't breathe in it, much less act in it. Please send some one up to cut off a few stones."

I went on with my part, and then, during a wait, two of Mrs. Nettleship's assistants came on to the stage and snipped off a jewel here and there. When they had filled a basket, I began to feel better!

But when they tried to lift that basket, their united efforts could not move it!

On one occasion I wore a dress made in eight hours! During the first week of the run of "The Merry Wives of Windsor' at His Majesty's, there was a fire in my dressing-room—an odd fire which was never accounted for. In the morning they found the dress that I had worn as Mrs. Page burnt to a cinder. A messenger from His Majesty's went to tell my daughter, who had made the ill-fated dress:

"Miss Terry will, I suppose, have to wear one of our dresses tonight. Perhaps you could make her a new one by the end of the week."

"Oh, that will be all right," said Edy, bluffing, "I'll make her a dress by tonight." She has since told me that she did not really think she *could* make it in time!

She had at this time a workshop in Henrietta Street, Covent Garden. All hands were called into the service, and half an hour after the message came from the theatre the new dress was started. That was at 10.30. Before 7 p.m. the new dress was in my dressing-room at His Majesty's Theatre.

And best of all, it was a great improvement on the dress that had been burned! It stood the wear and tear of the first run of "Merry Wives" and of all the revivals, and is still as fresh as paint!

225

That very successful dress cost no time. Another very successful dress—the white one that I wore in the Court Scene in "A Winter's Tale", cost no money. My daughter made it out of material of which a sovereign must have covered the cost.

My daughter says to know what *not* to do is the secret of making stage dresses. It is not a question of time or of money, but of omission.

One of the best "audiences" that actor or actress could wish for was Mr. Gladstone. He used often to come and see the play at the Lyceum from a little seat in the O.P. entrance, and he nearly always arrived five minutes before the curtain went up. One night I thought he would catch cold—it was a bitter night—and I lent him my white scarf!

He could always give his whole great mind to the matter in hand. This made him one of the most comfortable people to talk to that I have ever met. In everything he was *thorough*, and I don't think he could have been late for anything.

I contrasted his punctuality, when he came to see "King Lear", with the unpunctuality of Lord Randolph Churchill, who came to see the play the very next night with a party of men friends and arrived when the first act was over.

Lord Randolph was, all the same, a great admirer of Henry Irving. He confessed to him once that he had never read a play of Shakespeare's in his life, but that after seeing Henry act he thought it was time to begin! A very few days later he pulverised us with his complete and masterly knowledge of at least half a dozen of the plays. He was a perfect person to meet at a dinner or supper—brilliantly entertaining, and queerly simple. He struck one as being able to master any subject that interested him, and once a Shakespeare performance at the Lyceum had fired his interest, there was nothing about that play, or about past performances of it, which he did not know! His beautiful wife (now Mrs. George Cornwallis West) wore a dress at supper one evening which gave me the idea for the Lady Macbeth dress, afterwards painted by Sargent. The bodice of Lady Randolph's gown was trimmed all over with green beetles' wings. I told Mrs. Comyns Carr about it, and she remembered it when she designed my Lady Macbeth dress and saw to its making by clever Mrs. Nettleship.

Lady Randolph Churchill by sheer force of beauty of face and expressiveness would, I venture to prophesy, have been successful on the stage if fate had ever led her to it.

"BEEFSTEAK" GUESTS AT THE LYCEUM

The present Princess of Wales, when she was Princess May of Teck, used often to come to the Lyceum with her mother, Princess Mary, and to supper in the Beefsteak Room. In 1891 she chose to come as her birthday treat, which was very flattering to us.

A record of those Beefsteak Room suppers would be a pleasant thing to possess. I have such a bad memory—I see faces round the table—the face of Liszt among them—and when I try to think when it was, or how it was, the faces vanish as people might out of a room when, after having watched them through a dim window-pane, one determines to open the door—and go in.

Lady Dorothy Nevill, that distinguished lady of the old school—what a picture of a woman!—is as always a fine theatre-goer. Her face always cheered me if I saw it in the theatre, and she was one of the most clever and amusing of the Beefsteak Room guests. As a hostess, sitting in her round chair, with her hair dressed to *become* her, irrespective of any period, leading this, that and the other of her guests to speak upon their particular subjects, she was simply the *ideal*.

Singers were often among Henry Irving's guests in the Beefsteak Room—Patti, Melba, Calvé, Albani, Sims Reeves, Tamagno, Victor Maurel, and many others.

Calvé! The New York newspapers wrote "Salve Calvé!" and I would echo them. She is the best singer-actress that I know. They tell me that Grisi and Mario were fine dramatically. When I saw them, they were on the point of retiring, and I was a child. I remember that Madame Grisi was very stout, but Mario certainly acted well. Trebelli was a noble actress; Maria Gay is splendid, and oh! Miss Mary Garden! Never shall I forget her acting in "Griselidis". Yet for all the talent of these singers whom I have named, and among whom I should surely have placed the incomparable Maurel, whose Iago was superb, I think that the arts of singing and acting can seldom be happily married. They quarrel all the while! A few operas seem to have been written with a knowledge of the difficulty of the conventions which intervene to prevent the expression of dramatic emotion; and these operas are contrived with amazing cleverness so that the acting shall have free play. Verdi in "Othello", and Bizet in "Carmen" came nearest solving the problem.

To go back to Calvé. She has always seemed to me a darling, as well as a great artist. She was entirely generous and charming to me when we were living for some weeks together in the same New York hotel. One wonderful Sunday evening I remember dining with her, and she sang and sang for me, as if she could never grow tired. One thing she said she had never sung so well before, and she laughed in her delicious rapturous way and sang it all over again.

Her enthusiasm for acting, music, and her fellow-artists was magnificent. Oh, what a lovable creature! Such soft dark eyes and entreating ways, such a beautiful mixture of nobility and "câlinerie"! She would laugh and cry all in a moment like a child. That year in New York she was raved about, but all the excitement and enthusiasm that she created

227

only seemed to please and amuse her. She was not in the least spoiled by the fuss.

I once watched Patti sing from behind scenes at the Metropolitan Opera House, New York. My impression from that point of view was that she was actually a *bird*! She could not help singing! Her head, flattened on top, her nose tilted downwards like a lovely little beak, her throat swelling and swelling as it poured out that extraordinary volume of sound, all made me think that she must have been a nightingale before she was transmigrated into a human being! Near, I was amazed by the loudness of her song. I imagine that Tetrazzini, whom I have not yet heard, must have this bird-like quality.

The dear kind-hearted Melba has always been a good friend of mine. The first time I met her was in New York at a supper party, and she had a bad cold, and therefore a frightful *speaking* voice for the moment! I shall never forget the shock that it gave me. Thank goodness I very soon afterwards heard her again when she hadn't a cold!

"All's well that ends well." It ended very well. She spoke as exquisitely as she sang. She was one of the first to offer her services for my jubilee performance at Drury Lane, but unfortunately she was ill when the day came, and could not sing. She had her dresses in "Faust" copied from mine by Mrs. Nettleship, and I came across a note from her the other day thanking me for having introduced her to a dressmaker who was "an angel". Another note sent round to me during a performance of "King Arthur" in Boston I shall always prize.

> You are sublime, adorable *ce soir*. . . . I wish I were a millionaire—I would throw *all* my millions at your feet. If there is another procession, tell the stage manager to see those imps of Satan *don't chew gum*. It looks awful.
>
> Love, MELBA.

I think that time it was the solemn procession of mourners following the dead body of Elaine who were chewing gum; but we always had to be prepared for it among our American "supers" whether they were angels or devils or courtiers!

In "Faust" we "carried" about six leading witches for the Brocken Scene, and recruited the forty others from local talent in the different towns that we visited. Their general direction was to throw up their arms and look fierce at certain music cues. One night I noticed a girl going through the most terrible contortions with her jaw, and I thought I must say something.

"That's right, dear. Very good, but don't exaggerate."

"How?" was all the answer that I got in the choicest nasal twang, and the girl continued to make faces as before.

I was contemplating a second attempt, when Templeton, the limelight man, who had heard me speak to her, touched me gently on the shoulder. "Beg pardon, miss, she don't mean it. She's only *chewing gum!*"

One of my earliest friends among literary folk was Mr. Charles Dodgson—or Lewis Carroll—or "Alice in Wonderland". Ah, *that* conveys something to you! I can't remember when I didn't know him. I think he must have seen Kate act as a child, and having given *her* "Alice"—he always gave his young friends "Alice" at once by way of establishing pleasant relations—he made a progress as the years went on through the whole family. Finally he gave "Alice" to my children.

He was a splendid theatre-goer, and took the keenest interest in all the Lyceum productions, frequently writing to me to point out slips in the dramatist's logic which only he would ever have noticed! He did not even spare Shakespeare. I think he wrote these letters for fun, as some people make puzzles, anagrams, or Limericks!

Now I'm going to put before you a "Hero-ic" puzzle of mine, but please remember I do not ask for your solution of it, as you will persist in believing, if I ask your help in a Shakespeare difficulty, that I am only jesting! However, if you won't attack it yourself, perhaps you would ask Mr. Irving some day how *he* explains it?

My difficulty is this:— Why in the world did not Hero (or at any rate Beatrice on her behalf) prove an "alibi" in answer to the charge? It seems certain that she did *not* sleep in her room that night; for how could Margaret venture to open the window and talk from it, with her mistress asleep in the room? It would be sure to wake her. Besides Borachio says, after promising that Margaret shall speak with him out of Hero's chamber window, "I will so fashion the matter that Hero shall be absent." (*How* he could possibly manage any such thing is another difficulty, but I pass over that.) Well then, granting that Hero slept in some other room that night, why didn't she say so? When Claudio asks her: "What man was he talked with yesternight out at your window betwixt twelve and one?" why doesn't she reply: "I talked with no man at that hour, my lord. Nor was I in my chamber yesternight, but in another, far from it, remote." And this she could, of course, prove by the evidence of the housemaids, who must have known that she had occupied another room that night.

But even if Hero might be supposed to be so distracted as not to remember where she had slept the night before, or even whether she had slept *anywhere*, surely *Beatrice* has her wits about her! And when an arrangement was made, by which she was to lose, for one night, her twelve-months' bed-fellow, is it conceivable that she didn't know *where* Hero passed the night? Why didn't *she* reply:

But good my lord sweet Hero slept not there:
She had another chamber for the nonce.
'Twas sure some counterfeit that did present
Her person at the window, aped her voice,
Her mien, her manners, and hath thus deceived
My good Lord Pedro and this company?

With all these excellent materials for proving an "alibi" it is incomprehensible that no one should think of it. If only there had been a barrister present, to cross-examine Beatrice!

"Now, ma'am, attend to me, please, and speak up so that the jury can hear you. Where did you sleep last night? Where did Hero sleep? Will you swear that she slept in her own room? Will you swear that you do not know where she slept?" I feel inclined to quote old Mr. Weller and to say to Beatrice at the end of the play (only I'm afraid it isn't etiquette to speak across the footlights):

"Oh, Samivel, Samivel, vy vornt there a halibi?"

Mr. Dodgson's kindness to children was wonderful. He *really* loved them and put himself out for them. The children he knew who wanted to go on the stage were those who came under my observation, and nothing could have been more touching than his ceaseless industry on their behalf.

I want to thank you [he wrote to me in 1894 from Oxford], as heartily as words can do it for your true kindness in letting me bring D. behind the scenes to you. You will know without my telling you what an intense pleasure you thereby gave to a warm-hearted girl, and what love (which I fancy you value more than mere admiration) you have won from her. Her wild longing to try the stage will not, I think, bear the cold light of day when once she has tried it, and has realised what a lot of hard work and weary waiting and "hope deferred" it involves. She doesn't, so far as I know, absolutely need, as N. does, to earn money for her own support. But I fancy she will find life rather a *pinch*, unless she can manage to do something in the way of earning money. So I don't like to advise her strongly *against* it, as I would with any one who had no such need.

Also thank you, thank you with all my heart, for all your great kindness to N. She does write so brightly and gratefully about all you do for her and say to her.'

"N." has since achieved great success on the music-halls and in pantomime. "D." is a leading lady!

This letter to my sister Floss is characteristic of his "Wonderland" style when writing to children:

MY DEAR FLORENCE, Ever since that heartless piece of conduct of yours (I allude to the affair of the Moon and the blue silk gown) I have regarded you with a gloomy interest, rather than with any of the affection of former years—so that the above epithet "dear" must be taken as conventional only, or perhaps may be more fitly taken in the sense in which we talk of a "dear" bargain, meaning to imply how much it has cost us; and who shall say how many sleepless nights it has cost me to endeavour to unravel (a most appropriate verb) that "blue silk gown"?

Will you please explain to Tom about that photograph of the family group which I promised him? Its history is an instructive one, as illustrating my habits of care and deliberation. In 1867 the picture was promised him, and an entry made in my book. In 1869, or thereabouts, I mounted the picture on a large card, and packed it in brown paper. In 1870, or 1871, or thereabouts, I took it with me to Guildford, that it might be handy to take with me when I went up to town. Since then I have taken it two or three times to London, and on each occasion (having forgotten to deliver it to him) I brought it back again. This was because I had no convenient place in London to leave it in. But *now* I have found such a place. Mr. Dubourg has kindly taken charge of it—so that it is now much nearer to its future owner than it has been for seven years. I quite hope, in the course of another year or two, to be able to remember to bring it to your house: or perhaps Mr. Dubourg may be calling even sooner than that and take it with him. You will wonder why I ask you to tell him instead of writing myself. The obvious reason is that you will be able, from sympathy, to put my delay in the most favourable light—to make him see that, as hasty puddings are not the best of puddings so hasty judgments are not the best of judgments, and that he ought to be content to wait even another seven years for his picture, and to sit "like patience on a monument, smiling at grief". This quotation, by the way, is altogether a misprint. Let me explain it to you. The passage originally stood. "*They* sit like patients on the Monument, smiling at Greenwich". In the next edition "Greenwich" was printed short, "Green^h", and so got gradually altered into "grief". The allusion of course is to the celebrated Dr. Jenner, who used to send all his patients to sit on the top of the Monument (near London Bridge) to inhale fresh air, promising them that, when they were well enough, they should go to "Greenwich Fair". So of course they always looked out towards Greenwich, and sat smiling to think of the treat in store for them. A play was written on the subject of their inhaling the fresh air, and was for some time attributed to him (Shakespeare), but it is certainly not in his style. It was called "The Wandering Air", and was lately revived at the Queen's Theatre. The custom of sitting on the Monument was given up when Dr. Jenner went mad, and insisted on it that the air was worse up there and that the *lower* you went the *more airy* it became. Hence he always called those little yards, below the pavement, outside the kitchen windows, *"the kitchen airier"*, a name that is still in use.

All this information you are most welcome to use, the next time you are in want of something to talk about. You may say you learned it from "a distinguished etymologist", which is perfectly true, since any one who knows me by sight can easily distinguish me from all other etymologists.

What parts are you and Polly now playing?

Believe me to be (conventionally), yours affectionately

L. DODGSON.

No two men could be more unlike than Mr. Dodgson and Mr. J. M. Barrie, yet there are more points of resemblance than "because there's a 'b' in both!"

If "Alice in Wonderland" is the children's classic of the library, and one perhaps even more loved by the grown-up children than by the others, "Peter Pan" is the children's stage classic, and here again elderly children are the most devoted admirers. I am a very old child, nearly old enough to be a "beautiful great-grandmother" (a part that I have entreated Mr. Barrie to write for me), and I go and see "Peter" year after year and love him more each time. There is one advantage in being a grown-up child—you are not afraid of the pirates or the crocodile.

I first became an ardent lover of Mr. Barrie through "Sentimental Tommy", and I simply had to write and tell him how hugely I had enjoyed it. In reply I had a letter from Tommy himself!

DEAR MISS ELLEN TERRY, I just wonder at you. I noticed that Mr. Barrie the author (so-called) and his masterful wife had a letter they wanted to conceal from me, so I got hold of it, and it turned out to be from you, and *not a line to me in it!* If you like the book, it is *me* you like, not him, and it is to me you should send your love, not to him. Corp thinks, however, that you did not like to make the first overtures, and if that is the explanation, I beg herewith to send you my warm love (don't mention this to Elspeth) and to say that I wish you would come and have a game with us in the Den (don't let on to Grizel that I invited you). The first moment I saw you, I said to myself, "This is the kind I like," and while the people round about me were only thinking of your acting, I was wondering which would be the best way of making you my willing slave, and I beg to say that I believe I have "found a way", for most happily the very ones I want most to lord it over, are the ones who are least able to resist me.

We should have ripping fun. You would be Jean MacGregor, captive in the Queen's Bower, but I would climb up at the peril of my neck to rescue you, and you would faint in my strong arms, and wouldn't Grizel get a turn when she came upon you and me whispering sweet nothings in the Lovers' Walk? I think it advisable to say *in writing* that I would only mean them as nothings (because Grizel is really my one), but so long as they were sweet, what does that matter (at the time); and besides, *you* could *love me* genuinely, and I would carelessly kiss your burning tears away.

Corp is a bit fidgety about it, because he says I have two to love me already, but I feel confident that I can manage more than two.

Trusting to see you at the Cuttle Well on Saturday when the eight o'clock bell is ringing,

I am, your indulgent Commander,

T. SANDYS.

P.S.—Can you bring some of the Lyceum armour with you, and two hard-boiled eggs?

Henry Irving once thought of producing Mr. Barrie's play "The Professor's Love Story". He was delighted with the first act, but when he had read the rest he did not think the play would do for the Lyceum. It was the same with many plays which were proposed for us. The ideas sounded all right, but as a rule the treatment was too thin, and the play, even if good, on too small a scale for the theatre.

One of our playwrights of whom I always expected a great play was Mrs. Craigie (John Oliver Hobbes). A little one-act play of hers, "Journeys End in Lovers' Meeting"—in which I first acted with Johnston Forbes-Roberston and Terriss at a special matinée in 1894—brought about a friendship between us which lasted until her death. Of her it could indeed be said with poignant truth, "She should have died hereafter". Her powers had not nearly reached their limit.

Pearl Craigie had a man's intellect—a woman's wit and apprehension. "Bright", as the Americans say, she always managed to be even in the dullest company, and she knew how to be silent at times, to give the "other fellow" a chance. Her *executive* ability was extraordinary. Wonderfully tolerant, she could at the same time not easily forgive any meanness or injustice that seemed to her deliberate. Hers was a splendid spirit.

I shall always bless that little play of hers which first brought me near to so fine a creature. I rather think that I never met any one who *gave out* so much as she did. To me, at least, she *gave, gave* all the time. I hope she was not exhausted after our long "confabs". *I* was most certainly refreshed and replenished.

The first performance of "Journeys End in Lovers' Meeting" she watched from a private box with the Princess of Wales (our present Queen) and Henry Irving. She came round afterwards just *burning* with enthusiasm and praising me for work which was really not good. She spoiled one for other women.

Her best play was, I think, "The Ambassador", in which Violet

233

Vanbrugh (now Mrs. Bourchier) played a pathetic part very beautifully, and made a great advance in her profession.

There was some idea of Pearl Craigie writing a play for Henry Irving and me, but it never came to anything. There was a play of hers on the same subject as "The School for Saints", and another about Guizot.

February 11, 1898.

MY VERY DEAR NELL,   I have an idea for a real four-act comedy (in these matters nothing daunts me!) founded on a charming little episode in the private lives of Princess Lieven (the famous Russian ambassadress) and the celebrated Guizot, the French Prime Minister and historian. I should have to veil the identity *slightly*, and also make the story a husband and wife story—it would be more amusing this way. It is comedy from beginning to end. Sir Henry would make a splendid Guizot, and you the ideal Madame de Lieven. Do let me talk it over with you. "The School for Saints" was, as it were, a born biography. But the Lieven-Guizot idea is a play.

Yours ever affectionately,
PEARL MARY TERESA CRAIGIE.

In another letter she writes:

I am changing all my views about so-called "literary" dialogue. It means pedantry. The great thing is to be lively.

"A first night at the Lyceum" was an institution. I don't think that it has its parallel nowadays. It was not, however, to the verdict of all the brilliant friends who came to see us on the first night that Henry Irving attached importance. I remember some one saying to him after the first night of "Ravenswood": "I don't fancy that your hopes will be quite fulfilled about the play. I heard one or two on Saturday night——"

"Ah yes," said Henry very carelessly and gently, "but you see there were so many *friends* there that night who didn't pay—*friends*. One must not expect too much from friends! The paying public will, I think, decide favourably."

Henry never cared much for society, as the saying is—but as host in the Beefsteak Room he thoroughly enjoyed himself, and every one who came to his suppers seemed happy! Every conceivable type of person used to be present—and there, if one had the *mind*,[1] one could study the world in little.

One of the liveliest guests was Sir Francis Burnand—who entirely contradicted the theory that professional comedians are always the most gloomy of men in company.

[1] "Wordsworth says he could write like Shakespeare if he had the *mind*. Obviously it is only the mind that is lacking."—*Charles Lamb's Letters*.

234

A Sunday evening with the Burnand family at their home in The Bottoms was a treat Henry Irving and I often looked forward to—a particularly restful, lively evening. I think a big family—a "party" in itself—is the only "party" I like. Some of the younger Burnands have greatly distinguished themselves, and they are all perfect dears, so unaffected, kind, and genial.

Sir Francis never jealously guarded his fun for *Punch*. He was always generous with it. Once when my son had an exhibition of his pictures, I asked Mr. Burnand, as he was then, to go and see it or send some one on Mr. Punch's staff. He answered characteristically!

WHITEFRIARS,
LONDON, E.C.

MY DEAR ELLEN TERRY, Delighted to see your hand—"wish your face were with it" (Shakespeare).

Remember me (Shakespeare again—"Hamlet") to our Sir Henry. May you both live long and prosper!

GORDON CRAIG'S PICTURES

He opens his show
A day I can't go
Any Friday
Is never my day.

But I'll see his pictures
(Praise and no strictures)
'Ere this day week;
Yet I can't speak
Of them in print
(I might give a hint)
Till each on its shelf
I've seen for myself.
I've no one to send
Now I must end.
None I can trust,
So go I must.
Yours most tru*lee*
V'la F.C.B.
All well here,
All send love.
Likewise misses
Lots of kisses.

From all in this 'ere shanty
To *you* who don't play in Dante!

What a pity!
Whuroo-oo
Oo-oo-oo!

BITS FROM MY DIARY

What is a diary as a rule? A document useful to the person who keeps it, dull to the contemporary who reads it, invaluable to the student, centuries afterwards, who treasures it!

Whatever interest the few diaries of mine that I have preserved may have for future psychologists and historians, they are for my present purpose almost worthless. Yet because things written at the time are considered by some people to be more reliable than those written years afterwards when memory calls in imagination to her help, I have hunted up a few passages from my diaries between 1887 and 1901; and now I give them in the raw for what they are worth—in my opinion nothing!

July 1887—E. B.-J. (Sir Edward Burne-Jones) sent me a picture he has painted for me—a troop of little angels.

August 2—(We were in Scotland.) Visited the "Blasted Heath". Behold a flourishing potato field! Smooth softness everywhere. We must blast our own heath when we do Macbeth!

November 29—(We were in America.) Matinée "Faust"—Beecher Memorial. The whole affair was the strangest failure. H. I. himself took heaps of tickets, but the house was half empty.

The following Saturday—Matinée "Faust". House crammed. Why couldn't they have come when it was to honour Beecher?

January 1890—In answer to some one who had said that Henry had all his plays written for him, he pointed out that of twenty-eight Lyceum productions, only three were written "for" him—"Charles I", "Eugene Aram", and "Vanderdecken".

February 27—(My birthday.) Henry gave me a most exquisite wreath for the head. It is made of green stones and diamonds and is like a myrtle wreath. I never saw anything so simple and grand. It's lovely.

(During this year our readings of "Macbeth" took place.)

April—Visit to Trentham after the reading at Hanley. Next day to hotel at Bradford, where there were beetles in the beds!

I see that Bulwer, speaking of Macready's Macbeth, says that Macbeth

236

was a "trembler when opposed by his conscience, a warrior when defied by his foes".

August—(At Winchelsea.) We drove to Cliffe End. Henry got the old pony along at a spanking rate, but I had to seize the reins now and again to save us from sudden death.

August 14—Drove to Tenterden. Saw Clowes's Marionettes.

(Henry saw one of their play-bills in a shop window, but found that the performances only took place in the evening. He found out the proprietor and asked him what were the takings on a good night. The man said £5, I think. Henry asked him if he would give him a special show for that sum. He was delighted. Henry and I and my daughter Edy and Fussie sat in solemn state in the empty tent and watched the show, which was most ingenious and clever. Clowes's Marionettes are still "on the road", but ever since that "command" performance of Henry's at Tenterden their bill has had two extra lines:

Patronised by Sir Henry Irving
and
Miss Ellen Terry.

September—"Method," (in last act of "Ravenswood"), "to keep very still, and feel it all quietly and deeply." George Meredith, speaking of Romance, says: "The young who avoid that region, escape the title of Fool at the cost of a Celestial Crown." Good!

December—Mr. Gladstone behind the scenes. He likes the last act very much.

January 14, 1892—Prince Eddie died. Cardinal Manning died.

January 18—(Just after successful production of "Henry VIII.) H. I. is hard at work, studying "Lear". This is what only a great man would do at such a moment in the hottest blush of success. No "swelled head"—only fervent endeavour to do better work. The fools hardly conceive what he is.

February 3—Morell Mackenzie died.

March 1—Mother died. Amazing courage in my father and sisters. She looked so lovely when she was dead.

March 7—Went back to work.

October 6—Tennyson died.

October 26—A fine day. To call on the young Duchess of S——. What a sweet and beautiful young girl she is! I said I would write and ask Mrs. Stirling to give her lessons, but feared she could not as she was ill.

November—Heard from Mrs. Stirling: "I am too ill and weak to see any one in the way of lessons. I am just alive—in pain and distress always, but always anxious for news from the Lyceum. 'Lear' will be a great success, I am sure. I was Cordelia with Macready."

November 10—First night of "Lear". Such a foggy day! H. was just marvellous, but indistinct from nervousness. T. spoke out, but who cared! Haviland was very good. My Ted splendid in the little bit he had to do as Oswald. I was rather good tonight. It *is* a wee part, but fine.

December 7—Poor Fred Leslie is dead. Typhoid. A thunderbolt to us all. Poor bright, charming Fred Leslie!

December 31—This has been a dark year. Mother died. Illness rife in the family. My son engaged—but that may turn out well if the young couple will not be too hasty. H. I. not well. Business by no means up to the proper point. A death in the Royal Family. Depression—depression!

March 9, 1897—Eunice (Mrs. Henry Ward Beecher) is dead. Poor darling! She was a great friend to me.

April 10—First night of "Sans-Gêne". A wonderful first-night audience. I acted courageously and fairly well. Extraordinary success.

April 14—Princess Louise (Lorne) came to see the play and told me she was delighted. Little Elspeth Campbell was with her, looking lovely. I did not play well—was depressed and clumsy.

May 13—It's all off about "The Man of Destiny" play with H. I. and G. B. S.

May 15—To "Princess and Butterfly" with Audrey and Aimée. Miss Fay Davis better than ever.

May 17—Nutcombe Gould has lost his voice, and Ted was called upon at a moment's notice to play Hamlet at the Olympic tonight.

June 20—Thanksgiving Service at St. Paul's for the Queen's Jubilee. Went with Edy and Henry. Not at all adequate to the occasion was the ceremony. The Te Deum rather good, the sermon sensible, but the whole uninspired, unimpassioned and *dull*. The Prince and Princess looked splendid.

June 22—To Lady Glenesk's, Piccadilly. Wonderfullest sight I ever saw. All was perfect, but the little Queen herself more dignified than the whole procession put together! Sarah B. was in her place at the Glenesks' at six in the morning. Bancroft made a Knight. Mrs. Alma-Tadema's "at home". Paderewski played. What a divinely beautiful face!

July 14—The Women's Jubilee Dinner at the Grafton Galleries. Too ill to go. My guests were H. I., Burne-Jones, Max Beerbohm, W. Nicholson, Jimmy Pryde, Will Rotherstein, Graham Robertson, Richard Harding Davis, Laurence Irving, Ted and Edy.

December 11—(In Manchester.) Poor old Fussie dropped down a trap 30 feet and died in a second.

December 16—Willie Terriss was murdered this evening. Newspapers sent me a wire for "expression of sympathy"!!

January 22, 1901—(Tenterden.) Nine o'clock evening and the bell is tolling for our dearest Queen—Victoria, who died this evening just before seven o'clock—a grand, wise, good woman. A week ago she was driving out regularly. The courage of it!

January 23—To Rye (from Winchelsea). The King proclaimed in the Market Place. The ceremony only took about five minutes. Very dull and undignified until the National Anthem, which upset us all.

January 26—London last night when I arrived might have been Winchelsea when the sun goes down on all our wrath and arguments. No one in the streets . . . empty buses crawling along. Black boards up at every shop window. All the gas half-mast high as well as the flags. I never saw such a mournful city, but why should they turn the gas down? Thrift, thrift, Horatio!

February 2—The Queen's Funeral. From a balcony in St. James's I saw the most wonderful sight I have ever seen. The silence was extraordinary. . . . The tiny coffin on the gun-carriage drawn by the cream-coloured ponies was the most pathetic, impressive object in all that great procession. All the grandest carriages were out for the occasion. The King and the German Emperor rode side by side. . . . The young Duke of Coburg, the Duchess of Albany's son, like Sir Galahad. I slept at Bridgewater House, but on my way to St. James's from there my clothes were torn and I was half squeezed to death. One man called out to me: "Ah, now you know what it feels like at the pit door, Miss Terry."

April 15—Lyceum. "Coriolanus" produced. Went home directly after the play was over. I didn't seem to know a word of my part yesterday at the dress rehearsal, but tonight I was as firm as if I had played it a hundred times.

April 16—The critics who wrote their notices at the dress-rehearsal, and complained of my playing pranks with the text, were a little previous. Oh, how bad it makes one fee! to find that they all think my Volumnia "sweet", and *I* thought I was fierce, contemptuous, overbearing. Worse, I felt as if I must be appearing like a cabman rating his Drury Lane wife!

April 20—Beginning to play Volumnia a little better.

June 25—Revival of "Charles I". The play went marvellously. I played first and last acts well. H. was magnificent. Ted saw play yesterday and says I don't "do Mrs. Siddons well". I know what he means. The last act too declamatory.

June 26—Changed the "Mrs. Siddons" scene, and like it much better. Simpler—more nature—more feeling.

July 16—Horrible suicide of Edith and Ida Yeoland. The poor girls were out of an engagement. Unequal to the fight for life.

July 20—Last day of Lyceum season—"Coriolanus".

(On that night, I remember, H. I. for the first time played Coriolanus *beautifully*. He discarded the disfiguring beard of the warrior that he had worn during the "run" earlier in the season—and now that one could see

239

his face, all was well. When people speak of the evils of long runs, I should like to answer with a list of their advantages. An actor, even an actor of Henry Irving's calibre, hardly begins to play an immense part like Coriolanus for what it is worth until he has been doing it for fifty nights.)

> *November* 16—New York. Saw delightful Maude Adams in "Quality Street"—charming play. She is most clever and attractive. *Unusual* above everything. Queer, sweet, entirely delightful."

From these extracts, I hope it will be seen that by burning most of my diaries I did not inflict an unbearable loss upon present readers, or posterity!

I am afraid that I think as little of the future as I do of the past. The present is for me!

If my impressions of my friends are scanty, let me say in my defence that actors and actresses necessarily *see* many people, but *know* very few.

If there has been more in this book about my life in the theatre than about my life outside it, the proportion is inevitable and natural. The maxim is well-worn that art is long and life is short, and there is no art, I think, which is longer than mine! At least, it always seems to me that no life can be long enough to meet its requirements.

If I have not revealed myself to you, or succeeded in giving a faithful picture of an actor's life, perhaps I have shown what years of practice and labour are needed for the attainment of a permanent position on the stage. To quote Mrs. Nancy Oldfield:—

> Art needs all that we can bring to her, I assure you.